How the Tricolor Got Its Stripes

and other stories about flags

*To my parents, who were the first
to read this book and gave me plenty
of valuable advice; to my grandfather,
who implanted a love for books in me
and helped me develop writing skills;
and to my wife, who is my muse.*

First published in Great Britain in 2023 by
Profile Editions,
an imprint of Profile Books Ltd
29 Cloth Fair
London
EC1A 7JQ
www.profileeditions.com

First published in Ukrainian by Yakaboo Publishing

Copyright © Dmytro Dubilet, 2023

1 3 5 7 9 10 8 6 4 2

Printed and bound by Livonia Print, Latvia

The moral right of the author has been asserted.

All rights reserved. Without limiting the rights
under copyright reserved above, no part of
this publication may be reproduced, stored or
introduced into a retrieval system, or transmitted,
in any form or by any means (electronic,
mechanical, photocopying, recording or otherwise),
without the prior written permission of both the
copyright owner and the publisher of this book.

A CIP catalogue record for this book is available
from the British Library.

ISBN 978 1 80081 7609
eISBN 978 1 80522 0008

MIX
Paper | Supporting
responsible forestry
FSC® C002795

Dmytro Dubilet

How the Tricolor Got Its Stripes

and other stories about flags

PROFILE EDITIONS

About this book **7**
About the author **9**
Afterword **244**
Index **246**

01. The Tricolor Worldwide **10**

02. The Union Jack **24**

03. Bad Vexillological Omen **44**

04. When Flags are Crossed **56**

05. The Bird Heritage of the Romans **78**

06. Vexillological Tango **94**

07. American Dream **108**

08. Orange Stripes **120**

09. Grim Reaper Flags **134**

10. Six-pointed Stars **152**

11. Horizontal Stripes of Eastern Europe **162**

12. Pan-African Colours **174**

13. Pan-Arabic Colours **188**

14. Crescent on the Flags **204**

15. The Sun on the Flags **214**

16. Distinctive African Flags **224**

17. British Island Colonies **234**

About this book

This book comes with a warning. It's so fascinating you may need to alert your loved ones that you'll be unreachable for a bit. You might also think about taking some time off work.

This is a book about flags. More to the point, it's an invitation to immerse yourself in the stories of the nations all around us – the stories told by the flags they fly.

Most flags are fairly simple. Yet learning the why and the how of a nation's flag design can equip you with some interesting information on the history, geography and culture of the country that flies it.

To give some examples: the star on the flag of the Democratic Republic of the Congo is a reminder of what Sir Arthur Conan Doyle once called the greatest crime against humanity; the eagle on Mexico's flag recalls the Aztec sacrifice to their gods of the daughter of a rival tribal leader; and those stars on the flag of Tuvalu? They remind us of a strange contradiction in the country's name.

Flags are a life hack – ready information that can be fetched from your memory banks as needed. By now we're all aware that one of the quickest routes to memory is through visual images. You catch sight of the flag of India and an image of Mahatma Gandhi and his betrayed principles comes right with it.

I don't intend to give you an exhaustive treatment of the subject. In this book we will be talking about the flags of every nation, spending more time on some, less time on others. But my main objective in choosing the material contained here was to whet your interest in the topic.

Welcome to the wonderful world of flags.

Get comfortable and enjoy the view, as beautiful as watching the sun rising on the flag of Kiribati.

About the author

I admit it: I am not a professional writer or researcher. But wait – don't shut the book yet. I have produced written material before; I used to be a journalist. These days, I write one of the most popular blogs in Ukraine.

So what usually occupies my time? I'm a serial entrepreneur. I also did a stint recently as a minister in Ukraine's Cabinet of Ministers.

My fascination with flags began in childhood, during the 1994 FIFA World Cup. I was on holiday with my grandparents in Crimea and we were watching live broadcasts of football matches every night in our tiny hotel room on the slopes of Ayu-Dag.

A great deal has changed in my life since then. My passion for football has cooled and the Russian occupation has meant that our family can no longer travel to Crimea. But my fascination for flags, spawned during those FIFA matches, has stuck.

I'm at a loss to explain why those colourful rectangles next to the score in the corner of the television screen prompted such warm feelings in me. At the time, I was unaware of the whole other world that lay behind those flags. Or that the study of flags has a name: vexillology.

But even then I had an inkling that something was up. In the first match – between the United States and Switzerland – I noticed that the Swiss flag, unlike banners of all the other countries, was not rectangular but square (Vatican City hadn't sent a squad to that tournament). Then, in the second match (Italy against Ireland), what struck me was how similar their flags were. Only later did I find out that this was not a mere coincidence.

My passion for the subject gradually grew. I started noting down interesting details of flags that I came across. Later, I made occasional posts about flags on my social media pages, which took my 400,000 followers by surprise. They hadn't signed up for vexillology. Finally, I created a dedicated Telegram page: Flags with Dmytro Dubilet.

The idea of writing a book about flags had been with me for some years. I was surprised that the only books on flags that I could find were reference materials or children's books. I had to remedy that situation. But life got in the way, and I kept postponing the project.

At last, the ideal opportunity arose. Our Cabinet of Ministers resigned and then came the global coronavirus lockdown. Two years of work, and now you're holding the fruit of my toil in your hands. I hope you become as passionate about vexillology as I am.

01. The
Tricolor
Worldwide

Between 1789 and 1799, as the eighteenth century was drawing to a close, France was hit by a cataclysmic wave that we now call the French Revolution. These events turned Europe on its head. Absolute monarchies disappeared. Nations were engulfed by the Revolutionary Wars. The map of Europe was radically redrawn.

That revolution holds a prominent place in the science of vexillology, having endowed the world with the celebrated French tricolor – a flag of nearly unrivalled influence over the hearts and minds of revolutionaries the world over and the flags of scores of sovereign states. Only the British Union Jack can boast a comparable level of influence. But whereas Britain's standard secured its place through colonial expansion, the influence of the French flag lies more in the principles it symbolises: liberty, equality before the law, and democracy. *Liberté, égalité, fraternité.*

The origins of the tricolor are bound up with the year 1789 and the storming of the Bastille. Revolutionaries at the time adorned their hats with cockades in the colours of the City of Paris: blue and red. That same year the National Constituent Assembly, which was called under the pressure of the revolutionaries, adopted the national flag with a simplified design – one that would bear witness to the world of France's break with its past.

They based it on the revolutionaries' cockade, with a central strip in white (the colour of the Bourbon monarchy) flanked by the blue and red colours of the City of Paris (symbolising 'the people'). It would be the people, empowered by a constitution, who would control the monarch.

In its first few years, the order of the stripes on the French flag, from left to right, was red, white and blue. Then, in 1794, the colours were reversed, forming the current order. It is possible that the original red-white-blue was an attempt to reflect the colour arrangement on the flag of Paris; it may also have been a matter of aesthetic preference.

The French Revolution began with high ideals of human rights and turned into the Reign of Terror. At some point, the guillotines in Paris were working almost around the clock, and sometimes 'public enemies' were even put on a barge, taken to the Seine and shot from cannons. The Directory that ruled France from 1795 was aimed at ending the Reign of Terror, but was overthrown by Napoleon, who then also had a hand in the design of the flag. Initially, the three stripes of the flag were different widths, in the proportions 30 (blue), 33 (white) and 37 (red). Under Napoleon, the stripes were made of equal width.

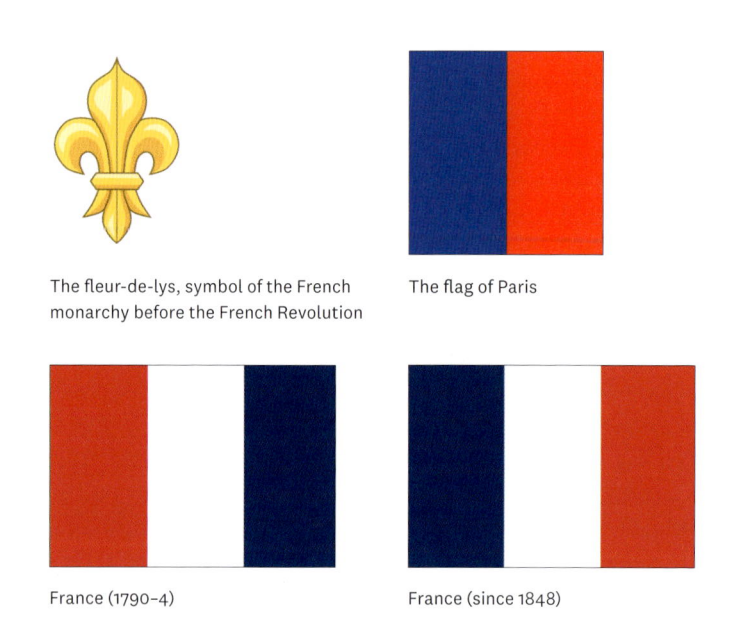

The fleur-de-lys, symbol of the French monarchy before the French Revolution

The flag of Paris

France (1790–4)

France (since 1848)

Napoleon made another contribution to world heraldry by announcing the creation of the French Empire, and proclaiming himself as its emperor. (Previously, he had been ardently against the monarchy, but temptation is hard to resist!) He forced the Pope to come to his coronation. And when His Holiness was about to place the crown on his head at the ceremony, Napoleon snatched it from the Pope's hands and put it on himself, as if to say: 'It was I who crowned me!'

Napoleon chose the eagle as his royal coat of arms – the image widely used in ancient Rome. And during the coronation he sat on a golden throne made in the form of an eagle. The Napoleonic eagle did not nest on the French flag, but we will soon see it in the heraldry of other countries.

After Napoleon was overthrown, Bourbon royalty was briefly restored in France, and the country returned to the flag with royal lilies instead of the revolutionary tricolor. Lilies are popular in European heraldry because of their significance in the Bible. In icons, the Virgin Mary often holds a white lily in her hands, as a symbol of her purity.

The French fleur-de-lys (which is probably a stylised yellow iris rather than a lily) has been the official symbol of the French monarchy since the reign of Louis VII in 1150. There are various legends about how it came to be on the royal coat of arms, most dating back to the fifth century and the first king of France, Clovis I. It was said that the fleur-de-lys had been a gift from heaven to Clovis by an angel on the eve of an important battle – a battle in which he was then victorious.

In 1337, the English king Edward III laid claim to the throne of France, and thus began the Hundred Years War between the two countries. Three years later, in 1340, Edward included French fleur-de-lys in his royal coat of arms. This act had much more significance than a mere copyright infringement – it was an unequivocal demonstration of British claims to French lands. Thanks to Joan of Arc France survived that war, and the royal French fleur-de-lys survived with it. The British kept the fleur-de-lys on their coat of arms for almost 500 years, removing them only in 1801, when George III abandoned his formal claim to the French throne.

In 1515, Pope Leo X decided to make a gift to the French king Francis I, and commissioned Leonardo da Vinci to make a large mechanical lion: a wooden, walking lion, whose chest opened to reveal a host of lilies. The flower symbolised French power, and the lion symbolised Pope Leo himself (the Leo in Leonardo da Vinci being a bonus).

But let's get back to post-Napoleonic France. The monarchy there did not last long, and the French restored their favourite tricolor soon enough.

In 1871, the French tricolor lost its official status once again, when the Paris Commune seized power in the country for seventy-two days. During this time, the French flag was a banner of solid red. Since then, red has become associated with communism and so the French flag was the precursor of the flags of the Union of Soviet Socialist Republics and China.

Another somersault with the French flag might have occurred in 1873. This story is unusual in vexillology, because flags are most often the result of historical events rather than the cause.

That year, the French, having overthrown Napoleon III and the Paris Commune, decided to give the monarchy another chance. Parliament offered the throne to Henri, Count of Chambord, heir of the Bourbon dynasty. But Henri insisted that the tricolor, which was associated with the French Revolution, be replaced with the pre-Revolution fleur-de-lys flag.

National deputies suggested a compromise: putting the fleur-de-lys on the white stripe in the centre of the tricolor, so the symbols of revolution and absolute monarchy would both be there. But the suggestion was beyond scandalous for Count Chambord. He also rejected a compromise whereby the fleur-de-lys would be his own personal standard, and the tricolor would remain the national flag.

And so he refused the throne. Plans to restore the monarchy were dropped, and the country remained a republic.

French 'Bourbon flag' (1589–1792 and 1815–48)

Compromise tricolor with the royal crown and fleur-de-lys, possibly designed by Count Chambord himself

The flag of France for the 72 days of the Paris Commune in 1871

If you visit Paris, note that two types of French flags can be found on the streets: darker and lighter ones. The fact is that in 1976 a tricolor of lighter shades was introduced into the national standards because it looked better on television. Since then, the lighter version of the flag has been used much more frequently by the French authorities, although in 2021 President Macron's administration unexpectedly began to use the flags with the original darker shades. Perhaps it was a symbolic gesture of returning to the ideals of the French Revolution, or perhaps the French rightly decided that modern media would be able to cope with transmitting the more subtle shades.

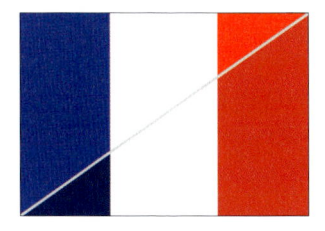

Comparison of the dark and light versions of the flag

Version of the French flag with the narrower white stripe

When it comes to heraldry, French television people are really inventive. Sometimes, when French presidents are addressing the public, you can see a strange version of the French flag in the background, with a very narrow white stripe. This is because, if you place a standard French flag against the background, close-ups of the speaker show only the white stripe, whereas if the white stripe is narrower, all three colours of the flag are visible in the shot.

And so the French flag, as the embodiment of the ideals of the French Revolution, began its victorious heraldic procession around the world, from the Caribbean to Africa.

Consider the Italian tricolor, which first appeared at the end of the eighteenth century – the period in which Napoleon identified a satellite state on the Italian Peninsula, known as the Cisalpine Republic. Napoleon felt little need to fuss with a new flag, and simply replaced the blue of the French flag with green, a colour that was used in the heraldry of the Duchy of Milan.

A few years later the Cisalpine Republic was transformed into the Italian Republic. The new country had a flag of a very uncommon format: red, white and green squares superimposed on each other. A few years later, when Napoleon declared himself emperor, he added his eagle to this flag, so had to abandon the square shape.

In the twentieth century, Mussolini – not worried about resting on Napoleonic laurels – incorporated that same eagle in the Italian flag of his regime. The Napoleonic bird would also find its way on to the standard of an African 'empire' that we will discuss later.

A few years of Napoleon's rule over Italy were enough for the Italians to appreciate the key ideas of the French Revolution, and also to feel like a single nation. Thus began the Risorgimento – the struggle with the Austrian Empire and the gradual process of uniting the different territories of the peninsula into a single Italy. It is understandable that the Italian revolutionaries made the green-white-red tricolor of Napoleon's era their official flag.

Interestingly, while Napoleon inspired the Italian Risorgimento, his nephew Napoleon III, who ruled France from 1852 to 1870, helped Italian unification in practice. Initially, Napoleon III had an alliance with Austria, but in 1858 an Italian terrorist made an unsuccessful attempt on his life – a bomb was thrown under his carriage, but the carriage was armoured and the plot failed. The terrorist was captured and sentenced to death. Before his execution, however, he wrote a letter to Napoleon III, urging him to support the Italians in their struggle against the Austrians. Surprisingly, the letter had the desired effect, and after a few years the French troops joined the Italians against the Austrians. Perhaps this is the only case in history when a terrorist has influenced the target of his own failed attack.

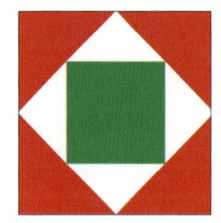

Italian Republic (1802–05)

Italian Empire (1805–14)

Flag of the Italian Social Republic of Benito Mussolini (1944–5)

Italian tricolor (since 1946)

Although there is no official interpretation of the three colours of the Italian flag, one explanation is that they represent faith, hope and love (coincidentally, the names that my great-grandfather gave to his three daughters). Another, more common, explanation is that green symbolises Mediterranean vegetation, white symbolises the snowy Alps and red the struggle for Italian unification. Given that the Italian flag has become one of the most recognisable in the world thanks to Italian cuisine, you might suggest that the green, white and red correspond to basil, mozzarella and tomato. Or you may choose any explanation you like.

Hungary (since 1957)

Romania (since 1848)

Belgium (since 1831). It is almost square

The story behind the Hungarian flag is surprisingly similar.

The wave of revolutions that swept through Europe in 1848 is often known as the Spring of Nations. Much like the Italians, the Hungarians were inspired by the French Revolution, rising up against the Austrian Empire. They too considered adopting the green–white–red vertically striped tricolor, only to discover that the Italians were several decades ahead of them, so instead chose horizontal stripes in those colours.

The Spring of Nations inspired revolutionaries on the territory of modern Romania to rise up against the Ottoman and Russian empires. Probably also influenced by the French tricolor, the insurgents began to use the blue–yellow–red tricolor, which eventually became the flag of modern Romania.

Some years earlier, in 1830, a revolt took place in Belgium, starting with the uprising at a Brussels opera house. That's right – at the opera, not the pub. Moved by the nationalistic performance they had seen that day, the Brussels opera crowd rioted, ransacking shops throughout the city. The rebellion spilled over into outlying regions, ending only a year later with the divorce of Belgium from the Netherlands. Belgian revolutionaries took their cue from the French, adorning their hats with cockades – their cockades being in black, yellow and red. When Belgian independence was declared, they chose the colours of their national revolution for their flag, in line with the design provided half a century earlier by the French.

So far so straightforward, yet make no mistake: the spirit of the French flag has reached well beyond the continent of Europe. As Napoleon was making his way around Europe the ideals of the French Revolution found a home on the other side of the planet among the people of Haiti – known, at the time, as the French colony of San Domingo.

Republic of Haiti (since 1986, and 1859–1964)

The flag of Paris, which was the predecessor of the French tricolor

The first flag of the Republic of Haiti (1806–11). Almost matching the flag of Paris!

The flag of Liechtenstein

Haiti was among the most prosperous of French colonies: the French colonists called it 'the pearl of the Antilles'. By the end of the nineteenth century, the island produced nearly half of all the sugar and coffee consumed in Europe (the Europeans called sugar 'the sweet salt'). And the local people of Haiti were almost all African slaves. A series of bloody clashes and the spread of yellow fever decimated the French military presence on the island; and Haiti became the world's first republic established by former slaves, providing neighbouring Latin American countries with an example of a successful uprising.

The newly established state took a simple approach to the matter of its flag. Tradition has it that rebel leader Jean-Jacques Dessalines took the French tricolor, tore out the white centre with his own hands – almost certainly it bore strong associations for him with the white colonisers – and asked his goddaughter to sew together the two remaining coloured strips. The inaugural flag of independent Haiti thus had two vertical stripes – one blue, one red – identical to the historical flag of the City of Paris. The connection is nothing less than wonderful. The Paris flag provides the basis for the French tricolor which added a white band. And then, on the other side of the world, the white band is removed, producing the flag of Haiti which resembles the banner of Paris.

Another interesting turn of events involving the Haitian flag occurred a century after the country's independence. However, in the days immediately before the 1936 Summer Olympics, the Liechtenstein delegates noticed that their flag was identical to the flag of Haiti and later Liechtenstein officially added a golden crown to its flag to avoid confusion.

So the French flag has influenced the flag of neighbouring Liechtenstein via the flag of distant Haiti. What a wonderful world!

In 1964, the Haitian flag underwent further change when the dictator François 'Papa Doc' Duvalier held a referendum on two issues: to make himself president for life, and to change the country's flag from blue and red to black and red, with the black band symbolising its ties to Africa. Conveniently, for the first question there was only one box to tick: 'Yes'. But in fact Duvalier's presidency lasted only as long as the black band on the flag – until 1986, when he was overthrown.

Elsewhere in the western hemisphere but somewhat to the south lies another country where the French flag has exerted its influence: Chile.

On gaining their independence from Spain, the Chileans, inspired by the French, adopted a flag of three horizontal stripes of blue, white and red, in 1817. (Incidentally, this was identical to the flag of the Kingdom of Yugoslavia.) And so the world endured the risk of yet another red-white-blue flag to confuse with those of the Netherlands, Russia and Paraguay.

The first flag of Chile – the Flag of Transition (five months in 1817)

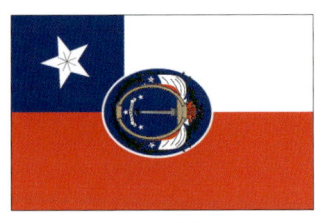

The original flag of Chile. Too complicated, perhaps

The current flag of Chile (since 1817)

It didn't take long before the Chileans decided to choose a more original design. Maybe, at first, a little too original. In the canton (the rectangular area at the top hoist corner of a flag) they added a white star and just below, to the right, overlaying the canton, another star symbolising the indigenous Mapuche people.

The flag's blue and white stripes adhered to the golden ratio of design (a mathematical formula that essentially gives the most pleasing proportions for the sides of a rectangle). At its centre was placed the Chilean coat of arms. Eventually the flag was simplified to its present form.

The Chilean flag was also the inspiration for the flags of two other republics: Texas (an independent state from 1836 to 1845) and Cuba. The Cuban flag would, in its turn, serve as the basis for the flags of both nearby Puerto Rico and the far-off Philippines.

Moving from the New World to Africa, we see that the French flag has also made its mark on this massive continent. And it influenced one of the most unusual national flags of a former French colony that is now the independent Central African Republic (CAR).

Of the four horizontal stripes on the CAR flag, the upper two were imported from the French flag and the lower two from the Ethiopian flag. The horizontal stripes are broken by a vertical red stripe symbolising the blood spilled in the quest for independence.

It's worth noting that red is the most frequent colour to appear on national flags, and nearly always represents blood.

The President of the Central African Republic from 1966 to 1979 was Jean-Bédel Bokassa – yes, the man who would be accused of acts of cannibalism, among other things. One account states that on one occasion Bokassa fed his Cabinet with one of its former members (perhaps, having served in my own nation's Cabinet, this is easier for me to imagine than it is for you). Bokassa converted to Islam in 1976 and, under the influence of Libyan strongman Muammar Gaddafi, decided to adopt for his nation a green flag with the crescent moon and star symbol often seen flying over Islamic nations. It was at this time that Bokassa recast the Central African Republic as the Central African Empire, declaring himself to be its emperor, Bokassa I.

Bokassa modelled himself on Napoleon, whom he revered. In 1977, he organised a lavish coronation ceremony for himself in a blow-by-blow recreation of Napoleon's self-coronation. But 'lavish' doesn't do justice to the indulgence of this event, which seriously depleted state funds in this poor country. A massive imperial throne was made of gilded bronze in the shape of a sitting eagle with wings outstretched. The eagle, in a clear imitation of the Napoleonic flag, would serve as the central element in Bokassa's imperial standard.

Central African Republic (since 1958)

Proposed flag of the Central African Republic after Bokassa converted to Islam

Bokassa, once again taking his cue from Napoleon and his beloved Josephine, crowned Catherine Denguiadé (his 'Number One Wife', of the nineteen women in his harem) as his empress. Later, during Bokassa's imprisonment, rumours circulated that Wife Number One had had an affair with the French president, Valéry Giscard d'Estaing.

Bokassa was overthrown in 1979 after mass demonstrations, initially organised by schoolchildren protesting against restrictive rules on school uniforms. The emperor had decreed that students had to purchase uniforms produced by the company belonging to one of his wives. More than a hundred children were killed in the regime's violent repression of the protests, and it was alleged that Bokassa had personally run over one protester with his car. The French, who had sheltered the Bokassa regime for geopolitical reasons, lost patience, and French paratroopers helped conduct a bloodless coup in the country. The former president, David Dacko, was returned to power; he restored the CAR, and the country retained its unique flag.

Chad (since 1959)

Mali (since 1961)

    Chad is another African country that has adopted a derivative of the French flag. The first president of Chad was a dictator named François Tombalbaye. When François was a teenager, he had to go through a rather cruel traditional rite of his tribe, which gave him scars on his face. One day Tombalbaye issued a decree strictly prescribing the horrific rite (which included flogging, burying alive and other delightful adventures) to the entire cabinet of ministers and thousands of officials throughout the country. The people of Chad had had enough, and in 1975 there was a military coup. Tombalbaye was killed.

    When the Chadians chose their flag, they initially wanted the simplest design: three vertical stripes in the pan-African colours of green, yellow and red. But the state of Mali had chosen that colour scheme a few months previously, so the green stripe of the Chadian flag was replaced with blue.

    However, Chad's flag still ended up being the same as another national flag. In 1989, Romania dropped socialism and subsequently the socialist coat of arms from its national standard, resulting in a flag nearly identical to that of Chad. There were even media reports that they were considering initiating an official hearing at the United Nations to resolve the matter before they ultimately resigned themselves to their fate.

The flag of Romania

Nevertheless, despite being seemingly everywhere, the French flag per se, is nowhere to be found represented on any flag of any sovereign nation.

The one flag on which the French tricolor conceivably could have remained is that of the African nation of Gabon. After winning autonomy from France in 1958, Gabon placed the French colours on its new flag's canton. Another defining characteristic of that flag was a thin yellow stripe that ran horizontally through the flag's centre – a symbol of the Equator, which runs through the territory of Gabon. (Gabon had been part of French Equatorial Africa in the colonial period.)

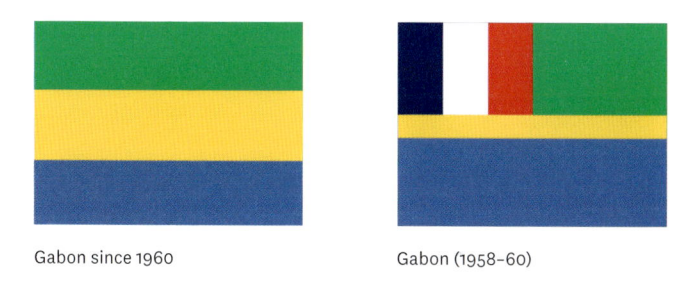

Gabon since 1960

Gabon (1958–60)

But two years later, with national independence fully ratified, Gabon made two changes to its flag: it removed the French colours entirely, and it made the central yellow stripe the same width as the blue and green stripes either side.

Indeed, the French flag is vaguely echoed on dozens of flags all over the world, but in its complete form it is present only once – in the French tricolor itself. In this arena the French can only stand back in envy of the British.

And Britain is exactly where we're going next.

02. The
Union Jack

Once upon a time, many centuries ago, a small settlement near Beirut in Lebanon faced a serious problem – a dragon settled next to it. The monster constantly demanded victims. Initially, the dragon was content with sheep, but at some point he decided he preferred eating people. Every day, the inhabitants of the city sacrificed their children to the dragon. Finally came the turn of the daughter of the local ruler. The unfortunate girl was dressed in a beautiful outfit, adorned with gold and taken to be devoured by the dragon. But, fortunately, at that very moment a Roman soldier and a devout Christian named George was passing by. He fought with the dragon, defeated it and dragged it to the village. There he announced that he would kill the monster if the locals converted to Christianity. All means are good in missionary work.

I cannot know whether this dragon story is true, but today George is one of the most revered saints in the Christian world, among Catholics and Orthodox. Moreover, George is also respected by Muslims.

We vexillologists also deeply revere St George. After all, it was the St George's cross that formed the basis of the English flag, as well as many other banners.

The origins of the English flag can be traced back to the Crusades, with the cross representing the country's link to Christianity. Henry II of England used a white cross, but at some point the English forces began to use a red cross instead. One legend has it that Henry's son, Richard the Lionheart, adopted the red cross for the Third Crusade to symbolise St George, as it was at about this time that St George was made the patron saint of England.

Richard spent almost all his money on equipping his army, but the campaign ended in failure, for he managed to quarrel with almost all his allies. Relations with the French king Philip II deteriorated after he refused to marry Richard's sister. And there was a quarrel with Leopold V, Duke of

Austria, after the fall of the Palestinian city of Acre; when the banners of the Kingdom of Jerusalem, England, France and Leopold's ducal flag were raised on one of the captured city's walls, but Richard ordered Leopold's colours to be removed.

This banner incident is another example of how flags can influence the course of history. It is believed that it was why Leopold arrested Richard a couple of years later, when he was finally returning home from the Crusade. Then almost all the inhabitants of England had to chip in money to ransom Richard.

The main rival of European kings in that campaign was the legendary Muslim ruler Saladin, who also left his mark on world heraldry. We will talk about him in another chapter.

Richard left another vexillological trace in history by giving the world three lions, which became the coat of arms of England. We will meet English lions in this book more than once, because they are not only on the British coat of arms but also on many flags around the world.

While visiting the Tower of London I was amused to see these lions painted on the mantelpiece in the bedroom of King Edward I, who lived a century after Richard. It was evident that the artist had only a rough idea of what lions looked like, so he depicted them very much like people with tails.

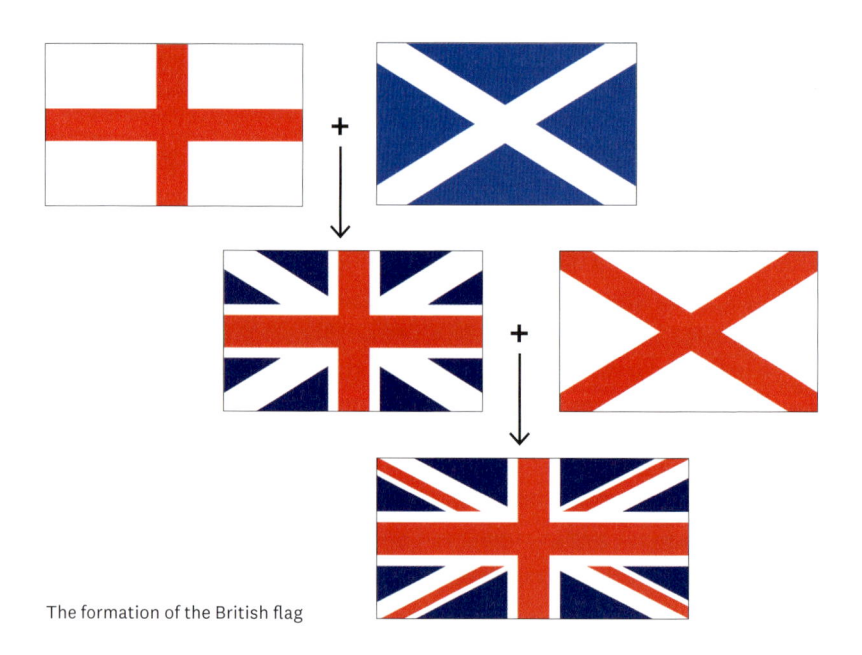

The formation of the British flag

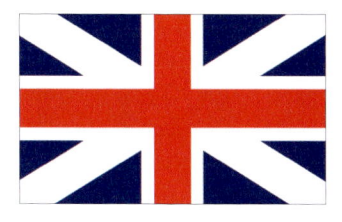

The flag of the union between England and Scotland, adopted in 1606

Scottish version of the Union Jack (Scottish cross of St Andrew over English cross of St George)

The flag of England with a red cross on a white background became the first layer (to use Photoshop terms) on the flag of Great Britain.

The next milestone in the development of the British flag came after Queen Elizabeth I died in 1603, without any direct heirs, and the Scottish king James VI came to the English throne as James I. So England and Scotland had the same monarch, while formally remaining separate countries. The flag of the new union was obtained by superimposing the English cross of St George on the Scottish cross of St Andrew.

According to the Bible, St Andrew was the first disciple of Christ (which is why he is sometimes known as Andrew the First-Called). He was crucified for his faith, just like Christ, but his cross was X-shaped.

The question of whose cross should be on top was far from a purely aesthetic issue. Although the union was formally equal, the English were somewhat 'more equal', so, in 1606, the English cross was placed on top of the Scottish one, which was not to the liking of many Scots at the time. That is why Scotland had an unofficial version of the union flag with the white cross over the red one. It is thought that Scottish ships flew flags with this unofficial design during the seventeenth century.

For me, the Scottish version looks more interesting, because it turns the red cross into red arrows pointing to the centre – which kind of brings out the additional symbolic meaning. Although it has to be said that the use of arrows in graphics did not exist at that time.

Initially, the flag was used only on warships as a jack (that is, a small flag flown from the mast). And so the term 'Union Jack' is based on these maritime roots.

Half a century later, in 1649, a revolution took place in Britain: the king, Charles I, was executed, and a Puritan landowner named Oliver Cromwell, who gave himself the title of Lord Protector, seized power. For eleven years, the country was a republic, and instead of the Union Jack, a flag consisting of four coats of arms became the national banner – the coats of arms of England and Scotland, repeating diagonally over each other. In heraldry, this design is called 'quartering'.

A couple of years later, a harp was added to the flag as a symbol of Ireland, which Cromwell had conquered with particular cruelty. His policy caused wars and famine, the Irish population was reduced by about a third, and their lands were settled by English Protestants. This laid the foundations for the conflict between Protestants and Catholics, which ultimately led to the division of the country.

One day, as Cromwell was returning home after his Ireland campaign, one of his entourage noticed how enthusiastically Cromwell was greeted by the people. Cromwell commented philosophically that the same people would also rejoice at his execution. The words turned out to be prophetic: when Cromwell died and the monarchy was restored, the people dug up his body, hung it on the gallows and put his head on a spear for all to see.

In those days, heraldic elements in Britain could be combined at the personal level as well as at the national level. If a man and a woman from noble families got married, their new coat of arms was created by combining the coats of arms of both families. So the number of coats of arms could grow exponentially. One British duke had 719 elements on his coat of arms.

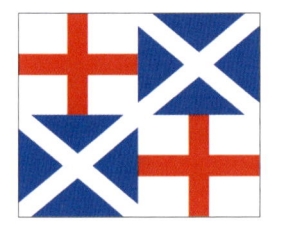

The flag of the Republic of Britain, adopted by Cromwell

The harp of Ireland was added to Cromwell's flag, as well as to his personal coat of arms

The British flag took its final form in 1801, when Great Britain and Ireland united to form the United Kingdom. St George of England and St Andrew of Scotland were joined by St Patrick of Ireland with his red cross. This decision disappointed many Irish people, who hoped that the harp would be added to the flag of the kingdom again. However, British heraldists probably rightly decided that placing a harp on an already complex flag would not be easy.

Since then, the British flag has not been changed.

Wales is not represented separately on the Union Jack, because when England and Scotland were united and the Union Jack was created, Wales was already ruled by the English Crown. Anyway, if the Welsh dragon were to be put on the British flag, the symbolism would be awkward because St George is famous for killing a dragon.

The flag of Wales with the red dragon

A variant of the British flag with the element of Wales added

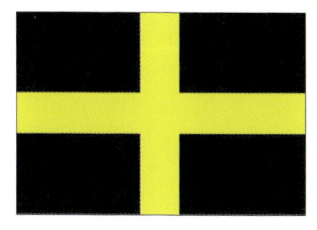

One of the variants of the flag of Wales is the flag of St David

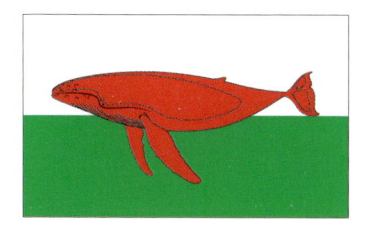

The reaction to Donald Trump's mistake: the dragon is substituted by a whale on the Welsh flag

By the way, in 2019, Donald Trump tweeted that he met with 'the Prince of Whales'. Pranksters responded to the mistake with a Welsh flag that had the dragon replaced by a whale.

Another potential question arose in 2014, when Scotland held a referendum on independence. What would the flag look like if Scotland had left the union? Fortunately for the unionists, the No campaign won by a small margin, and British heraldists did not have to address the problem.

The flag of Great Britain is on the flags of four other states: Australia, New Zealand, Fiji and Tuvalu. No other national flag can boast of its presence on the flags of other nations. This is clear evidence that the British know how to 'divorce' peacefully. (It's rather like your ex-wife still 'liking' your photos on Instagram.) And this does not detract from the fact that the other fifty-one countries in the Commonwealth of Nations, having become independent, chose to get rid of the Union Jack.

The history of the Australian flag in its modern form began in 1901, when the sovereign Australian Union was created out of six British colonies. The same year, there was a contest to design a flag. There were significant prizes for winning, which attracted 32,823 submissions. The conditions stipulated that the flag must have the Union Jack and the Crux constellation (the Southern Cross) on it. Given that one of the sponsors of the prizes was a local tobacco company, we can be thankful that a cigarette did not appear on the flag.

Under such strict stipulations, it is no wonder that most of the proposals were quite similar. In the end, the contest was won by five participants (including two teenagers and a resident of New Zealand) who submitted almost identical designs. They divided the winnings.

Among the unsuccessful designs was a flag that had Australian animals playing cricket.

So, this is how they chose the option that you and I see today.

The stars on the Australian flag are symbolic. The Commonwealth Star is on the left side. On the right are five stars representing the Crux constellation, and symbolising the southern hemisphere of the planet. We will come across this constellation many times again in this book.

The modern flag of Australia (since 1908)

Initial version: with a six-pointed star of Commonwealth and stars with different number of points

Flag of the Australian Anti-Transportation League (1851–2)

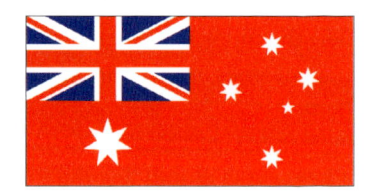

A variant of the Australian flag with the red background

So, there are six stars on the flag, which represent the six British colonies that formed the federation. For the same reason, the Commonwealth Star originally had six points, similar to the Star of David. However, a few years later, the six-pointed Commonwealth Star was replaced by a seven-pointed star. This happened after another territory was joined to Australia: Papua. In fact, Papua later separated from Australia, in 1975, but the Australians decided to keep the seven-pointed star anyway.

The shape of the stars on the right side of the flag was not always as it is now. At first, the number of points on each star (between five and nine) was related to the brightness of each star in the sky. Later, the design was simplified and all the stars became seven-pointed, except for the smallest star.

The flag of Australia is also a reminder that this country was first formed by British criminals who were exiled to the 'southern land'. Half a century before the creation of the national flag, the Australian Anti-Transportation League, which fought to stop sending British convicts to the continent, had almost the same flag.

Until the middle of the twentieth century, there were two versions of the Australian flag: one with a blue background and one with a red background. Both versions were considered official; the flag with the red background was slightly more popular. However, in 1953, the Australian government issued a decree making the blue flag the only official one. It is believed that blue was chosen because red was associated with communism.

In all countries that have the Union Jack on their flag, there are periodic attempts to change it. Canada is a good example of how difficult the process of changing the national flag can be. This nation managed to replace its flag featuring the Union Jack with a new one depicting a maple leaf.

For most of Canada's new history, the Canadian territories were administered by Britain and France. The influence of these two countries left its mark on Canadian flags. For example, the two main heraldic colours of Canada come from the English St George Cross (red) and French royal heraldry (white).

Until 1965, the flag of Canada had a fairly typical design for the British dominions – a red background, a Union Jack in the upper left part (the canton) and a coat of arms that changed every time a new province joined Canada. As new provinces were added, so the Canadians updated their coat of arms in the same way that British aristocrats did after marriage – they added the coat of arms of a new province through quartering.

The Canadian coat of arms began with four provinces, and by 1907 had nine. This was soon considered too complicated, and a committee was set up to design a new coat of arms – finally approved and adopted in 1921. Instead of the coats of arms of the provinces, the new Canadian flag had the symbols of the main founders – England, Scotland, Ireland and France (three lions, a

1868–70, quartering the arms of the four founding provinces

1870–3, addition of Manitoba

1873–97, addition of British Columbia and Prince Edward Island

1907–21, addition of Saskatchewan and Alberta

lion, a harp and a fleur-de-lys) – with the maple leaves underneath, as the symbol of Canada. The leaves were initially green, but were redrawn in red in 1957.

Another detail on the coat of arms also changed at around that time - the shape of the crown on the lion on top of the image. On her coronation in 1953, Queen Elizabeth II opted for a stylised version of the St Edward's Crown to be used on her coat of arms, rather than the Tudor crown, which had been used for centuries previously. British heraldists had to update the coat of arms not only of Great Britain, but also of Canada and several other countries whose heraldry used the British crown. After the death of Elizabeth II in 2022 and the accession of King Charles III to the throne, the Tudor crown has once again returned to the royal coat of arms.

Another feature of the present coat of arms of Canada is two flags flying: the Union Jack and the French fleur-de-lys. The British flag is reflected from left to right (this can be seen by the location of the red stripes). A few chapters later, we will see the same reflected placement of the Union Jack on one of the most unusual flags in the world.

The year 1963 saw the Great Flag Debate in Canada. That year, the Canadian Conservatives lost the election, and the Liberals came to power, led by the energetic Lester Pearson. Pearson was an experienced politician and diplomat; he had received the Nobel Peace Prize for his part in resolving the Suez crisis in 1956. During the crisis, there was an incident when the Egyptian authorities prevented a Canadian ship from going into the Suez Canal, mistaking its flag for a British one.

Later, Pearson repeated this story as proof that Canada needed its own flag. As leader of the opposition, he included the case for the new flag in his pre-election programme. The Conservatives opposed the idea; the Liberals, whose electorate mainly lay in the French territories of Canada, supported it.

After coming to power, Pearson pursued the initiative. His favourite design was one with blue edges and three red leaves in the middle, which the opposition contemptuously called 'Pearson's Pennant'. This flag embodied Canada's motto 'From sea to sea' (the blue stripes on both sides symbolise the Pacific and Atlantic oceans). There is a similar idea on the flags of some Central American nations.

Then the seemingly endless process of choosing a new flag began. The opposition tried to take the Liberals by siege. First, they created a special flag committee, which held thirty-five long meetings. When the committee finally chose the flag, the Conservatives resorted to a filibuster, attempting to drag out the parliamentary debate by an endless series of speeches.

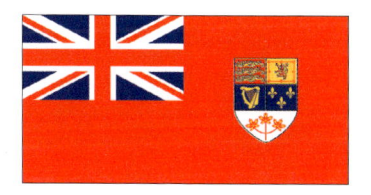

Canada (1921–65)

Pearson's Pennant: 'From sea to sea'

The Coat of Arms of Canada

Official flag of Canada (since 1965)

The Canadian public was also invited to submit designs. Altogether, the committee considered 3,541 options. Sixty per cent of suggestions had a maple leaf, and about 11 per cent featured a beaver. The design that was ultimately adopted (a single red maple leaf on a white plain background, flanked by two red borders, and designed by George Stanley) was submitted to a committee at the last minute and made it to the finals along with the Pearson Pennant. The Conservative MPs on the committee voted unanimously for the maple leaf option, thinking that the Liberals would vote for the Pearson Pennant. However, the Liberals voted for the maple leaf flag too and the result was unanimous.

Queen Elizabeth II of Great Britain signed a royal proclamation in 1965 that finally approved Canada's new national flag. It was signed while the Canadian prime minister Pearson was in London for the funeral of Winston Churchill.

This is how Canada got its flag, which is perhaps one of the most recognisable and stylish flags in the world.

Note that the white section in the middle of the flag is square. This new element in vexillology, whereby the centre band of a triband flag covers half the length of the flag, was named a 'Canadian pale'. (We will also see it on the flags of Saint Vincent and the Grenadines.)

The maple leaf on the flag has eleven points, though there is no symbolism behind this number. There is a story on Wikipedia that this shape was chosen after special experiments on maple leaves in air tunnels to determine which shape bends the least, but I doubt this is true. Another explanation is that the original design had thirteen points on the maple leaf, but this was hard to recognise when the flag was fluttering in the wind, so the number of points was reduced to eleven.

But apparently, the shape of the leaf was chosen for purely aesthetic reasons.

Changing a flag – especially making radical changes – is a risky undertaking. As soon as a design becomes a national symbol, it immediately acquires a special meaning in the eyes of the population (especially if the country went through a war under that flag). Canadians managed to change their flag because part of the population of the country is from France. If Canada were as homogeneous as Australia or New Zealand, this would probably not have happened.

However, the Union Jack can still be seen on the flags of four out of ten Canadian provinces. Two of these flags (British Columbia, and Newfoundland and Labrador province) are particularly distinctive.

British Columbia placed the Union Jack not on the canton, as has become a sort of tradition, but stretched it across the entire flag. Let the residents of this glorious province forgive me, but I find this distortion terrible. It makes the hair on my head stand on end, like the rays of the sun at the bottom of the flag.

Newfoundland and Labrador went even further and made their flag look like an unfinished drawing. It was created by local artist Christopher Pratt, who incorporated many symbols into the design. However, I can't help imagining how cute it would be if the flag featured Newfoundland and Labrador dogs!

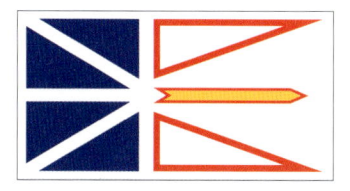

British Columbia province

Newfoundland and Labrador province

Newfoundland joined Canada only in 1949. Before then, it was a separate British dominion along with Canada, Australia, New Zealand and some others. If not for the crisis of 1932, when Newfoundland defaulted, it could have become an independent state, like the other dominions.

Bermuda

After Canada adopted the new flag, there was only one significant flag with the Union Jack on a red background left in the world – that of Bermuda. On the right of the flag is a coat of arms, which deserves a whole book dedicated to it. There we see a red English lion in a very uncharacteristic pose for heraldry; he is holding a shield in his paws, looking rather like someone holding up a billboard. The picture of a sinking ship on the shield reminds us not only about the mysterious Bermuda triangle, and the danger to ships, but also about the history of how the islands were discovered.

The ship on the coat of arms is a real ship, named *Sea Venture*. In 1609, she set sail from Plymouth in England, bound for the New World. After a month at sea, *Sea Venture* ran into a heavy storm, began to leak, and was steered into some reefs to prevent her sinking at sea. And so the ship's 150 passengers and one dog were saved, landing on what later turned out to be eastern Bermuda.

Among the survivors was the ship's captain, Christopher Newport. Having reached the shores of North America, he organised the first successful British enterprise in the cultivation of tobacco, thereby undermining the long-standing monopoly of the Spaniards. For this, Newport had to smuggle tobacco seeds from the island of Trinidad (a crime punishable by death under Spanish law). After settling in America, Newport married a local Indian girl named Pocahontas, made famous through the animated Disney film.

But let's return to Australia, where there is a movement to remove the Union Jack from their flag. Proponents of the movement cite three main arguments. First, the flag of Australia is forever confused with the flag of New Zealand at international events. Secondly, it is strange that the flag of an independent state contains the image of another country's flag. And thirdly, the flag does not include the symbols of Indigenous Australians.

The flag of Aboriginal Australian
(since 1995)

The Australian government addressed the last point in 1995, by making the Australian Aboriginal flag one of the official flags of Australia. This flag – a yellow disc on a black and red background – was drawn in 1971 by the Aboriginal Australian artist Harold Thomas. The flag is often used at official and unofficial events. For example, in 2000, the Australian sprinter Katie Freeman wrapped this flag over herself, celebrating her victory at the Olympic Games.

Many alternative Australian flags contain images of established national symbols, such as the kangaroo and the boomerang

There is an amazing story associated with the Aboriginal flag. Harold Thomas owns the copyright to it and is successfully selling the image for commercial use. For example, in 2020, a scandal broke out in Australia when the rights to the flag were bought by a clothing brand that began to make sure that no one else uses this flag in their products (the brand itself belongs to a non-Aboriginal Australian).

In Australia there is an organisation called Ausflag, which has actively advocated changing the flag since 1981. Some works are quite stylish and original, but surveys show that more than two-thirds of Australians do not want to change the flag.

New Zealand (since 1904)

There is a similar movement for a new flag in New Zealand. Many people don't like the fact that their flag is often confused with the Australian one (the New Zealand flag has fewer stars than the Australian flag, and the stars are red). They also want to display the symbols of the indigenous people on their flag instead of the Union Jack.

The New Zealanders have gone further than the Australians, in that they held two referendums on this issue in 2015 and 2016. The main instigator of the process was the prime minister, John Key. Key was just as zealous as his counterpart in Canada, and tried to involve the whole country in the discussion about a new flag.

The referendum took place in two stages. First, citizens were asked: 'If the New Zealand flag changes, which flag would you prefer?' Voters were presented with five options. A design with a fern instead of the British flag with the upper left corner painted black was the most popular choice. (In second place was the same design but with the upper left corner painted red.)

First choice in the first referendum

Second choice

Third choice

Fourth choice

Fifth choice

In the second referendum, three months later, voters were given two options: keep the current flag or change it to the design that was most popular in the first referendum. The existing flag won, by a majority of

57 to 43 per cent. Despite their defeat, supporters of changing the New Zealand flag believe that 43 per cent is a pretty good result (especially when compared with the plebiscite in Australia).

The fact that the flags of Australia and New Zealand are often confused still annoys many. After their referendum ended in no change, New Zealanders have periodically called for the Australians to change their flag, on the grounds that New Zealand was the first to adopt the design. For example, in 2018, this grudge was voiced by the acting prime minister Winston Peters.

An attempt to change the flag of Fiji also ended in failure. Among other countries with the Union Jack on their flags, Fiji stands out because it is a republic, and as such is not formally subject to the British Crown. So it is even more remarkable that the Union Jack remains on the banner of this island nation.

On this banner, in addition to the British flag, we see the cross of St George (so St George is present twice on the flag of Fiji). Another British footprint is the lion, but with a local flair – he holds a coconut in his paws, which makes him look like a cat frolicking with a ball of thread.

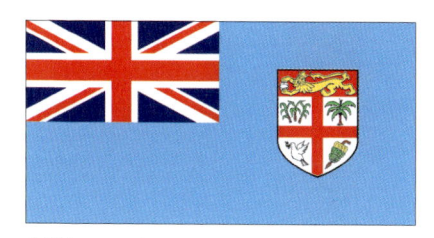

Fiji (since 1970)

Respect for Britain, and for British heraldry, has remained in Fiji since the nineteenth-century Fijian chief named Seru Cakobau, who united the islands into one single kingdom. He is considered the first and last king of Fiji. In his youth, Cakobau practised cannibalism, but then converted to Christianity and essentially delegated his power voluntarily to the British Crown.

Fiji's current prime minister Frank Bainimarama, who organised two successful military coups, suggested changing the national flag in 2013 to emphasise the country's new course and say goodbye to the colonial past. Perhaps this plan was also prompted by the suspension of

Fiji's participation in the British Commonwealth from 2006 to 2014 for violating democratic principles.

For two years, the Fijian government held a competition for the best flag design, constantly postponing the results, until it finally abandoned its plans in 2016. Again, maybe that had something to do with Fiji being re-admitted to the Commonwealth by that time.

In 2016, Fiji won its first ever Olympic medal, winning gold in rugby sevens, which greatly increased the popularity of the current flag. After that, there were no more discussions about a new flag.

Meanwhile, the oceanic state of Tuvalu got further than others in its plans to change the flag. Unlike others in the 'British vexillological problem', the Tuvalians did succeed in changing the flag, albeit for a short time.

The islands of Tuvalu became fully independent from Great Britain in 1978. The national flag consisted of a sky-blue cloth with the Union Jack on the canton and nine stars, symbolising the nine Tuvalu islands.

And here we have a contradiction — perhaps one of the most surprising in the history of naming independent states and the design of their flags. The name 'Tuvalu' actually means 'eight standing together', because there are eight inhabited islands. However, there is also one uninhabited island, represented by the ninth star on the flag.

In 1995, the Tuvalans decided to eliminate this contradiction, and remove one of the stars from the flag. The next year, the country's coat of arms was placed on the flag instead of the Union Jack. But in 1997 the Union Jack was returned, because the islanders respected the British monarchy, and the ninth star was reinstated as well, thus restoring this strange contradiction between the country's name and its flag.

The flag of Tuvalu

In 1995, one star was removed from the flag

The 1996–7 flag of Tuvalu without one of the stars and the Union Jack

Actually, the flag of Tuvalu can be considered a vexillological symbol of the problem of global warming. Scientists predict that the Tuvalu Islands may become uninhabitable due to rising sea levels in the next hundred years.

However, the name of the country has one important advantage. Thanks to it, Tuvalu received the right to domains in the .tv domain zone. Sales of these domains to television companies in some years provided up to 10 per cent of state budget revenues.

Niue

Here it is appropriate to mention the island of Niue, which is not far from Tuvalu. Although Niue formally belongs to New Zealand, it has its own domain zone and flag. Niueans seized the .nu domain zone and are also making good money selling domain names. This zone is popular in the Scandinavian countries and the Netherlands, where nu means 'now'.

The island of Niue also has the Union Jack on its flag, but stands apart in the vexillological world because of the dominant yellow colour. Placing the Union Jack on a yellow background is very unusual, though we have to remember that this flag was designed by the wife of the premier rather than by a professional heraldist. As explained in the official document, the yellow symbolises 'the bright sunshine of Niue and the warm feelings of the Niuean people towards New Zealand and her people'.

02. The Union Jack

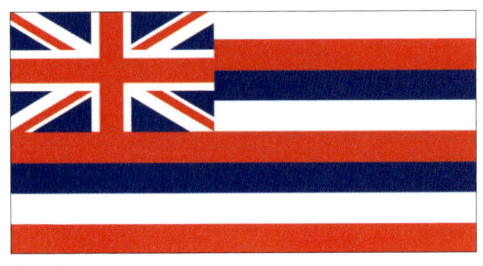

Hawaii

The Union Jack is also found on the flags of many countries and territories that previously were or still are under the rule of Great Britain. However, there is one unusual exception: the US state of Hawaii.

After James Cook discovered the Hawaiian Islands for Europeans (and later met his death there), Hawaii remained independent – until it became a US state. However, in 1845, the local king approved the official flag with the Union Jack. This was either out of respect for the British crown, or due to lack of imagination, and after Hawaii became the fiftieth state of the United States in 1959, the flag was not changed. So it can be said that former US president Barack Obama, a native of Hawaii, was born under the British flag.

The eight stripes on the Hawaiian flag symbolise the eight islands. Originally, there were nine stripes, to symbolise nine islands, which resonates beautifully with the history of the Tuvalu flag.

03. Bad
Vexillological
Omen

In the previous chapters, we learned why the flags of France and Great Britain have become so influential. Several other flags in the world have influenced other countries, including those of Ethiopia and Colombia. We will talk about them later. In this chapter we will discuss an influential banner that is not a national flag – the flag of the United Nations.

The concept of a new international organisation arose during the Second World War. Winston Churchill describes in his memoirs how, during his visit to Washington, US president Franklin Roosevelt first had the idea of calling it the United Nations. In response, Winston recalled a line from Byron: 'Here, where the sword united nations drew, Our countrymen were warring on that day!' Churchill liked the name much more than a previous suggestion – the Allied Powers.

If you are fond of vexillology, then you will certainly be interested in walking beside the UN headquarters in New York. Next to it is a row of massive flagpoles with the banners of the member states. There are 194 flags in total: the flags of the 193 member countries, placed in alphabetical order, from Afghanistan to Zimbabwe; plus the UN flag, which flies a little higher than the rest. Every weekday the flags are raised at 8 a.m. and lowered at 4 p.m., except in bad weather. At weekends, only the UN flag is raised.

The United Nations came into existence in 1945, when representatives of fifty nations met in California for a conference to create an organisation that would take care of keeping the peace on our planet – and do so better than the ineffective League of Nations. At first, there were no plans to create a UN flag. The organisers of the conference merely wanted to create an emblem that could be used on the participants' badges. But they quickly realised that this temporary emblem might become a permanent one, and set up a committee to create a design.

The UN flag

The first version of the UN emblem – with North America in the centre and some countries not visible

The creator of the design was the US architect Donal McLaughlin. During the war, he was engaged in preparing graphic materials on military operations, including geographical maps. He was also involved in designing the courtroom used for the Nuremberg trials.

Everything about the emblem and flag of the UN serves to express the main goals of this organisation: peace and prosperity. That is why blue was chosen as the main colour as the opposite of red, the war colour. This shade of blue even got its own name, 'UN blue'.

The white design on the UN flag is a map of the world in the azimuthal projection. The angle of this map (the view from the North Pole) symbolises equidistance from all countries. However, the map in the first version was different. Originally, the North American continent was in the centre and the map did not show countries closer to the South Pole (Argentina and South Africa). Now the Greenwich meridian, or longitude zero, is in the centre.

Around the map of the world on the UN flag are two olive branches, which have been a symbol of peace since the time of the ancient Greeks. Later, the olive migrated to Christian culture, where it was associated with doves. The theme of birds with an olive branch was also picked up by US heraldists, who placed an eagle on the Great Seal of the United States, which has an olive branch in its right talon and a bundle of arrows in its left.

The olive branch was already on the flags of Bolivia and Paraguay, but thanks to the UN, it was put on the flags of three more states: Cyprus, Eritrea and Turkmenistan. Unfortunately, it has not yet brought peace to either Cyprus or Eritrea. Some, in their vexillological wisdom, say that traces of the UN on the flag of a country can be a sign of a thorny path.

The modern history of Cyprus begins in 1960, when Great Britain, Greece and Turkey agreed to create a new independent state on the island.

Cyprus (since 1960)

In the same year, the official flag of Cyprus was approved. Its structure is similar to that of the United Nations: a map in the centre with two olive branches below. Everything on the flag of Cyprus is subordinated to the idea of peace – just as on the UN flag. The Cypriot constitution states that the design of the flag must be neutral, so the flag's creators were tasked with using neither blue nor red (the colours of Greece and Turkey respectively). It also prohibited the use of a Christian cross (as on the flag of Greece) or a Muslim crescent (as on the flag of Turkey).

The winning design was created by a Turkish teacher and artist, Ismet Güney. He put a silhouette of the island on the flag, in a copper-orange colour, to symbolise its rich copper deposits. (The name Cyprus is said to be derived from the Latin word for copper – *cuprum*.) Beneath the image of the island are olive branches.

Professional vexillologists disapproved of the flag of Cyprus. In heraldry, the colour orange on a white background is considered unacceptable. And the jokers nicknamed the flag of Cyprus 'fried eggs' (olive branches, apparently, being some kind of seasoning). An olive branch also appears on the coat of arms of Cyprus, held in the beak of a dove.

The fact that the first president of Cyprus, Makarios III (who was previously the archbishop of the Cypriot Autocephalous Orthodox Church), chose a design created by a Turk, inspired hopes for peace. Güney was apparently promised £20 per year for life for his design, but was never paid. He planned to sue the government, but died in 2009. It is a pity that the designer of the flag of the Australian Aborigines did not share his commercial experience with him.

03. Bad Vexillological Omen

At the time when Cyprus gained independence, almost 80 per cent of its population were Cypriot Greeks, and 20 per cent were Cypriot Turks. The Cypriot Greeks were discussing *enosis* – unification with Greece. The Cypriot Turks stressed their difficult situation after the neighbouring island of Crete became part of Greece and demanded that Cyprus be divided.

Throughout Cyprus' history, there have been clashes between the Greeks and the Turks, often ending in casualties on both sides. In 1974, the junta of the colonels, who had already seized power in Greece, added fuel to the fire: they organised a military coup to depose Makarios, and replaced him with a new president who tried to join Cyprus to Greece. In response, Turkey sent its troops to the north of the island, and established the Turkish Republic of Northern Cyprus – a state that is recognised only by Turkey.

Since then, there have been several attempts to reunite the island, most recently by the UN in 2004. The peace plan, which would have reunified Cyprus as a federation of two politically equal states, was put to a referendum. The Turkish Cypriots voted in favour of the plan, but the Greek Cypriots rejected it.

One of the new national flags proposed for the United Cyprus Republic

Among other things, the UN plan provided for the creation of a new flag for a united Cyprus, and announced a competition. More than 1,000 designs were submitted (one of which is shown here), but as the reunification plan was rejected, there was no need for a new flag.

Eritrea – one of the youngest countries in the world – was another nation whose flag received the UN olive branch. Before the Second World War, this African state was an Italian colony (there are many beautiful Italian buildings in Asmara, the capital of Eritrea). After the war, the victorious

Allies could not decide what to do with this territory. The local population demanded independence, but the Allies had to respect the Ethiopians, who were on the side of the victors and claimed Eritrea as their own. Eritrea was made a British protectorate.

Finally, in 1952 the UN made a compromise decision, and Eritrea was made an autonomous part of Ethiopia for ten years. The design of the Eritrean flag during those federation years was inspired by the UN flag: a blue background with a wreath of two olive branches around an upright olive branch – a powerful vexillological symbol of peace and prosperity. Unfortunately, it was not enough. In 1961, an armed independence movement arose. The war of independence lasted for thirty years, until finally Eritrea became an independent state in 1993.

The flag of Eritrea when it was part of a federation with Ethiopia (1952–62)

Eritrea (since 1993)

The official flag of Eritrea has three triangles and still has the wreath and the upright olive branch. The thirty leaves in the wreath symbolise the thirty years of war before independence with Ethiopia. The triangles were taken from the flag of the Eritrean People's Liberation Front, which fought during the civil war and then became the country's only political party – the People's Front for Democracy and Justice.

The red of the largest triangle is said to suggest the blood shed during the liberation war. But has a different, double symbolism to me. Firstly, it roughly resembles the shape of the country (hello Cyprus!). Secondly, the word 'Eritrea' comes from the Greek word *erythros*, which means 'red' (as the ancient Greeks called this region beside the Red Sea). But these are just my fantasies.

The Eritrean flag is based on the banner of a political organisation, which is a sad symbol. Today Eritrea is a totalitarian one-party state and one of the poorest countries in the world.

03. Bad Vexillological Omen

Turkmenistan (since 2001)

The coat of arms of Turkmenistan featuring the president's horse

The third country in our olive hit parade is Turkmenistan. The flag was adopted almost immediately after the collapse of the USSR. The first version did not have olive branches, but in 1995 these were added to commemorate the fact that the Turkmens proclaimed 'permanent neutrality'. Permanent neutrality is an interesting phenomenon in the world of international relations. Even the UN General Assembly officially voted to support the Turkmens in this status. In addition to Turkmenistan, neutral status is assigned at the international level to five other countries: Switzerland, Austria, Laos, Cambodia and Malta.

In the capital of Turkmenistan is the Monument of Neutrality. On top of this monument is a golden statue of President Niyazov, the first president of Turkmenistan. Until the monument was moved in 2010, the statue rotated during the day so that it always faced the sun.

Also on the Turkmen flag are five carpet designs, symbolising the five Turkmen regions. We see the same designs on the state coat of arms, placed around a beautiful horse. This is not just some abstract heraldic horse, but a specific horse – Niyazov's pet horse.

But let us get back to East Africa. Next to Eritrea is another state with an unhappy fate and traces of the UN on its flag: Somalia.

After the Second World War, in 1950, British Somaliland and Italian Somaliland were merged, forming the independent Somali Republic. French Somaliland remained as a neighbouring country.

As with Eritrea, the UN played an important role in the fate of this country, and the flag of Somalia, adopted in 1954, has blue as its main colour. The country of Djibouti, which gained independence in 1977, also has blue as one of the main colours on its flag, in tribute to its neighbour.

Somalia (since 1953)

Djibouti (since 1977)

Around the same time that the modern political map was being drawn up in eastern Africa, another independent state called Micronesia appeared on the opposite side of the planet, in the Pacific Ocean. As its name implies, this is a tiny country – slightly smaller than Singapore in area.

Until 1944, these islands belonged to Japan, which used them for military purposes during the Second World War. Then the UN formed the Trust Territory of the Pacific Islands (TTPI) there. The flag of the TTPI was a blue background with six stars, symbolising the territory's six geographical districts.

The flag of the Trust Territory of the Pacific Islands

Micronesia (since 1978)

Thirty years later, when the already independent Micronesia created its own flag, the TTPI flag was chosen as the basis. In doing so, the shade of blue was changed slightly to match that of the UN, and the six stars were reduced to four. One star represented the Federated States of Micronesia (of the six states of the TTPI, only three became part of Micronesia). The other three stars represented the republics of Palau and the Marshall Islands, and the Northern Mariana Islands (now under US administration).

In the previous chapter, I wrote about the luck of Tuvalu and Niue, who got the .tv and .nu domain zones. In this regard, Micronesia also got lucky – it got the .fm domain, which is in demand from radio stations.

Cambodia's development was also deeply influenced by the UN. For most of the second half of the twentieth century, the country was torn apart by civil wars. The violence came to a head in 1975 when the Khmer Rouge, led by General Pol Pot, entered the capital, Phnom Penh. Within a few days, the Khmer Rouge evacuated almost all the city's 2.5 million residents, forcing them to work in the fields as part of an agrarian revival. (Pol Pot referred to cities as 'abodes of vice' and wanted to make everyone peasants.) With the same passion, Pol Pot began to destroy the national minorities of the country, including the Vietnamese in the border areas.

Pol Pot called himself a disciple of Stalin, and in terms of the rate of destruction of his population, he turned out to be a very gifted student. During his few years in power, about two million Cambodians died (up to a third of the population). Finally, in January 1979, Vietnamese troops managed to capture Phnom Penh, and Pol Pot and the Khmer Rouge retreated into the jungle.

In 1991, a peacekeeping conference was held in Paris, after which the administration of Cambodia was temporarily transferred to the United Nations. This was the first time that the United Nations had ever had direct responsibility for the administration of an independent state. The UN transitional authority lasted for eighteen months, during which time the country's official flag was UN blue with a map of Cambodia that had the word *Kâmpŭchéa* (Cambodia) in beautiful Khmer script.

UN Transitional Authority in Cambodia (1992-3)

Cambodia (1948-70 and since 1993)

A good indication of the history of a country, peaceful or turbulent, is the history of its flag. Frequent changes to the flag are a sure sign that the fate of the country has not run smoothly. In Cambodia, the flag was changed eight times in the last century. Each time it had some variation of the image of the Angkor Wat Temple – the largest religious building in the world by area. This makes Cambodia one of only five countries with buildings on its flag, the others being Spain, Portugal, San Marino and Bolivia.

Not far from Micronesia is the youngest state in Asia: East Timor (also known as Timor-Leste). The word 'Timor' is derived from the Malay word for 'east'. So one can say the name 'East Timor' is a tautology. Not a contradiction as in the case of Tuvalu, but unusual nevertheless.

East Timor

For almost three centuries East Timor was a colony of Portugal. But after the Carnation Revolution in Portugal in 1974, troops from neighbouring Indonesia invaded the territory. During the twenty years of occupation, about 200,000 Timorese died, out of a population of one million. Eventually, the international community intervened and the country was under UN administration for three years before gaining independence in 2002.

Thus, for three years the official flag of East Timor was the UN banner. Then the new official flag was adopted – a red flag with a star on a black triangle. Red here symbolises the suffering of the East Timorese people. The symbolism of the black is interesting: it represents 'the obscurantism that needs to be overcome'. And the dynamic yellow triangle to the right of the black triangle stands for the struggle for independence.

Another feature of the symbols of East Timor is the Kalashnikov assault rifle on its coat of arms, which creates an affinity with Zimbabwe and Mozambique.

But let's get back to Europe. In the early 1990s, six countries were formed on the territory of the former Socialist Federal Republic of Yugoslavia. One was Bosnia and Herzegovina. If there is a postmodern trend in vexillology, then the flag of Bosnia and Herzegovina is a good example.

Bosnia and Herzegovina (since 1998)

An early UN blue version of the flag

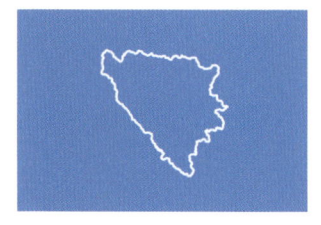

One of the alternative versions of the flag proposed by the UN

To understand why Bosnia and Herzegovina has such an unusual flag, we must remember that a military conflict raged here between 1992 and 1995, between the Bosniaks, Serbs and Croats. The war finally ended with the Dayton Agreement, after which the warring parties agreed to peace and to a single sovereign state: Bosnia and Herzegovina.

Among their new tasks was to decide on a national flag. This they were unable to do. So in 1998, the UN introduced its own version of the flag. One of the three options in the first proposal was to make a standard blue flag with a white map of the country, but then the UN team decided to offer something more special.

And so a yellow triangle appeared on the new flag of Bosnia and Herzegovina, which is very similar to the political map of the country (hello Eritrea!). Its three sides symbolise the three main ethnic groups who until recently fought so desperately among themselves – the Bosniaks, Serbs and Croats.

The triangle is not the only unusual element on this banner. Stars, representing Europe, run along the left side of the triangle. The line of stars is cut off at each end – to symbolise that there is not an exact number.

In the original version of the flag, the triangle and stars were set on UN blue, but this was changed to darker blue, which is a reference to the EU flag.

There is another flag in the world that bears the imprint of the UN: the unofficial flag of Antarctica. (There is no official flag for Antarctica, because it has no single governing body, but several designs have been created to represent it.) As you might guess, it is a white map of this continent on a background of UN blue. And you can use this picture for the Rorschach test, to see what image you perceive in the design. (Personally, I see a furry rhinoceros.)

Interestingly, the author of this flag is Graham Bartram, the chief vexillologist of the UK Flag Institute, who also played a part in creating the flag of Bosnia and Herzegovina. It turns out that vexillologists do have such a thing as their own style.

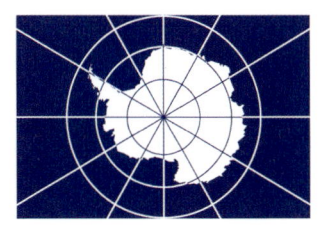

The flag of Antarctica, as proposed by the Antarctic Treaty

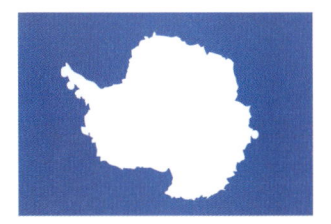

Graham Bartram's proposal for the flag of Antarctica

The flag of Antarctica proposed by the Antarctic Treaty Organisation, adopted in 2002, has the map of Antarctica, but on a darker background and with the main lines of latitude and longitude. But it is Graham Bartram's design that you will see on the 'flag for Antarctica' emoji.

04. When Flags
are Crossed

The cross on the flag is as old as the concept of a national flag itself. The flag of Denmark (*Dannebrog* in Danish) is the oldest continuously used national flag in the world, and has a white Scandinavian cross on a red background.

More than a thousand years ago, the Danish king Harald 'Bluetooth' Gormsson made Christianity the official religion of Denmark. (Bluetooth technology was named after this king because its creators said it would unite the gadgets as Harald had united Denmark and Norway.) After that, the wars waged by Denmark were considered not barbarian quarrels but holy deeds in the name of the Christian faith.

In 1219, the Danes were fighting against Estonians near Tallinn. The Danes were near to defeat but then, so the story goes, a red banner with a white cross suddenly fell from the sky. After that, the inspired Danes won, and the white cross on a red background was adopted as the royal banner.

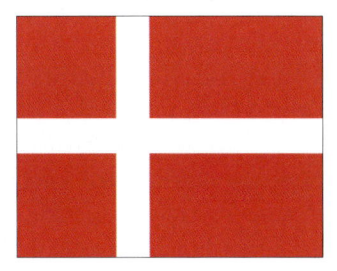

The flag of Denmark with the traditional Scandinavian cross shifted to the left

4. When Flags are Crossed

According to a more earthly version, the cross on the Danish flag has the same roots as the St George Cross of England, from the times of Richard the Lionheart and the Third Crusade.

If you like symmetry, you might not appreciate the shift of the Scandinavian cross to the left. To justify the design, I will say that initially the Danish flag was not strictly rectangular. It was often flown on ships in the form of a pentagon with two tails (the dovetail) and therefore looked symmetrical.

Dannebrog is remarkable not only because it is the oldest national flag in the world, but also because it has never officially changed in its long history. No wonder Danish companies often use it on their product packaging.

Denmark is an unusual country in many ways. It consists of more than 440 islands; one of them, Greenland, is the largest island in the world. You can tease your friends by asking them which European country is the largest in terms of area. They probably won't think of Denmark (which is the correct answer).

The territory of Denmark could be larger still if it had retained Schleswig-Holstein – the land that has been part of Germany since 1948. The history of this territory is one of constant skirmishes between the Danes and Germans. At the beginning of the twentieth century, the Germans forbade the Schleswig-Holstein Danes from flying the Danish flag. In response, Danish farmers bred a special breed of pigs, nicknamed the Danish Protest pig. These pigs were red with large white stripes on their backs and did indeed resemble the Danish flag.

Denmark has also a rather atypical flag law which is one of the special vexillological features of the country. Countries usually forbid any desecration of their national flag. But the Danish penal code, on the contrary, prohibits burning the flags of any country in the world, except for the flag of Denmark itself. There's a similar law in Japan.

At this point, you might ask why anyone would even think of burning the flag of this peaceful northern European country. But in 2006, the Danish flag became one of the most burned flags in the world, possibly even more than the US flag. At that time, radical Muslims around the world were protesting against the fact that a Danish newspaper had published a caricature of the Prophet Muhammad on its pages.

Sweden

The flag of neighbouring Sweden has a similar origin to Denmark's. According to legend, in the twelfth century, the Swedes defeated the Finns in a battle. At first the Swedes were losing, but after the Swedish king saw a solar cross in the blue sky, the course of the battle changed.

Well, at least this version sounds a little more plausible than the Danish one. It's quite common to see images in the clouds.

Like the *Dannebrog*, the flag of Sweden has hardly changed during its history. The only exception was in the nineteenth century, when Sweden was in alliance with Norway for almost a century. As a result, the flags of these states became a mesh of crosses, similar to the British one. Then a vexillological compromise was reached by putting the sign of the union in the upper left corner – the canton. This was not popular with the Swedes, who called it *Sillsallaten*, which is a traditional Swedish dish made from herring, red beets and apples.

After the collapse of the union, the Swedes regained the good old flag, but changed the dark blue colour to a lighter shade.

Union sign of Sweden and Norway. Aka *Sillsallaten* (herring salad)

The Swedish flag with the union sign (1844–1905)

4. When Flags are Crossed

Finland (since 1918)

Alternative red flag of Finland that could have become the national flag

Next to Sweden is another happy northern European state: Finland. The border between these two countries is considered one of the strangest and most confusing in the world. The Finns once mistakenly built a lighthouse on the Swedish side of the border on a tiny uninhabited island, after which the two countries quickly had to agree to redraw their boundaries.

Unlike their neighbours, the Finns cannot boast of a long history of either an independent state or their own flag. When the country gained independence from Russia in 1917, a competition was held for the design of the national flag. Public discussions focused around two main options: a blue cross on a white background, and a yellow lion on a red background (judging by its appearance, the lion on the flag was clearly out of his mind).

A third option was a white cross on a blue background, but that was considered too similar to the Greek flag of the time, so was discounted.

In the end, the blue cross was chosen. The country had just survived civil clashes between the White Guard (supporters of the bourgeois parties) and the Red Guard (socialists), after which the colour red fell out of favour with the public. (Remember how the Australians abandoned the red flag for a similar reason?)

It is worth remembering that even though the Scandinavian cross is flaunted on the flag of Finland, the Finns themselves are not considered Scandinavians.

A couple of years after the adoption of the new flag, the Finns decided to change the colour of the flag from light blue to dark blue – at the same time as the Swedes did exactly the opposite with their flag.

Another banner with a Scandinavian cross is the flag of Norway. During its history, Norway was in an alliance with Denmark, then with Sweden, which all had an effect on the country's banner.

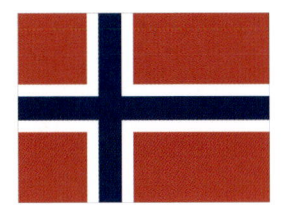

Norway (since 1821)

'The Swiss knife of all flags'

The official flag was approved in 1821. Its author was a member of the Norwegian parliament, Fredrik Meltzer. I remember a guide telling me, during a tour of Oslo, that Meltzer's son painted a blue cross on the Danish flag, and that gave his father the idea. Unfortunately, the story appears to be just that – a story.

But what is not fiction is the fact that Meltzer's choice was significantly influenced (surprise, surprise!) by the French tricolor.

The German geographer Simon Küstenmacher once called the Norwegian flag 'the Swiss knife of all flags' on Twitter. He noted that it is possible to discern the flags of six more countries in it: Indonesia, Poland, Finland, Netherlands, Thailand – and the flag of France, which inspired Meltzer. I would add that Monaco can also be included in the mix of flags represented.

Almost as many countries can be distinguished on the flag of Iceland. In 1944, this small but proud country gained independence, after a referendum in which 98 per cent of the population voted to abolish the union with Denmark. That same year, the national flag was adopted. The red colour on the Icelandic flag does not symbolise blood, as is often the case in heraldry, but volcanic lava, because volcanoes are prominent in the history of the country. For instance, in 2010, the eruption of a volcano with an unpronounceable name (Eyjafjallajökull) stopped air traffic in Europe for about a week. However, this is a trifle compared with a volcanic eruption at the end of the eighteenth century, which lasted two years and led to global cooling. A consequence of that cooling was total crop failure in Europe, and a result of that, it is said, was the French Revolution.

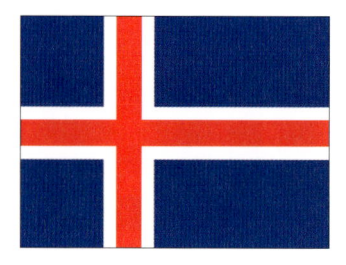

The flag of Iceland: bird's eye view of the picturesque landscapes of Iceland

The flag of Switzerland: inspiration for the Red Cross logo

The flag of Switzerland is similar to the Danish flag. Unlike the Danish and other Scandinavians, the Swiss have a perfectly symmetrical banner. The Swiss flag is one of the two square national flags of the world, the other being the flag of Vatican City. (The flag of Belgium, with proportions of 13:15, is quite close to joining this club.)

I still remember the bewildered face of the Swiss president, who in 2014 came on an official visit to my native Kyiv, and was greeted with a large flag … of Denmark.

The roots of the logo of the international organisation of the Red Cross, which we see on hospitals and pharmacies around the world, also lie in the flag of Switzerland. The Red Cross was created in Geneva in 1864, and is simply the reverse of the colours of the Swiss flag.

As grateful as we are to the Swiss for the Red Cross, the choice of a cross for the logo of an international humanitarian organisation was not such a good idea – even though no religious meaning was intended. Non-Christian countries around the world began to modify this emblem in their own way. In 1876–8 during the Russo-Turkish war, the field doctors of the Ottoman Empire used a red crescent as their sign. Today, the Red Crescent is used in thirty-three Muslim countries, and Israel has the Red Star of David.

In 2006, an attempt was made to replace the Red Cross with something more neutral. An emblem called the red crystal – a red square on its edge on a white background – was proposed as a compromise. However, as is often the case when international unanimity is needed, the idea was voted down.

The Red Cross logo

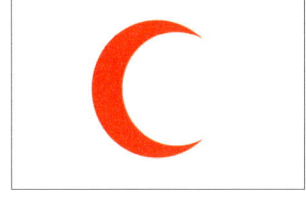

The Red Crescent adopted in thirty-three countries

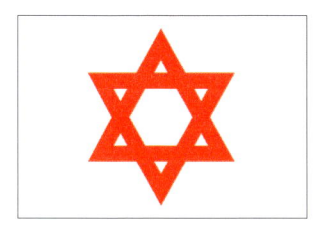

The Red Star of David adopted in Israel

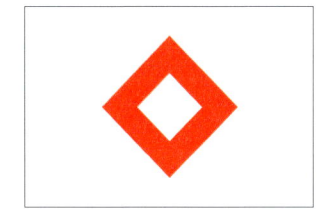

The Red Crystal, the failed religiously neutral version of the International Humanitarian Movement logo

The Red Cross logo has another interesting story behind it. In 1862 (two years before the First Geneva Convention), a new state was created on the opposite side of the planet – the miniature monarchy of Tonga. Like many other lands in the Pacific region, these islands were discovered by Captain Cook, after which British missionaries quickly converted the local population to the Christian faith. In fact, Christianity is so influential in Tonga that local laws still prohibit any work on Sundays.

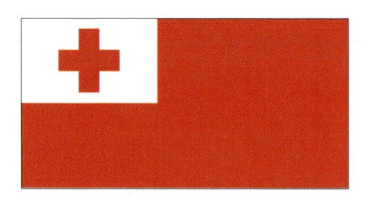

Tonga (since 1866)

Tonga (1862–6)

In 1862, the leadership of Tonga adopted a red cross on a white background as its flag. A few years later, they discovered that the same sign had become the emblem of the international organisation the Red Cross. The League of Nations did not yet exist, there was no one to complain to, so the Tongan flag had to be changed.

An ancient Transcaucasian state, Georgia, also has a red cross on its flag. In fact there are five crosses: one large and four small ones. This heraldic pattern is called the Jerusalem cross. It was first seen on the banner of the Kingdom of Jerusalem, which was created about 1,000 years ago as a result of the First Crusade. The five crosses symbolise the five wounds of Christ.

Although the design has been around for almost 500 years, the current Georgian flag is comparatively young. In 2003, the Rose Revolution took place in Georgia under the leadership of Mikheil Saakashvili. The flag with the Jerusalem cross became the main symbol of the protests and was adopted when Saakashvili became president.

Georgia (since 2004)

There is another country in the world that could have a white cross on a red background on its flag: Malta. The flag, which looks something between the flags of Switzerland and Denmark, was the official banner of the Order of Malta, which was based in Malta until the beginning of the nineteenth century.

The Order of Malta is unusual. Although it has no land, it regards itself almost as a sovereign entity. It has official observer status at the UN and the Council of Europe, prints its own currency and stamps, issues passports, and has ambassadors in most countries. Confusingly, its capital is no longer in Malta but in Rome.

The Order of Malta was formed in the eleventh century in Jerusalem. At first, members of the order provided accommodation and hospitals for poor pilgrims in the Holy Land. It was because of this that the order became known as the Knights Hospitaller. The fact that the flag of the 'hospital' order is similar to the flag of Switzerland, from which the Red Cross originated, is a beautiful vexillological coincidence.

After the Muslims captured Palestine, the Hospitallers moved to the Greek island of Rhodes. Then in 1522 the Ottoman Empire under the rule of Suleiman the Magnificent captured Rhodes, and the order eventually found a base in Malta, changing its name to the Order of Malta. The knights were expelled from Malta by Napoleon in 1799.

Malta played an important role in the Napoleonic Wars. The fact is that the Order of Malta had one very influential member: the Russian tsar, Paul I. The tsar was so proud of his membership of the order (which was unusual, because the order was Catholic) that he added the Maltese cross to the Russian coat of arms. When Napoleon was destroying the European monarchies, the Russian Empire tried not to get involved, but when Napoleon captured Malta, Russia did enter the war, which ultimately led to Napoleon's defeat.

At one time, Malta was even considered one of the Russian provinces. Who knows, if Tsar Paul had not been killed during a palace coup, history could have turned out differently, and Malta would have remained part of Russia. But in reality, after the overthrow of Napoleon, the island came under the protectorate of Great Britain.

During the Second World War, Malta again played a major role in the Allied victory, this time over Hitler. Winston Churchill called the island an 'unsinkable aircraft carrier', and King George VI awarded the George Cross to the protectorate.

It was this cross that became part of the modern flag of Malta, after it gained independence in 1964. If you look closely, you can distinguish the words 'For Gallantry' on it, as well as the figure of our old friend St George, slaying a dragon with his sword. Apart from Malta, only the Central American state of Belize has a human figure on its flag.

Sovereign Military Order of Malta

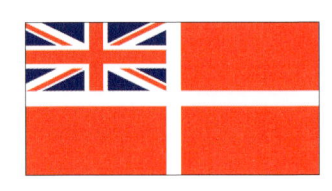

Crown Colony of Malta (nineteenth century)

Crown Colony of Malta (1875–98)

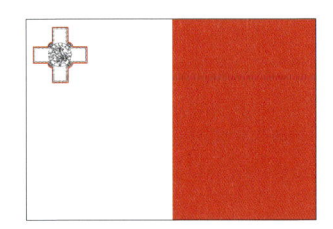

Malta (since 1964)

Having mentioned Rhodes, it's time to talk about Greece. From the fifteenth century to the nineteenth, the Greek territories were under the rule of the Ottoman Empire, until the independent Kingdom of Greece was formed as a result of the revolution against the Turks in 1830.

The modern state has had two official flags. One is a white cross on a blue background (the one that indirectly influenced the flag of Finland). The second – the one we know today – has a cross on the canton and nine stripes of alternating blue and white.

As strange as it seems, there is no official reason for the nine bands. According to one explanation, it's because there are nine syllables in the phrase 'Freedom or death' in Greek – or nine letters in the Greek word for freedom. Another explanation is that there were nine muses (goddesses) in ancient Greek mythology.

It is interesting to look at the evolution of the blue colour on the Greek flag, which reflects the history of the country's independence.

The first king of independent Greece was the Bavarian Prince Otto.

The flag's light blue hue comes from the heraldry of Bavaria. You might be familiar with the Bavarian flag because of the BMW logo. Some say that the logo represents a propeller, referring to the roots of BMW in making aircraft engines. In fact, the logo has the state colours of the flag of Bavaria.

And so there is a historical connection between BMW and the flag of Greece. Who would have thought!

The flag of Greece. Adopted in 1822; the only official one since 1978.

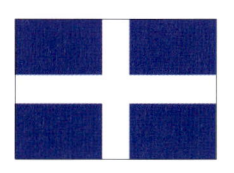

The second official flag of Greece from 1822 to 1969 and from 1975 to 1978. The Finns could have accepted the same flag.

Flag adopted by the Greek junta (1970–5)

The maritime ensign of Greece with Bavarian pattern and crown on cross (1833–58)

The flag of the Free State of Bavaria

BMW logo based on the flag of Bavaria

Another interesting evolution of the blue shade of the Greek flag was caused by a change in politics. After the Second World War, an explosive cocktail of monarchy and left and right political forces emerged in Athens. In the end, in 1967 a military coup brought the colonels (aka the Greek junta) to power. The colonels ruled the country as dictators, with a great deal of repression and many arrests. But, because of their reforms, the Greek economy began to grow. During their time in power, the colonels adopted a new flag in 1970 with a tinge of blue that was so dark it was almost black.

In 1973, Greece was hit by a global economic crisis, provoked by Saudi Arabia, which sharply reduced oil sales in order to weaken Israel's allies. The United States was forced to cut off its aid to the Greeks, and

4. When Flags are Crossed

the economic situation in the country began to worsen. To distract the population from its economic woes, the junta instigated a military coup in Cyprus, aiming to unify the island with Greece. However, as we saw in the previous chapter, they underestimated Turkey's reaction. Turkey's invasion of Cyprus led to the collapse of the colonels in Greece, and the general who temporarily seized power, Constantine Karamanlis, ensured that democratic elections were held.

The blue colour and the cross are also present on the flag of one of the tiniest and oldest states in the world: San Marino. This country, which is one of three enclave states along with Vatican City and Lesotho, was founded at the beginning of the fourth century by a Christian named Marino, who was persecuted for his faith.

San Marino (since 1862)

The coat of arms is in the centre of the blue and white bicolour of San Marino. There are three towers in the centre of the coat of arms, which today are the main sights and symbols of the country. Above the coat of arms is a crown with a cross – a symbol of independence. The fact that there is a crown on the country's flag and on the coat of arms is somewhat paradoxical, because San Marino is considered the oldest republic in the world.

Well, the country with the largest number of crosses on the flag is, naturally, Vatican City.

Vatican City

In antiquity, the Roman emperor Caligula built a hippodrome for his mother Agrippina on the Vatican Hill, where St Peter was later crucified. It was to Peter that Christ said, according to the Bible: 'And I will give you the keys of the kingdom of heaven' (Matthew 16:19). And it is these keys – in gold and silver – that are depicted on the flag of Vatican City.

Above the keys is a triple crown: the papal tiara. In fact, the tiara was initially a rather modest headdress. Until the eighth century, the popes wore 'phrygian caps'. Then the jewellers took up these caps – and away we go! First a valuable ruby appeared on it, and, step by step, this modest cap evolved into a jagged crown.

An important change in the tiara occurred under Pope Boniface VIII. Boniface was unlucky enough to become pope in a crucial era for Europe, when feudal fragmentation was a thing of the past, and European monarchs were gathering more and more power in their hands. Contesting the French king Philip IV, the Pope issued a bull in which he outlined his concept of the supremacy of the throne over any secular power. To emphasise this, Boniface added a second layer to the tiara. However, this did not save him. In the end, the French king managed to arrest the Pope, accusing him of usurpation and sodomy, and, as an added extra, started a rumour that he kept a little devil as a pet.

Forty years later, another pope named Benedict XII added a third level to the papal tiara. The exact motives are lost in history, but, of course, the number three is an important concept in Christianity.

The tradition of wearing the papal tiara during the coronation was interrupted in 1978, when the Italian John Paul I entered the Holy See. He professed a modesty and simplicity not usually seen in the Vatican. John Paul's reign was one of the shortest papacies, as he died after only a month in post. Of course, this gave rise to theories that he was poisoned by the treacherous inhabitants of the Vatican who were afraid of his radical reforms.

None of the popes since John Paul I has worn the tiara. In 2005, for the first time, Benedict XVI placed a more modest mitre on the personal coat of arms of the pope. Francis, who became the next pope, followed his example. Who knows, maybe someday the tiara will disappear not only from personal papal coats of arms, but also from the flag of Vatican City.

Interestingly, the colours of the flag could have been yellow and red, which were historically used by the guards of the Vatican, but in 1808 Pope Pius VII changed the red colour to white to distinguish his troops from those Italian troops that were part of Napoleon's army. And thus Napoleon's influence has even spread to the flag of Vatican City.

As part of the Italian reunification (Risorgimento) movement in the nineteenth century, the Papal States were annexed to Italy. For half a century, the Holy See ruled this domain from the Vatican, until in 1929 the Italian leader Benito Mussolini signed the Lateran Treaty with Pope Pius XI, declaring Vatican City as an independent state.

In our time, an amazing incident occurred with the Vatican flag. In 2023, flag enthusiasts suddenly noticed that an incorrect version of it had spread worldwide! It turned out that for many years, Wikipedia had been displaying the flag of the Vatican City with a red disk inside the tiara (instead of white, which is correct). From there, the mistake spread across the internet, and even to Google and Facebook emoji libraries.

Another country with many Christian symbols on its flag is the Dominican Republic. This country is on the same island as Haiti. Actually, the Dominican Republic was originally part of Haiti. And its flag is an interesting evolution of the flag of Haiti, which itself evolved from the French tricolor.

The flag of Haiti (1820–1949) was obtained by eliminating the white stripe from the French tricolor

The flag of the secret society whose activities led to the independence of the Dominican Republic

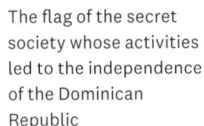

The flag of the Dominican Republic (1844-9) on which the cross of the flag on the left is enlarged

Dominican Republic (since 1844)

Dominica (since 1990)

Comparing the flags (and fates in general) of Haiti and the Dominican Republic is as interesting as comparing the fates of classmates at a reunion. Being on the same island, these two countries started with equal opportunities. Just like Haiti, the Dominican Republic was ruled by a brutal dictator (Rafael Trujillo) for much of the last century. His family's income reached 40 per cent of the country's national income; his lust and love for women, who were delivered to him daily, earned him the nickname *El chivo* ('goat'). However, the Dominican Republic is now ten times richer than Haiti in terms of GDP per capita.

In the same Caribbean Sea, not far from the Dominican Republic, is the country of Dominica. These two names are always confused, but their etymology is quite different. The Dominican Republic was named after the founder of the Dominican Order (whose members are sometimes also referred to as the 'Dogs of the Lord' – a Latin pun on *Domini canes*). And Dominica got its name from the Latin word *dominica* (Sunday), because Christopher Columbus discovered the island on a Sunday.

The flag of Dominica also has a cross, which is unique in that it has purple on it (another country with purple on its flag is Nicaragua). Purple is the colour of the plumage of the sisserou, a parrot of which the Dominicans are so proud that they placed it on both the flag and the coat of arms. In 2019, it was estimated that there were only about fifty mature birds of this species in the world.

Another European country with a cross on its flag is Portugal. Unlike the flags of other countries, the cross is not in such an obvious form, but the Portuguese flag could have lost it altogether. But first things first.

The flag of Afonso I (1143)

Portugal (1830–1911)

Portugal (since 1911)

4. When Flags are Crossed

The flag of Portugal can be studied like an onion, layer by layer. And behind each layer is an interesting story. The central place on the flag is occupied by the coat of arms, in the centre of which is the Portuguese shield, which, in turn, consists of five shields, each of which has five solid circles (known in heraldry as bezants). As on the Georgian flag, the number five symbolises the five wounds of Christ. According to legend, the Portuguese shield became the coat of arms of the Portuguese king Afonso I in the twelfth century, after Christ appeared to him on the eve of an important battle.

Divine manifestations before military operations have had a great deal of influence on world heraldry.

Around the Portuguese shield are seven golden castles on a red background. These elements came to Portugal, most likely from Castile. The same castle is on the flag of Spain.

Finally, the outer part of the coat of arms is occupied by an armillary sphere, an astronomical instrument used by sailors to determine the coordinates of celestial bodies. The armillary sphere appeared on the coat of arms after the Portuguese royal family fled from Napoleon in 1807 and moved to Brazil. After Brazil became independent, it kept the armillary sphere in its heraldry.

So that is the explanation of the Portuguese coat of arms. We now look at the red and green colours of the flag, where the explanation is not as straightforward.

Until the beginning of the twentieth century, the main colours of the Portuguese flag were white and blue. These two colours were strongly associated with the Portuguese monarchy; the white also symbolised the Virgin Mary and Christianity in general.

The monarchy in Portugal lasted until the twentieth century. In 1908, Republican terrorists assassinated King Carlos I and his eldest son in Lisbon. So the Portuguese throne went instead to Carlos' second son, who was more interested in art than in politics. Eighteen months later, the young king was deposed and Portugal was proclaimed a republic.

These events of course are reflected in the Portuguese flag. First, the Republicans removed the royal crown from the flag, but this did not seem enough and they decided to replace the blue and white colours with green and red, which were used in their party symbols. It is surprising that the revolutionaries did not remove all Christian symbols from their flag, because they left the shields in the form of a cross.

Over the next sixteen years after the overthrow of the king, there were seventeen attempts at a military coup in Portugal, and the government changed forty-four times. In 1926, the next military coup took place, and Antonio de Salazar, a professor at the Catholic University, became minister of finance in the Portuguese government. As a young man, Salazar planned to become a Catholic priest, but instead he became the dictator of his country for thirty-six years.

The Portuguese are ambivalent about Salazar. He was a dictator with fascist tendencies, but he did achieve impressive economic growth in a country that was one of the most backward economies in Europe.

In 1968, the elderly Salazar swayed in his chair, fell out of it and hit his head hard. After that, he lived for another two years, but he no longer ruled the country, although he did not realise this. He continued to hold pointless cabinet meetings in his hospital room. His friends even printed a single copy of the government newspaper for him, removing any news that might upset him. And a few years later, the Carnation Revolution took place in Portugal, which led to a parade of independence for many Portuguese colonies.

Despite the turbulent history of Portugal in the twentieth century, its flag has not changed since 1911. It has the same symbols of Christianity as well as revolutionary republican colours.

Portugal, as we have seen, had lost its main colony, Brazil, in 1822.

When the Portuguese royal family was fleeing from Napoleon to Latin America, it led to the unique situation of the capital of a European country being located outside Europe – in Brazil.

Empire of Brazil (1853–89)

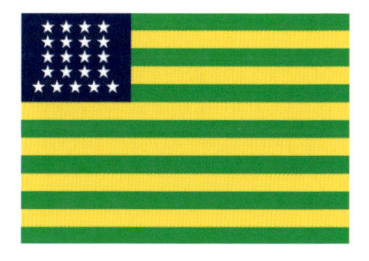

Provisional flag of the Republic of the United States of Brazil (1889)

4. When Flags are Crossed

First flag of the Federative Republic of Brazil, with 21 stars (1889–1960). A star has been added for every new state

After Napoleon was defeated, the Portuguese king Juan returned from exile in Brazil to Portugal and left his son Pedro in Rio de Janeiro as the viceroy. But a year later, Pedro proclaimed the independence of Brazil from Portugal and was crowned as the first Brazilian king, Pedro I.

Pedro I was an energetic and versatile ruler. He was fond of music, and even wrote two hymns – for Brazil and Portugal. He was also involved in horse training, blacksmithing and wood carving and spoke many languages.

One of his first decrees concerned the new national flag. It featured the coat of arms in the middle of a yellow diamond on a green background. Branches of coffee and tobacco are also depicted on the coat of arms. They were the main Brazilian export items of that period (and a good illustration of bad office habits). The central place is occupied by the same armillary sphere as on the flag of Portugal, as a symbol of the common roots of the two countries.

After the death of the Portuguese king Juan, the Portuguese throne passed to his son Pedro I, who was already the king of Brazil. So Portugal and Brazil had a chance to reunite, forming a single country. Pedro, however, understood that Brazil did not want to lose its independence, and so abdicated the Portuguese throne in favour of his seven-year-old daughter Maria. Moreover, he tried to arrange a marriage between his daughter and his brother Miguel (that is, between an uncle and a niece). Uncle Miguel at first pretended to agree with the plan, but then seized power and proclaimed himself the sole king of Portugal. So now you know where the creators of Brazilian TV shows get their stories.

Before his death, Pedro requested that his body be buried in Brazil, but that his heart be preserved in Portugal. In 2022, Brazil celebrated its 200th anniversary, and in honour of this, Portugal temporarily sent Pedro's heart, preserved in formaldehyde, to Brazil. The son of Pedro I, also called Pedro, became the second and last emperor of Brazil. In 1889 the country became a republic. The causes of this event can be seen on the Brazilian flag of the time: the coffee and tobacco.

Brazil at that time was one of the last large countries that still had slavery. South America was one of the corners of the triangular trade, whereby European merchant ships travelled between the three peaks of the 'golden triangle'. First they sailed to Africa, where they bought slaves; then they sailed to Latin America, where they sold these slaves and bought coffee, tobacco and other goods; and then they returned to Europe with these goods.

Traditionally, British merchants made the most money on this scheme, but then the British government banned its citizens from participating in the slave trade. After that, Britain began to put pressure on Brazil and other nations to abolish slavery in their own countries (not only out of humanitarianism, but also so that the slave owners would not have a competitive advantage over the British colonies). In the end, in 1889, Brazil adopted the 'Golden Law', which had only two points:
1. From this date, slavery is declared abolished in Brazil.
2. Any dispositions to the contrary are revoked.

This law allowed Brazil to turn over the shameful page of its history, but it caused dissatisfaction among large Brazilian landowners, and the king was removed from power. Brazil became a republic, and the question of choosing a national flag arose once again.

For the first four days, the Brazilian Republic used a flag inspired by the US flag. However, the provisional president vetoed this design because of that similarity. Instead, he suggested that the flag of the new republic should resemble the old imperial flag, to show continuity.

The flag of the new republic had the same yellow rhombus as the imperial flag, also on a green background. In the centre was a blue disc with a starry sky and a curved white band with the inscription *Ordem e Progresso* (Order and Progress) – the national motto of Brazil, taken from the writings of the French philosopher Auguste Comte.

There are many interesting symbols embedded in the starry sky, so let's have a look in more detail.

The number of stars on the flag corresponds to the number of Brazilian states. When the flag was first adopted, it had twenty-one stars. Then the number of stars gradually increased with the increase in the number of states. However, because the adoption of a new flag required the consent of Parliament, the flag could be out of sync with the number of states for years, or even a decade. Today, the Brazilian flag has twenty-seven stars.

The location of the stars on the flag corresponds to the position of the stars in the Brazilian sky on 15 November 1889: Independence Day. In 1992 Brazilian astronomers changed the location of the stars on the flag slightly, to match more accurately the position of the stars in the sky on that day.

The stars on the flag are of different sizes – the larger the state, the brighter the corresponding star. Let me remind you that Australia also intended to have stars of varying degrees of brightness on its flag, according to the size of each state, but then decided not to add this complication. The Brazilian heraldry experts were less timid.

Another element that the flags of Brazil and Australia have in common is the constellation of the Southern Cross. It can be seen on the Brazilian flag if you look closely.

Australia

The constellation of the Southern Cross on the flag of Brazil

The only thing that might confuse the observer is that on the Brazilian flag this constellation is depicted with a small star on the left, and not on the right. This is not a mistake: the stars on the flags of Australia and other countries are shown as if they were looked at from below, from the ground. In contrast, the stars on the Brazilian flag are located as if the observer was located infinitely far away in space – that is, looking at the constellation from the other side.

To conclude the star theme, I would like to draw your attention to the fact that there is just one star on the flag that is above the white curved band. This star symbolises the state of Pará, the only Brazilian state in the northern hemisphere. In Pará, there is a town called Fordlândia, founded by Henry Ford when he unsuccessfully tried to create his own rubber production facility for his car tyres.

Here's another geographical puzzle for you. Which country has the longest border with France? The correct answer is Brazil, bordering French Guiana.

05. The Bird
Heritage of the
Romans

According to legend, Mars, the Roman god of war, once raped a temple priestess named Rhea Silvia, who then gave birth to twin boys, called Romulus and Remus. Rhea was a Vestal Virgin, sworn to celibacy: she was sentenced to death after the birth, and a servant was ordered to abandon the babies by the side of a river so that they would die from exposure. Instead, he set them adrift in a basket down the river.

Fortunately, the river god Tiberius took pity on them all. He married Rhea and his waters carried the boys down the river, handing them over to a she-wolf who nursed them. They were then adopted by a shepherd, who brought them up. Then, when the brothers were young adults, they decided to found a city near the place where the she-wolf had found them. In quarrelling over which hill to build on, Romulus killed Remus. He founded the city on his own, and named it after himself: Rome.

Vexillum (standard) of the ancient Roman army

Double-headed eagle of Byzantium

The eagle of the Holy Roman Empire

5. The Bird Heritage of the Romans

The flag of the Austrian Empire

The flag of Austria-Hungary

The coat of arms of Austria-Hungary

Austria (since 1945)

The coat of arms of Austria – with the socialist sickle and hammer in the eagle's talons

It is customary to use this legend as an introduction to the history of ancient Rome – a civilisation that perhaps has had the greatest influence on our civilisation. Of course, it has also influenced our heraldry. The eagle – one of the most frequent inhabitants of flags and coats of arms – has its roots in ancient Rome.

The geese, who are known to have saved Rome from the barbarians, must feel a little hurt.

In general, neither flags nor coats of arms in their modern sense existed in the Roman Empire. But they still had something conventionally heraldic – the standards of the military legions. Originally, each Roman legion carried five standards, with emblems of a wolf, a bull, a horse and a boar, as well as the eagle. But later, a military commander named Gaius Marius made the eagle the supreme symbol, because it was associated with the god Jupiter, and abolished the others.

So the Roman eagle is a pagan symbol. It is all the more interesting that Christian countries adopted it into their heraldry. First, it alighted on the banners of the fragments of ancient Rome, and from there it travelled around the world. Sometimes an interesting mutation occurred: the eagle grew an additional head, and occasionally more than one. The official standard of the president of Turkmenistan, for example, has an eagle with five heads.

The eagle is an important symbol in Christian religion. The Old Testament describes the vision of one of the prophets, in which a single figure derived from four creatures appears – a human, a lion, a bull and an eagle. Today in Christianity, these four creatures are associated with the four evangelists (the authors of the four gospels). The eagle is the symbol of John the Evangelist. Thus, Christian countries that had an eagle on their flags and coats of arms could relate these to the Holy Scriptures, and not to some ancient Roman paganism.

In the fourth century, the Roman emperor Constantine split the empire into two. The western part, centred in Rome, bore the onslaught of the barbarians and lasted for a relatively short time. The eastern part, known as Byzantium, and centred in Constantinople, existed for more than a thousand years.

The Byzantines made Constantinople their capital, but called themselves Romans (although Rome itself was not part of the Byzantine Empire for most of its history). So it is not surprising that they used an eagle in their symbolism. This eagle had two heads looking in different directions, symbolising the influence of Byzantium in both Europe and Asia.

After the Ottoman Sultan Mehmed II conquered Constantinople in 1453, many members of the Byzantine church took refuge in Russia, calling Moscow the 'Third Rome' (Constantinople being the second Rome), and a double-headed Byzantine eagle solemnly flew into the coat of arms of the Russian Empire.

Interestingly, today the double-headed eagle can be found in Kyiv. Its image flies on one of the main architectural monuments of the Ukrainian capital – St Sophia Cathedral. Ever since Russia launched a war against Ukraine in 2014, puzzled posts periodically appear on the Ukrainian internet asking what this 'two-headed chicken' (as Ukrainians affectionately call the Russian eagle) is doing there. Historians and heraldists patiently explain that this eagle is Byzantine, not Russian, and St Sophia Cathedral was built in Kyiv in the eleventh century, when Moscow did not even exist, let alone the Russian coat of arms.

The eagle occupies an honourable place in the heraldry of Western Europe. It also flew here from the Roman Empire, alighting along the way on the emblems of the German kingdom and the Holy Roman Empire.

The German kingdom was formed at the beginning of the tenth century as a result of the unification of several German duchies, and Henry I the Fowler became its first king. According to legend, he got this epithet because when the messengers brought him the news that he had become king, he was mending his birding nets. Which is a nice link with the flag and coat of arms of the kingdom - a black eagle on a yellow background.

Of course, when Henry approved the flag and coat of arms of his kingdom, he did not know about his nickname.

Half a century later, the German kingdom became the Holy Roman Empire under the leadership of Henry's son Otto the Great. In 960, Pope John XII turned to Otto with a request to help him in the political struggle and send troops to Rome. Otto responded and within two years had conquered most of Italy. For this, the pope crowned him as emperor. So the German kingdom turned into the Holy Roman Empire, and the eagle on its flag grew a second head just like the Byzantine one.

A year later, Otto overthrew John XII from the papal throne, putting an end to the period that historians call 'pornocracy' or 'the rule of prostitutes' when the popes were mired in lust and debauchery.

The Holy Roman Empire, like Byzantium, lasted almost a thousand years - although, at the end of its existence, 'The Holy Roman Empire was neither holy, nor Roman, nor an empire,' as Voltaire wrote. Formally, it ceased to exist in 1806, when its troops were defeated by Napoleon. Emperor Franz II was forced to announce the dissolution of the empire (and at the same time gave his beloved daughter in marriage to this Corsican monster).

So, instead of the Holy Roman Empire, the Austrian Empire appeared on the map of Europe. The same double-headed eagle became the Austrian coat of arms, but the flag became simpler: a black and yellow bicolour. The colours were taken from the previous flag with a black eagle on a yellow background.

However, neither the Austrian Empire nor its flag lasted for long. Soon Vienna was forced to make concessions to Hungary, where the national liberation movement had been raging since the Spring of Nations, and Austria-Hungary was formed in 1867. It included the territories of modern Austria, Hungary, Bosnia and Herzegovina, Slovakia, Slovenia, Croatia, the Czech Republic, Romania and Ukraine. The flag of the new state was unusual, consisting of two flags and two coats of arms with crowns (two crowns might be considered a natural consequence of the bird having two heads). But all this pales before the coat of arms of Austria-Hungary, which absorbed the heraldry of almost all the collected lands. This coat of arms can be contemplated for hours. There are fourteen eagles on it, of which three are double-headed. (Maths problem: how many eagle heads are there on this coat of arms?)

Perhaps it was then that the joke arose about the Austrian archduke who shot an eagle while hunting and was surprised to discover that it had only one head.

After the First World War, the empire broke up into many separate states. Austria itself, in the end, received the red–white–red flag that we see today. A flag of this design has been used by the Austrians since the thirteenth century, when Duke Leopold, after one successful battle, removed the belt from his white cloak covered with blood and saw a white stripe underneath. He liked the sight and decided to use the bloodied cloak as a flag.

However, the double-headed eagle in Austrian symbolism remained – today it is on the Austrian coat of arms holding a sickle and a hammer in its talons. Appreciate the twist: the coat of arms of the capitalist Austrian republic depicts a royal eagle with a socialist hammer and sickle.

Modern Germany – another descendant of the Holy Roman Empire – also has an eagle in its heraldry. But only on the coat of arms, not the flag – just like Austria. However, unlike the Austrian bird, the German eagle is not holding anything. But under Hitler the eagle took a fascist swastika surrounded by an oak wreath (another ancient Roman symbol) into its talons.

German Confederation (from 1848), Germany (1919–33), West Germany (since 1949), East Germany (1949–59)

German Empire (1871–1919), Germany (1933–5)

Germany (1935–45)

The current coat of arms of Germany

The emblem of the German Reich (1935–45)

The emblem of one of the Nazi military units of the SS: the *Wolfsangel*

As for the flag itself, the vexillological history of Germany has wavered between two tricolors: black–red–gold (which we see today) and black–white–red.

5. The Bird Heritage of the Romans

The black-red-gold colours of the modern German flag have their roots in the uniform of one of the German military units that fought against Napoleon. The choice of colour was not symbolic, but was simply a result of the most accessible materials at the time. So, in 1848, when the confederation of thirty-eight German states adopted its first flag, it had those three colours.

The next milestone in the unification of the German lands occurred in 1871, when Germany was united under the rule of Prussia. The black-white-red tricolor became its flag.

Then the First World War broke out. Germany expected the war to be over in a few months. (Otto von Bismarck said that he would not need military forces to defeat Great Britain – German policemen would be enough.) In fact, Europe plunged into a bloody slaughter for four years. In Germany itself, imminent defeat sparked a revolution, and the Weimar Republic replaced the German Empire, returning the black-red-gold tricolor.

But this did not last long. When the Nazis came to power in 1933, Hitler brought back the black-white-red flag as a symbol of Germany's former greatness and established the party's own flag, which carried the swastika, as another national flag. Two years later the Nazi Party flag was made the only official one.

Another symbol adopted by the Nazi Germany was a stylised crossed-out letter Z, known as the *Wolfsangel*, because mediaeval pagans believed that it had magical powers and could ward off wolves. By some blasphemous coincidence (coincidence?), the letter Z became the main symbol of Russian aggression against Ukraine in 2022.

After the Second World War, Germany was divided into West Germany (the Federal Republic of Germany) and East Germany (the communist German Democratic Republic). For a time, both countries had the same Weimar flag, but in 1959 East Germany added its coat of arms to it, showing a hammer, compass and wreath of wheat.

There are three Balkan countries with an eagle on their flags: Serbia, Montenegro and Albania.

Serbia (since 1882)

Montenegro (since 2004)

We don't know how the Serbian flag came to be created, though there are various stories about it. One is that, in the First Serbian Uprising against the Ottomon Empire, a Serbian delegation went to Russia to ask for help. A parade was organised, and the Serbs quickly needed a flag. So they simply took the flag of Russia and turned it upside down.

After the First World War, Serbia united with the Croats and Slovenes, forming the new state of Yugoslavia. The country's flag was the same red–blue–white tricolor. After the Second World War, a red socialist star was added.

From 1991 to 2001, there was a series of wars in Yugoslavia, which led to the emergence of six independent countries matching the six former republics of Yugoslavia: Serbia, Montenegro, Slovenia, Croatia, North Macedonia, and Bosnia and Herzegovina.

After the collapse of Yugoslavia, Serbia and Montenegro was a single state (called the State Union of Serbia and Montenegro) until 2006, when an independence referendum was held in Montenegro. It was approved by 55.5 per cent of Montenegrins, just passing the required 55 per cent. And here's an amusing fact: as part of Yugoslavia, the national top-level domain for Montenegrins was .yu, and on independence it became .me.

From 1993 till 2004, when Montenegro was in union with Serbia, its flag was the longest in the world. (Its aspect ratio was 1:3 – that is, its width was three times its height.) In 2004, it adopted as its flag a red field with golden borders, and the Byzantine double-headed eagle, as well as the Lion of Judah, which we will meet on the flag of Ethiopia. Paradoxically, Montenegrins also placed a crown on their flag and coat of arms, despite the country being a republic.

Albanian Kingdom (1928–39) with the helmet of Skanderbeg

Albania (since 1992)

The double-headed eagle on the flag of Albania is somewhat different from its feathered friends on other European flags. Here it is depicted as a black silhouette, without crowns, sceptres or other accessories. On some

5. The Bird Heritage of the Romans

versions of the Albanian flag, adopted before the Second World War, there was another unusual attribute above the eagle – the helmet of Skanderbeg, hero of Albanian history, who fought against the Ottoman Empire. A distinctive feature of this helmet is the head of a mountain goat, in gold.

After the Second World War, when Albania became a socialist country, the helmet with a goat was replaced with a socialist star. In 1992 the star was removed, and the flag took on a modern, laconic appearance.

The use of the Christian Byzantine eagle on the flag of Albania is also interesting because the majority of the Albanian population is Muslim. It turns out that the pagan eagle from ancient Rome not only became widespread on the flags of Christian nations, but even alighted on one Muslim one. I love these cross-religious borrowings!

We can find eagle prints on the flag of another major European country: Spain. Spain is one of those countries whose history is particularly reflected by the changes in its flag.

The history of modern Spain usually starts from the marriage between Ferdinand II of Aragon and Isabella of Castile in 1469. Ferdinand and Isabella were second cousins, and therefore this marriage required special permission from the pope (the document was 'signed' by Pope Pius II, who had died five years previously, so someone must have forged it). As a result, Aragon and Castile united into a single state, and the country received a coat of arms, which, with some changes, has remained on the Spanish flag ever since.

The coat of arms of the Catholic monarchs Isabella and Ferdinand

The coat of arms of modern Spain – without an eagle, but with columns from ancient Greek myth and lilies in the centre

Spain (since 1981)

The coat of arms of the Kingdom of Castile – the yellow castle

The coat of arms of the Kingdom of León – the lion being the symbol of León

The coat of arms of the Kingdom of Aragon. It seems that this is where the colours of the modern Spanish flag came from

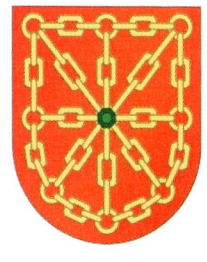

The coat of arms of the Kingdom of Navarre. The Muslim chains were broken during the Reconquista

The coat of arms of the Kingdom of Granada. The conquest of the Emirate of Granada was the last stage of the Reconquista

The coat of arms of the Bourbon-Anjou dynasty. A little bit of France on the Spanish flag

The most prominent place on this coat of arms belongs to the eagle of St John the Evangelist with a halo. In its talons, the bird holds a shield, on which there are many interesting things.

Here we see castles as a symbol of Castile (Castilla is translated as 'a castle'). We have already seen these castles on the Portuguese flag. Next comes the lion, as a symbol of León (León was united with Castile even before the marriage of Ferdinand and Isabella). Vertical yellow and red stripes are the symbol of the Kingdom of Aragon. They are the basis for the colours of the modern Spanish flag. We will see these stripes on the flag of Andorra. And finally, the fourth coat of arms – the smaller eagles, a symbol of the Kingdom of the Two Sicilies, which united with Aragon earlier.

Later, when Isabella and Ferdinand conquered the Emirate of Granada in 1492 and thus completed the Reconquista (the recapturing of the Iberian

5. The Bird Heritage of the Romans

peninsula from the Moors), the image of a pomegranate was added at the bottom of the coat of arms. After the Spanish conquest of Navarre in 1512, the coat of arms of Navarre was added. The gold chains on the Navarre coat of arms had been placed there to represent the protective chain that surrounded the tent of the Moorish king three centuries earlier, and which the Navarrese king broke with his sword.

The final element added to the Spanish coat of arms was the lilies, which everyone associates with France. This was in 1700, when Philip V, the grandson of the French king Louis XIV, came to the throne, and added the arms of Bourbon-Anjou to the Spanish coat of arms. It is interesting that there are French lilies on the flag of Spain, and not on the flag of France itself.

The coat of arms also holds the Gordian knot (which, according to legend, Alexander the Great cut with his sword) and a bundle of arrows, to illustrate that it is much more difficult to break a bundle of arrows than each arrow individually.

There is another interesting feature hidden in these images of the knot and arrows. The Spanish words for yoke and arrows (*yugo* and *flechas*) have the same initial letters as the names of Ysabel (the alternative spelling of Isabella) and Ferdinand.

Another symbol later added to the Spanish coat of arms is dedicated to the geographical discoveries of Spain. The two columns framing the coat of arms represent the Pillars of Hercules – the two promontories on either side of the eastern end of the Strait of Gibraltar. The name comes from the ancient Greek myth about one of the twelve labours of Hercules, when the hero was challenged to drive the cows of the giant Gerion to Mycenae. To do this, Hercules had to go to the western edge of the world. In one version of the legend, Hercules cut the Strait of Gibraltar through the mountains; in another, he narrowed an existing strait so that monsters from the ocean could not get into the Mediterranean Sea.

These pillars took on a special meaning in Spain when Spanish navigators began to discover new territories. It is believed that in antiquity, in the Gibraltar region, at the outlet to the ocean, there was a Latin inscription '*Non plus ultra*' ('Nothing further beyond'). But then the Spanish king Charles I – on whose empire the sun never sets – removed 'non' from this phrase and made it his personal motto. *Plus ultra* can be translated as 'Further beyond'. After some time, this was adopted as the national motto of Spain.

The discovery of the New World made Spain one of the richest countries of the time. The Spaniards received a significant part of their wealth from the largest silver deposits in the city of Potosí (modern Bolivia). Even today, the Spanish expression *valer un Potosí* (literally, 'as valuable as Potosí') is used to refer to something very valuable. At one time, the city of Potosí had an extremely unusual coat of arms: the double headless eagle of the Holy Roman Empire.

Unusual coat of arms of Potosi – the double-beheaded eagle

The Pillars of Hercules may have made another interesting contribution to world symbolism. One theory is that they were the inspiration for the dollar sign. As we have seen, these columns, with their S-shaped banners wrapped around them, first featured on the Spanish coats of arms. Then they appeared on Mexican pesos. This image gradually evolved into the $ symbol, to denote the Mexican currency, and then it became a symbol of the US dollar.

Until the eighteenth century, Spanish ships simply used the coats of arms on a white background as a flag, but in 1760 the Spanish king, Charles III, observed that the ships of most European countries flew banners that were mainly white, which sometimes led to confusion. So he instructed his minister of the navy to put forward proposals for a new flag whose design could be visible from afar. Twelve designs were shown to the king: he chose the triband with red–yellow–red horizontal stripes, in which the yellow band was twice the width of the red bands, and with the coat of arms to the left. So Spain received a naval ensign, which then evolved into its national flag.

The naval ensign of Charles III

Yoke and arrows – the emblem of Franco's Phalanx

The flag of Franco, who ruled Spain until 1975 – with the yoke and arrows of Isabella and Ferdinand

In 1936, a mutiny in Spain led to a bloody three-year civil war. The main instigators of the rebellion were the political party Falange Española Tradicionalista (Traditional Spanish Phalanx) led by General Francisco Franco. The yoke and arrows taken from the coat of arms of Isabella and Ferdinand became the symbol of the Falange. When General Franco finally established himself in power, he reinstated the eagle of Isabella and Ferdinand on the Spanish flag as a symbol of the Catholic faith.

Under Franco, although there were signs of Spain gradually evolving from backward agrarian nation into a country with a developed industry and tourism, there were tens of thousands of victims of political repression. Franco died in 1975, and democracy resumed under King Juan Carlos, which called for a new coat of arms, so in 1981, that new coat of arms was put on the flag (and is still there today): the shields of the four old Spanish kingdoms, the French lily, the Pillars of Hercules, motto *Plus ultra*, topped with a crown, to symbolise the monarchy. As for the eagle, there was no place for it on the banner.

Just as the Canadian flag gave vexillology the term 'Canadian pale', the Spanish flag gave rise to the term 'Spanish fess'. This is because the middle horizontal strip is twice the width of bands above and below it. We will meet the Spanish belt again on the flags of Lebanon, Libya and Laos.

Between Spain and France lies the small state of Andorra. Not surprisingly, the Andorran flag is a mixture of the Spanish and French ones. At the beginning of the nineteenth century, Andorrans had a yellow-red bicoloured flag, but at the insistence of Napoleon III, a third blue stripe was added to the flag, to symbolise France.

Andorra (1806–66)

Modern flag of Andorra (officially adopted since 1993)

The modern version of the flag was officially adopted in Andorra in 1993, when the country approved its constitution. Interestingly, the three vertical stripes on this flag may look the same width, as is common for many tricolors, but in fact the central stripe is just a little wider (the proportions of the stripes are 8:9:8) to make room for the coat of arms.

The Andorran coat of arms reflect the unusual political structure of this country, which was a co-government in which the two co-princes of the country were a bishop in Spain and a ruler of France. So in the upper left of the shield is a golden mitre (the arms of the Bishop of Urgell), and in the upper right are the three vertical red stripes that were arms of the Count of Foix, who was among the rulers of royal France. This system of co-government in Andorra still holds; today, the formal co-princes are the Bishop of Urgell and the president of France (Emmanuel Macron, at the time of writing).

When Andorra adopted its constitution in 1993, the country not only adopted the current flag, but also defined exactly what privileges these co-rulers have. For example, they have the right to grant an amnesty. After the adoption of the constitution, Andorra also stopped paying annual tribute to Spain and France. Until then, the country paid a tribute of about $460 to the French ruler in odd-numbered years, and in even-numbered years, paid about $12 to the Spanish bishop, plus six hams, six rounds of cheese and six live chickens.

There are surprising echoes of the Andorra flag on the flag of another European state: Moldova. First, the Moldovan flag has three vertical stripes in the same combination of colours – blue, yellow and red. Second, the eagle is holding a shield with the head of a bull on it (similar to the coat of arms of Romania). To be more precise, this is not the head of a bull, but of its ancestor the aurochs. It is said that the image of the aurochs comes from the pagan rite of sacrifice. If so, this is another example of a pagan symbol on a modern flag.

Aurochs became extinct in the seventeenth century but attempts are periodically made to revive them. For example, scientists in Nazi Germany carried out back-breeding experiments with other animals, with some success. The German plan was that aurochs would populate the territories of the conquered Belarusian lands.

The eagle – which is also present on the flag behind the shield with the aurochs – is a direct reference to ancient Rome. The symbol emphasised the Latin origin of the Moldovan people.

Until 2010, Moldova was one of the two countries (the other being Paraguay) whose flag had a different image on the reverse – the coat of arms was on one side only. But in 2010, the flag was changed, the coat of arms was added to the reverse side, and the shade of blue was made brighter to distinguish it from Romania, Chad and Andorra. This shade is called 'Berlin blue'. So there is an unexpected German trace on the Moldovan flag.

Moldova (since 1990) – the flag with an eagle and the head of an aurochs

The coat of arms of Romania

There are eagles on the flags of countries outside Europe, but they have their origins in other symbols and not from the ancient Roman or Christian eagle.

Let's look at the flag of Mexico. We also see an eagle there, with an amusing mythological background.

Before the arrival of the Spanish colonists, the territory of Mexico was inhabited by constantly warring tribes, the Aztecs being the most numerous. A few centuries before the Spaniards arrived, the Aztecs lived in another region. One day the leader of a neighbouring tribe married his daughter to the leader of the Aztec tribe. The Aztecs sacrificed the unfortunate girl to their gods, for which they were exiled. According to legend, the Aztecs travelled for a long time in search of a new home until they saw an eagle perched on a cactus, holding a snake in its talons. This was where they settled, and the settlement eventually became Mexico City.

When the Mexicans won independence from Spain in 1821, the flag of the new country was a red-white-green tricolor with an eagle, a cactus and a snake from the Aztec legend. However, it is possible that the choice of an eagle was also influenced by the popularity of eagles in European heraldry.

After the expulsion of the Spaniards, the history of independent Mexico did not run smoothly. There was a series of uprisings, as a result of which Texas and some other parts of northern Mexico separated from the country. There was also a war with France, which began with the complaint of a French pastry chef. He had a shop on the outskirts of Mexico City, and in 1832 Mexican officers looted it, taking away cakes worth 1,000 pesos. The French king made demands to Mexico for significant compensation. When his demands were refused, he went to war with the Mexicans. This became known as the Pastry War.

The internal affairs of Mexico were also unsettled. From 1824 to 1857, the head of state changed twenty-six times, often as a result of military coups (for example, the Mexican general Santa Anna, who called himself the Napoleon of the West, was president eleven times). Although the flag was changed almost as often as the country's leaders, the main element – the Aztec eagle on a cactus – remained unchanged. At first, the eagle was depicted with a crown on its head, but when Mexico became a republic, the crown was removed.

Mexico (1821–23)

(1823–62)

(1893–1916)

(since 1968)

At some point, the eagle on the Mexican flag proudly spread its wings, to avoid looking like its relations on European coats of arms. And in the twentieth century, the eagle was depicted sideways on, which is the position in which we see it today.

5. The Bird Heritage of the Romans

06. Vexillological Tango

One winter evening in 1785, the German poet Johann Wolfgang von Goethe had an interesting conversation. He was talking to Francisco de Miranda, a resident of Caracas, the capital of modern Venezuela, which was a Spanish colony at the time. During his turbulent life, Miranda took part in three revolutions – American, French and Latin American ones – and became one of the main characters in the history of Latin America. During the conversation, Goethe explained his theory of colour to Miranda, which he published twenty-five years later. From the point of view of physics, it was largely incorrect, but it played an important role in discussions about optics of that time.

According to Goethe's theory, all colours can be split into three basic ones – red, yellow and blue. On hearing about Miranda's exploits, Goethe told him: 'Your destiny is to create a place in your homeland where these basic colours are not distorted.' After that meeting, Miranda took part in the French Revolution, got disillusioned with it, almost died in a French prison and eventually became an exile for taking part in a military conspiracy.

Returning to his homeland in Latin America, Miranda organised the struggle against Spain. In 1811, Venezuela gained independence, and Miranda became its supreme chief. A year later, the Spaniards regained control of the lost territory and Miranda was put in prison, where he died a few years later.

It is easy to guess what kind of flag Miranda chose for the new state. Under the influence of the French, it was a tricolor. Under the influence of Goethe, yellow, blue and red became his colours. Miranda put these meanings into this flag: the blue colour symbolises the ocean; yellow represents the riches of the country and the sun; and the red represents the blood spilled during the battle of independence.

Miranda's struggle became the forerunner of events that caused Spain to lose its Latin American colonies. In 1819, a new independent state called Gran Colombia (also known as Great Colombia) appeared on the territory of modern Colombia, Ecuador, Venezuela and Panama. In those days, it was simply called Colombia, but later, to distinguish it from its modern namesake, historians added the adjective 'Gran'.

Miranda (1806)

Gran Colombia (1821–31)

The flag of Gran Colombia was the Miranda tricolor with the coat of arms in the centre. The coat of arms depicts the Roman fasces which is found in the heraldry of many countries. (The Latin word *fasces* refers to a bundle of elm or birch rods, usually with an axe, and is where we get the word 'fascism'.) The fasces was a symbol used in Italian heraldry of Mussolini's time, and is still the central element of the national emblem of France.

Gran Colombia did not last long. Twelve years later, in 1831, torn apart by internal conflicts, it broke into three new states: New Granada (the modern territory of Panama and Colombia), Venezuela and Ecuador. A glance at their flags is enough to show that these countries have a common history.

Colombia (since 1861)

Ecuador (since 1900)

Venezuela (since 2006)

State Flag since 2006

The tricolors of Colombia and Ecuador have a feature that you will not find on the flags of other countries of the world: the upper stripe is twice as wide as each of the other two stripes.

The Ecuadorian flag has another interesting feature. Its emblem depicts the sun (the Incan sun god) with the signs of the zodiac for Aries, Taurus, Gemini and Cancer, representing the months from March to June. This was to symbolise the duration of the March Revolution of 1845, a military coup in which the first president of independent Ecuador was overthrown.

Whereas the flags of Colombia and Ecuador have not changed for 150 years or so, the flag of Venezuela has changed relatively recently. Hugo Chávez ruled Venezuela from 1999 to 2013. He was a rabid socialist and, as is often the case with such leaders, was more interested in historical achievements than the country's economic development.

Before Chávez came to power, the Venezuelan flag had seven stars – representing the seven Venezuelan provinces that had signed the declaration of independence in 1811. In 2006, Chávez added an eighth star to the flag, as a very late fulfilment of Simon Bolívar's decree from 1817. This eighth star represented the province of Guyana, which was initially loyal to Spain but then joined the independent Venezuela, so the Guyanese were really bothered by the new design of the Venezuelan flag.

Another detail on the flag was also changed: the white horse on the coat of arms began to run towards the left, and not to the right. Perhaps this change was supposed to demonstrate the country's commitment to leftist ideas. If so, then from a heraldic point of view, Chávez was wrong: in heraldry, the sides are considered not from the viewer, but from the view of the coat of arms itself. What is 'left' to the viewer is actually 'right'.

According to the *Economist* magazine, Chávez decided to change the direction of the horse on the coat of arms and flag at his daughter's suggestion, after she noticed that on the previous coat of arms the horse seemed to be looking back.

Coat of arms of Venezuela

1864–1954
The Venezuelan horse rushing to the left

1954–2006
The horse is distracted

Since 2006
The horse rushing to the right

If we put the last three Venezuelan coats of arms in a row, you can see the progression: first the horse runs rapidly in one direction; then something behind it catches its attention; and then the horse starts running rapidly in that other direction. A beautiful and sad metaphor for the fate of Venezuela itself.

The opposition rejected Chávez's flag, and now the flag with seven stars is considered oppositional in the country. Perhaps, when the opposition in this long-suffering country does come to power, Venezuela will again have to change its flag. In creating a personality cult of Simon Bolívar, Chávez not only changed the flag of his country but also renamed the country itself. Now the full name of Venezuela is the Bolivarian Republic of Venezuela. So the name of Bolívar appears in the names of two countries. The etymology of the name 'Venezuela' is interesting, as it means 'Little Venice' in Spanish. It was the Italian navigator Amerigo Vespucci who gave this name to the region when he arrived here in 1499 with the first conquistadors. The watery area with its many bridges reminded him of Venice.

Another important cluster in Latin America in terms of vexillology are the countries whose flags are derived from the Argentinian flag.

In 1810, the aristocrats of Buenos Aires organised an uprising against Spain. As a result of this week-long May Revolution, a new independent state called the United Provinces of the Río de la Plata emerged, which included the territories of modern Argentina, Uruguay and several provinces of Bolivia and Brazil.

One of the leaders of the military resistance against Spain was the Latin American politician Manuel Belgrano. At some point, Belgrano realised that his soldiers needed their own colour for cockades to distinguish themselves from the Spanish troops. The colours of Spain then (as now) were red and yellow, so Belgrano chose the opposite: blue and white.

Let me remind you that this was the same reason for choosing blue as the colour for the UN flag: it needed a colour that was the opposite of red.

Argentina (since 1861)

Flag of the United Provinces (1819–20)

Argentina (1829–35)

Flag of the Argentine Confederation (1835–50)

Initially, the flag of Argentina was just three stripes: two blue stripes divided by a white stripe. Later, in honour of the May Revolution, the May sun was added – the emblem of the Incan empire. It is said that when the new government declared the independence of the Río de la Plata, the sun shone through the clouds in the Argentine sky.

The blue and white colours of the Argentinian flag have another interesting symbolic meaning – the association with silver. *Río de la Plata* translates from Spanish as 'silver river' and the word 'Argentina' itself comes from the Latin *argentum* – silver. This etymology from the Latin word for a metal is a link between Argentina and Cyprus.

As is often the case with blue flags, the blue has changed hue several times over its history. In 1829, the territories of Bolivia and Uruguay left the Río de la Plata, and the Río de la Plata was renamed the Argentine Confederation. The first Argentine dictator, Juan Rosas, changed the blue tint of the flag to purple, which is a very unusual colour for heraldry.

Later, the sun on the flag of Argentina became frighteningly red, and red caps appeared in the corners: phrygian caps. We have already come across the phrygian caps of the popes, which evolved into papal tiaras.

In fact, the phrygian cap is a cute cone-shaped headdress, dating from antiquity, which came to signify freedom and the pursuit of liberty. It became a symbol first in the American struggle for independence and then the French Revolution, and many wars in Latin America.

This cap has become one of the most common elements on the flags and coats of arms of the world: it appears on those of Bolivia, Colombia, Cuba, El Salvador, Haiti and Nicaragua as well as Argentina. Phrygian caps can even be found on the coat of arms of New York. Initially, the Statue of Liberty was supposed to wear this cap, but at the last moment the Americans asked the French, who gave them the statue, to remove it, because 'American freedom is genuine, and not the result of the fight against slavery'.

Uruguay (since 1828)

Paraguay (obverse)

Paraguay (reverse)

Uruguay, which gained independence in 1829, has a similar flag: white and blue and also with the sun of May. The design was inspired by the US flag. Initially, it consisted of nine blue stripes – for the nine original departments of the republic. But then the number of stripes was reduced to four, so that the design was not so crowded.

The structure of Paraguay's flag was also inspired by that of Argentina, and the colours were inspired by the French tricolor.

The Paraguayan flag is unusual in that its obverse (front) is different from its reverse. On the obverse is the coat of arms; on the reverse is the sea of the treasury. Previously, only Moldova (until 2010) and the USSR had different sides to their flag (both countries had the national coat of arms only on the front side).

Also on the flag of Paraguay is a symbol of peace – an olive branch. Contrary to its symbolism, this often turns out not to be a good omen for a country. Twenty-two years after it adopted a flag with an olive branch, Paraguay launched the Great War against Brazil, Argentina and Uruguay, in which it lost half of its territories and 70 per cent of the adult male population. These losses were so significant that the Paraguayan government was forced to legalise polygamy in the country for a while.

The third country to depict the May sun on its flag was Peru. In 1820, Peru began a war against the Spanish colonists and soon declared its independence. According to legend, General José de San Martin, on his arrival in Peru in 1820, saw a flock of flamingos with red and white plumage. He liked the show so much that he chose these colours for the flag of the new state. Two years later, a new flag of Peru was approved, which was a 'red copy' of the flag of Argentina. However, its similarity to the flag of Spain caused confusion in battle, and the horizontal stripes were replaced by vertical stripes.

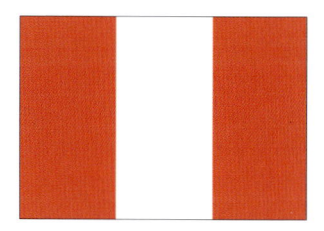

Peru (since 1825)

Red sun, horizontal stripes – too reminiscent of the flag of Spain

In 1822 the stripes became vertical

Peru-Bolivian Confederation (1836–39) – the meeting of two alpacas

06. Vexillological Tango

Another interesting event in the history of the flag of Peru was also reflected in its design. In 1824, Simon Bolívar conquered the country and divided it into two parts – Peru and Bolivia, created in 1825 and named after him. Bolívar himself ruled Peru, and not Bolivia. Under Bolívar, Peru received a new flag – the one we see today.

Peru

Between 1836 and 1839, Peru was in a confederation with Bolivia. Its flag was red with the coats of arms of the two countries under the May sun. The flag could be described as 'the meeting of two alpacas under the scorching sun' – after all, this animal with winsome eyes is present on the coats of arms of both countries.

The Bolivian flag is made in colours that are not typical of Latin America. These three colours are usually called pan-African, and we will discuss them later. The centre of the flag features the coat of arms of the country, which, in turn, has six flags of Bolivia (though these flags no longer have coats of arms). And in 2009, Bolivia adopted a second national flag of a very unusual design. It is called the Wiphala, and represents the indigenous peoples who lived there before the Europeans. Wiphala was adopted at the initiative of Evo Morales – the country's first president to come from the indigenous population.

Bolivia (since 1851)

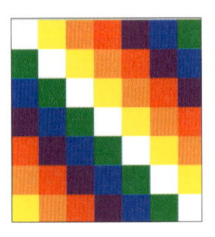

Wiphala

Naval ensign

We see the Bolivian Wiphala on another flag – the Bolivian naval ensign. The Bolivian Navy has about 5,000 personnel, even though the country has been landlocked since the end of the nineteenth century, after the war with Chile. The large yellow star on the flag represents the country's right of access to the Pacific Ocean. In 2013, Bolivia filed a lawsuit with the International Court of Justice (ICJ), seeking to force Chile to grant it maritime access. On the eve of the verdict, in 2018, the Bolivian authorities unfolded a long strip of naval flags sewn together, stretching for 200 kilometres. Unfortunately for the Bolivians, the ICJ ruled in favour of Chile.

In Bolivia, I came across an interesting case of how a television picture can influence national heraldry. In the first chapter, I mentioned that French had created a special version of their tricolor with a narrow white stripe to make it look good on a television screen. The administration of the president of Bolivia went further, and created a version of the flag with the coat of arms placed at an angle. So when the flag hangs at an angle, the coat of arms is straight. Nothing will prevent you from admiring the llamas on the coat of arms!

But back to Argentina. Traces of the Argentinian flag appear on the flags of five other countries in the region. This is because there was a democratic state called the Federal Republic of Central America from 1823 to 1841.

Federal Republic of Central America (1824–39)

6. Vexillological Tango

The federation's flag was inspired by the flag of Argentina, but instead of the sun, it featured a coat of arms so unusual that it can be assumed that it was drawn after an ayahuasca ceremony. In the centre of the coat of arms is a phrygian cap, from which rays diverge, and there is a rainbow in the sky, all against the backdrop of a beautiful landscape of five volcanoes – one for each of the five states in the federation.

As with Gran Colombia, this country did not last long. After fifteen years, the federation descended into civil war, and the union officially ended when the five provinces became the independent republics of Honduras, Costa Rica, Guatemala, Nicaragua and El Salvador.

The history of these five countries is a series of wars, military coups and changes of dictators who were guided either by the United States or by socialist powers. These countries also regularly fought among themselves. For example, in 1969 there was a brief military conflict between Honduras and El Salvador, which became known as the Football War, as it began after the El Salvador national team beat Honduras in the qualifying stages of the 1970 FIFA World Cup. Despite constant wars, each of these five countries keeps the essence of the Federal Republic of Central America on their flags.

El Salvador (since 1912)

Nicaragua (since 1908)

Costa Rica (since 1848)

Most similar to the banner of the Federal Republic are the flags of El Salvador and Nicaragua. Both have the same emblems in the centre – the images of a cap, a rainbow and five volcanoes.

The flag of Nicaragua has another unusual detail – purple in the rainbow. The other country with purple on its flag is Dominica, with its parrot.

The flag of Costa Rica also has Central American volcanoes on it (although there are three volcanoes, not five), though the flag is very different from the others because it uses red. This flag was created by the wife of the Costa Rican president in 1848. Inspired by the French tricolor, she took the flag of the Federal Republic and added a red stripe through the middle.

Guatemala (since 1871)

Guatemala (1851–8)

Guatemala (1858–71)

There are no volcanoes on the flag of Guatemala, but the historical connection with the Federal Republic of Central America on the flag can be traced even more clearly. In the centre of the flag is the inscription (in Spanish) 'Freedom 15 September 1821' – the date of Central America's independence from Spain.

Had history taken a slightly different turn, the flag of Guatemala might have had a red stripe like the flag of Costa Rica, although it would be Spanish red rather than French red. In 1851, a pro-Spanish faction seized power in the country, and added the Spanish colours of red and yellow to the flag. The result is a very unusual design, somewhat reminiscent of Mondrian paintings.

Honduras (since 2022)

Honduras (1949–2022)

Honduras is the only one of the five countries that does not have a coat of arms on its flag. To show its common history with its neighbours, the flag has five stars to represent the five members of the former Central American federation. The stars are placed in the shape of a cross, which is also the shape of an H – the initial letter of the country's name.

At the time of publication of this book, Honduras is the country that has changed its flag most recently. In 2022, the colour of the flag was changed from dark blue to turquoise, when Xiomara Castro became the president of the country. (Incidentally, she was the First Lady of the country in 2006-9, which means that her husband, the former president of Honduras, has become the First Gentleman.)

Neighbouring Belize has had a far more peaceful existence than its Central American neighbours. It was a British colony from 1783, known as British Honduras, and then became a self-governing colony, later renamed Belize, before gaining full independence in 1981. If not for the British, Belize would certainly have been mired in a conflict with neighbouring Guatemala, which renounced claims to the territory only in 1981 on its independence.

Belize (since 1981)

Guyana (since 1966)

Because of its isolation from the hot geopolitics of Central America, the flag of Belize has become very distinctive. First, it depicts people. And secondly, it is the most colourful flag in the world, with twelve different colours.

No less distinctive is the flag of another former British colony in Latin America: Guyana.

This country has quite an unusual name: Co-operative Republic of Guyana (which reflects its initial communist politics). Guyana stopped pursuing Marx's ideas after the collapse of the Soviet Union, but the unusual name stayed – as did its flag, known as the Golden Arrowhead.

This flag was designed by the famous American vexillologist Whitney Smith (who actually invented the term vexillology). Smith's original design didn't have black and white dividing stripes (known in vexillology as fimbriations: they were added later. According to official interpretation, the black border symbolises 'the perseverance needed to reach the goal'. In 2020 and 2021 Guyana's average GDP growth was an astonishing 30 per cent, thanks to the development of new oil reserves, so these black lines have developed a whole new meaning.

07. American Dream

One December day in 1773, thousands of Americans took to Boston Harbour to protest against taxes imposed by Great Britain on tea imports. The protests were led by members of an organisation called the Sons of Liberty. The protests came to a head when about a hundred angry men, some dressed as Mohawk warriors, rushed aboard ships waiting to be unloaded and dumped all 342 crates of tea into the water.

This event went down in history as the Boston Tea Party and was the harbinger of the American Revolution. The motto of the Sons of Liberty was 'No taxation without representation' (meaning representation in the British Parliament), and its flag had nine red and white vertical stripes.

The tea that was destroyed that day belonged to the East India Company, a private organisation with a monopoly on the import of tea and many other tradeable goods. The East India Company's flag had red and white horizontal stripes, with the Union Jack on the canton.

Today's US flag also has red and white horizontal stripes, and a popular explanation is that it is derived from the flag of the East India Company. Others say that the red and white stripes come from the Sons of Liberty flag. Whatever the case, the red and white stripes are one of the most recognisable elements in the world of heraldry today.

As for the flag of the East India Company itself, it probably comes from the flag of the Majapahit Empire, which existed from the late thirteenth century to the sixteenth century, and was based on the island of Java, now in Indonesia. It was from this region that the East India Company began to import coffee to Europe. The naval jack of the Indonesian Navy, of nine equal horizontal stripes of red and white, is inspired by the flag of the Majapahit Empire.

It is interesting to think that the US flag may be derived from the Indonesian one.

East India Company flag

Sons of Liberty flag

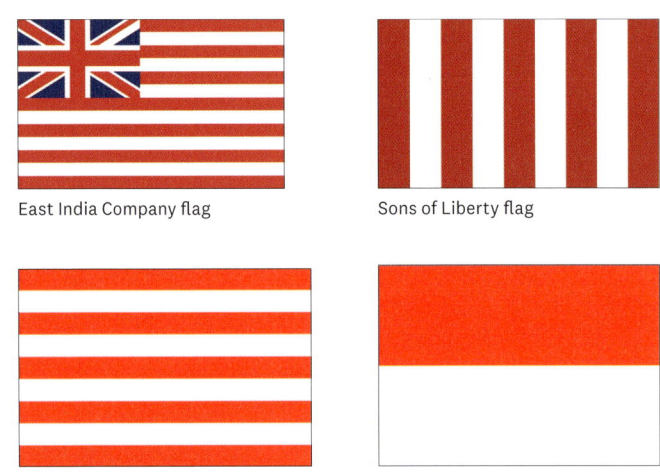

Royal colours of Majapahit Empire

Flag of Indonesia (from 1945)

The US flag was officially adopted in 1777, a year after independence was declared. It had thirteen stars and thirteen stripes, representing the thirteen British colonies that become the first states in the new union. Surprisingly, the flag of the East India Company also had thirteen stripes. One of the conspiracy theories explains this by the fact that the founders of the company were freemasons, and the number thirteen is considered significant by them.

Alternative arrangemenst of stars on early US flags.

There were no rules to state how to place the stars on the blue background of the new flag, so they were arranged in various ways. Sometimes they were placed in rows, sometimes in a circle, sometimes in the shape of a star. In fact, the Flag Act of 1777 did not even specify whether the red and white stripes should be vertical or horizontal.

After the United States expanded by two more states – Vermont and Kentucky – two more stars and two stripes were added to the flag. As the number of states continued to grow, the flag was getting crowded and, in 1818, the Americans returned to thirteen stripes, only increasing the number of stars with each new state.

Today, the United States has fifty states. Its flag is the most frequently changed national flag in the world, now in its twenty-seventh design. The flag underwent the last change in 1959, when Hawaii became part of the United States.

When the White House was holding the contest to choose the design for the fifty-star flag, more than 1,500 design proposals were submitted to the president from all over the country. At least three were the design that was ultimately accepted. One was from a seventeen-year-old schoolboy, Robert Heft, who prepared the design as part of a school project. He received a B minus for his work. Robert's teacher jokingly said that he would upgrade this if the design was accepted – and did indeed change Robert's grade to an A.

It is possible that the number of stars on the flag will continue to increase. For example, in 2017, Puerto Ricans voted (by 97 per cent) to become a state of the United States. And in 2020, Congress voted to make the District of Columbia the fifty-first state. In celebration of the idea, the mayor of the district hung US flags with fifty-one stars on the streets. The vote passed along party lines, but the measure was declared unconstitutional.

In the United States, there is still a ritual Pledge of Allegiance to the US flag, which is recited on solemn days in US government agencies, educational institutions and private companies. During the ceremony, people swear allegiance to the US flag and the country that it represents, while putting their hand to their hearts. At first it was customary to raise the hand towards the flag, palm downwards; however, the gesture was similar to the Nazi salute, and was therefore changed in 1942.

One of the most famous historical figures associated with the US flag is William Driver. In 1824, he became the captain of a merchant ship and sailed the seas. He always hoisted the US flag, which he called Old Glory. At the end of his naval career, Driver took the flag back with him to his home in Tennessee. When the American Civil War began, Tennessee formally separated from the northern states. Driver's two sons went to fight for the South, and Driver himself remained loyal to the North. When southerners came to his house and tried to seize the flag, he declared: 'Only over my dead body!' After this, the flag was sewn into a coverlet for safekeeping.

After the war, the story of Driver and his flag gained fame, and the US flag is often called Old Glory.

The official shades of the colours of the flag are derived from this nickname: Old Glory Red and Old Glory Blue. Other flags that have their own named colours are the flag of the United Nations (with its UN blue), and the flag of India (India saffron and India green).

Another unofficial name for the flag is the Stars and Stripes. It comes from a phrase in a poem written by US lawyer and amateur poet Francis Scott Key. Key wrote his poem, originally called 'Defence of Fort M'Henry', on the night of 1814 while watching the bombardment of Fort McHenry in Baltimore Harbour during a battle in the war of 1812. Key was inspired by the sight of the US flag flying proudly over the fort. Soon, the poem was set to the tune of a popular drinking song, written by a British composer. The patriotic song gradually gained popularity in the United States. First, it became the official song of the US Navy, and in 1931 it was officially recognised as the national anthem of the United States of America.

Today, Key's grave is one of several places where it is officially legal not to lower the US flag at night. Another place is the Moon, where the Americans left six US banners. Key was one of the wealthiest Americans of the day, and owned many slaves himself. Some believe that there is racism in the third verse of the anthem: 'No refuge could save the hireling and slave, From the terror of flight'. This phrase refers to the fact that the British promised the American slaves freedom and their own land if they escaped the Americans and fought on their side. The British kept their word: African Americans who later defected to the British side received land in the territory of the modern state of Trinidad and Tobago.

It is believed that one of the manifestations of Key's racism was his membership of the American Colonisation Society (ACS). Members of this organisation were afraid that the growing number of blacks freed from slavery was a threat to American society, and advocated their return to Africa. To this end, in 1822, the society bought a small territory on the west coast of Africa from the leaders of local tribes and organised the transportation of freed slaves there. The settlement was named Liberia, and its capital is Monrovia, named after James Monroe, the fifth US president, also a member of the ACS.

The freed slaves arriving in Liberia considered themselves primarily Americans, and there is some evidence that their behaviour was hostile towards the local black population. They brought many traditions and attributes from the United States, including the imperial measurement system. Liberia remains one of just a few countries in the world that do not have a metric system, others being the United States and Myanmar.

Liberia (since 1847)

The flag of Liberia was adopted in 1847, when the country declared independence. Not surprisingly, it is very similar to the US flag. But there is only one star on the canton, representing the first independent republic in Africa, and instead of thirteen stripes, there are eleven, to reflect the number of signatures of the declaration of independence.

Today Liberia is one of the poorest countries in the world. Its history is a continuous train of coups, civil wars and military conflicts with its neighbours. In 1980, Sergeant Samuel Doe came to power, having led a coup in which the previous president was killed. Ten years later, military rebels killed Doe himself, after twelve hours of torture. The Liberian dictator's arms were broken, he was castrated, his ear was cut off and he was forced to eat it – all on video.

The organiser of those tortures was the rebel leader Prince Johnson, who later became a senator, and also ran for the presidency of the country, gaining 12 per cent of the vote. As I write this in 2023, George Weah, one of the best football players in African history, is the president of Liberia. I remember how I rooted for Weah when he played in the Italian FC Milan along with Andriy Shevchenko. I root for him even now, though the sad news from Liberia indicates that so far he has handled the country much worse than a soccer ball.

The flag of Liberia is the second most commonly seen flags in international waters, flown as a 'flag of convenience' by cargo ships. Because of simplified flagging regulations, more than 10 per cent of the world's fleet sail under the Liberian flag. The ships simply pay a fee to be registered in Liberia and thus fly the Liberian flag, which is a huge source of revenue for the country. Before the 1990s Liberia was top of the list of flag states, but was displaced by Panama, because of its many wars.

So let's talk about Panama now.

The history of the Republic of Panama, and of its flag, is closely entwined with that of the Panama Canal. After the expulsion of the Spaniards in 1821, Panama first became a part of Gran Colombia and then, after its collapse, a part of Colombia.

The idea that Panama is the perfect place for a canal between the Atlantic and Pacific oceans first arose in the sixteenth century. Later, both the UK and the United States attempted to develop a canal; however, it was the French who won the concession to build the canal, although work did not start until 1882. The French company on the project was led by a diplomat who managed to raise considerable funds for the project because of his experience in constructing the Suez Canal.

Panama (since 1925)

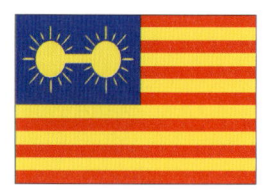

Bunau-Varilla design

A French company cheerfully took up the project, but soon went bankrupt. The project turned out to be much more difficult than expected, mainly because of the high mortality rate of the workers. By the time work was stopped in 1889, about 22,000 people had died – mainly from yellow fever and malaria, the climate, spiders and snakes.

The United States entered into negotiations with the French to buy the stalled project. Negotiations on the French side were led by energetic manager Philippe Bunau-Varilla, an engineer. The Americans were also exploring the possibility of building a canal through Nicaragua, though Bunau-Varilla vigorously persuaded them to stick with the canal through Panama.

Part of the reason may have been that the potential site in Nicaragua was twenty miles from a volcano. In fact, in 1902, the Mount Pelée volcano erupted, and its lava and gas destroyed the city of Saint Pierre and its

30,000 inhabitants. It turned out to be the deadliest volcanic eruption of the twentieth century. This led to volcanophobia in the United States. One month after the eruption, the US Senate voted in favour of building a canal through the Isthmus of Panama instead.

At first, the Americans were offered the project for $100 million, but then the parties bargained for $40 million. However, the deal almost fell through at the last moment – the Colombian senate rejected the proposed treaty with the United States that would enable a canal to be built through Panama.

And then the cunning Bunau-Varilla suggested that the United States support the Panamanian rebels, who were planning to break away from Colombia. The US president Theodore Roosevelt agreed with the plan, US troops supported the Panamanian independence movement, and in 1903 Panama became an independent country.

The canal was completed in 1914, after ten years of work. The Americans organised the opening ceremony on a grand scale. President Woodrow Wilson, in his White House office, pressed a symbolic button that sent a signal to Panama via telegraph to set off explosives. The dam was blown up and water filled the canal, connecting the two oceans.

Bunau-Varilla's wife decided to take part in the creation of the state symbols of the new republic. She proposed a design inspired by the US flag but with the colours of Spain, but her design was rejected. The most original part of this flag was the canton: two interconnected suns, symbolising North and South America. The twin sun motif is reminiscent of a shot from *Star Wars*. Had this design been accepted, the flag would certainly have stood out from all others.

The design that was approved is also unusual, and was created by the wife and son of the first president of Panama. Blue and red symbolised the two opposing political forces in the country at that time; white quarters with stars symbolised peace and purity.

Control of the Panama Canal Zone lay with the Americans. However, in 1977 a treaty prepared the way for handover to Panama. It was the Panamanian flag that became the reason for this landmark event.

In 1963, President John F. Kennedy agreed to fly Panama's flag alongside the US flag on non-military sites in the Canal Zone, but he was assassinated before these orders were carried out. Riots erupted near the canal after Panamanian students attempted to fly the Panamanian flag on a local school building. In the ensuing skirmish with the police, the flag was accidentally torn (later investigation showed that it was made of flimsy silk). This caused a flurry of indignation among the Panamanian population. Mass demonstrations began, and twenty-eight people were killed.

Although there was no unequivocal evidence that it was the US military that was guilty of these killings, a wave of indignation against them swept the world. All countries – both socialist and capitalist – merged in a single outburst of anger against the 'damn Yankees'. These events, commemorated in the annual Martyrs' Day, served as the catalyst for the United States to transfer control of the canal to Panama.

From Panama, let's now move to the Pacific Ocean, to the flag of Bikini Atoll, which is part of the Marshall Islands. This small atoll is known for giving its name to the women's two-piece swimsuit (in fact, if you enter 'Bikini flag' into Google, the search engine will bombard you with images of sultry girls in flag swimsuits), as well as the fact that it was here that the Americans tested the first hydrogen bomb in 1954. Alas, the swimsuit did not find its place on the flag, but traces of the hydrogen bomb explosion are there.

Bikini Atoll

Marshall Islands (since 1979)

Nauru (since 1968)

The flag is very similar to the US one. But there is additional strong symbolism of the great debt that the United States government owes the Bikini islanders, for testing the fifteen-megaton bomb on their atoll. That explosion completely destroyed the three islands, as eloquently evoked by the three black stars in the upper right corner. The Marshallese words in black mean 'Everything is in the hands of God'. This is said to be the reply that the leader of Bikini philosophically gave when the Americans asked them to vacate the islands so that they could test their bomb.

As for the flag of the Marshall Islands, I find its design aesthetically pleasing. Its symbolism is similar to that of the Brazilian flag: the orange and white diagonal line symbolises the equator, and the star above it represents the position of the islands in the northern hemisphere. The star has twenty-four points; no other star on any national flag has as many.

The Pacific island nation of Nauru, once also part of the Republic of the Marshall Islands, has similar symbols on its flag. The yellow line on the banner symbolises the equator, and the star below this line symbolises the country's position just south of the equator.

But back to the red and white stripes of the US flag. Remember, one explanation is that they came from the banner of the Majapahit Empire. The world owes this empire the design of the flags of several other countries: Indonesia, Malaysia and Singapore.

The flag of Indonesia was officially adopted in 1945 – immediately after the expulsion of the Japanese, who occupied the region during the Second World War, as well as the Dutch, who had administered it as a colony (the Dutch East Indies) since 1800. One one occasion in 1945, during the Indonesian war of independence against the Dutch, some Indonesian youths tore down the colonial Dutch flag flying over a hotel, tore off the blue stripe at the bottom, and re-hoisted it as the flag of Indonesia. This story would be even better if the flag of Indonesia had arisen from this event, but it was simply a coincidence.

After Indonesia's independence was recognised officially, the state of Monaco complained that the Indonesian flag was the same as the Monaco flag, except for a slightly different shade of red. The people of Monaco, the Monégasques, were outraged because they had been using their red and white bicolour since the fourteenth century; the response was that the Majapahit Empire began in the thirteenth century.

For the first twenty years of independence, Indonesia was ruled by an extravagant autocrat called Sukarno. During his presidency, he quarrelled with, then reconciled with, the USSR and the United States in turn. Under him, the country left the UN, invaded neighbouring Malaysia, and at some point a civil war broke out there. If you flip the flag of Indonesia, you get the flag of Poland. But here's another exact opposite between these two countries: the word *tak* means 'yes' in Polish and 'no' in Indonesian. What a beautiful parallel between vexillology and linguistics.

Indonesia (since 1945)

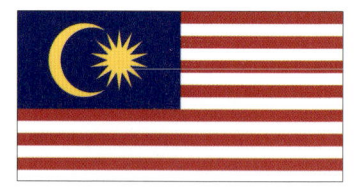

Malaysia (since 1957)

Singapore (since 1959)

Malaysia, which is next to Indonesia, gained its independence in 1957. Its flag also resembles the US flag, although it has no direct connection with it. Fourteen alternating red and white stripes and fourteen points on the star on the flag symbolise the administrative structure of the country. One stripe and one end of the star on this flag symbolised Singapore, which became fully independent from Malaysia in 1965.

Singapore is a rare example of a country that gained independence involuntarily. At that time, the Malaysian government was nervous about the declining percentage of Malays in the population. Singapore was inhabited mostly by ethnic Chinese. As a result there were constant conflicts between Malaysia and Singapore, until eventually the Malaysian parliament voted to exclude Singapore from the country. The prime minister of Singapore, Lee Kuan Yew, was initially fearful when he received the news of independence. However, Singapore has become one of the richest and most prosperous countries in the world.

When Singapore designed its flag, it was decided to respect both the Malay minority and the Chinese majority of the population. And so the flag has both a crescent moon, for Islam, and five stars, based on the flag of the People's Republic of China.

Finally, another country whose flag was influenced by Indonesia is Madagascar, off the coast of Africa. It is thought that the first settlers of this island were a small group from Indonesia. Among other things, they brought red and white banners with them, which have found their way into the heraldry of Madagascar.

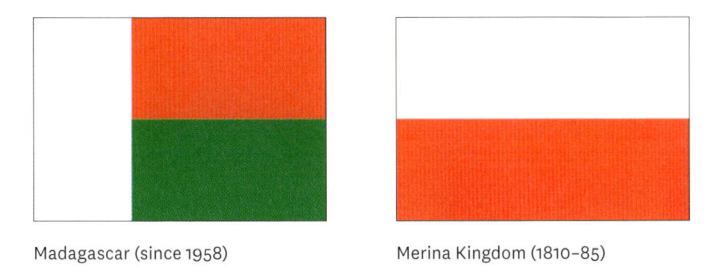

Madagascar (since 1958)

Merina Kingdom (1810–85)

In the late eighteenth and the nineteenth centuries, the island was part of the Merina kingdom (or kingdom of Malagasy); its flag was a white and red bicolour, like that of Poland. Madagascar was later colonised by France, and in 1960, having gained independence, it adopted a white-red-green tricolor, with the red and white of Indonesia. The name Madagascar was given by the Venetian explorer Marco Polo, who is said to have misheard the name of Mogadishu, in Somalia, and used it by mistake for Madagascar.

It turns out that the flag of the United States and the flag of Madagascar may have common roots with Indonesia. I love these incredible vexillological correlations.

08. Orange
Stripes

Once, while watching a soccer game, I had an argument with my friend. He, being a passionate sports fan, claimed that the flag of the Netherlands has an orange stripe. I, being a lover of vexillology, just laughed. We bet on it and turned to Google, which quickly proved me right.

To comfort my somewhat upset friend, I explained to him that he was far from alone in his delusion. In fact, so many Dutch people were convinced that there was orange on their flag that Queen Wilhelmina issued a special decree in 1937. It was just one sentence: 'The colours of the flag of the Kingdom of the Netherlands are red, white and blue.' This was the shortest decree in the history of the country.

How is it that many people still associate the Netherlands with the colour orange?

In the first half of the sixteenth century, the Holy Roman Empire was ruled by a representative of the Habsburg dynasty, Charles V. (Charles V is considered one of the most influential monarchs in European history. We met him earlier as Charles I of Spain, with his motto *Plus ultra*.) The first transatlantic empire in history, which included a significant part of Europe, was consolidated under his crown. But in 1556 he abdicated and retired to a monastery, having divided his empire into two parts between Spain and Germany.

At that time Protestantism was gaining momentum in Northern Europe, while the Spanish kings stayed devout Catholics (it was they who introduced the Inquisition to Europe). But after the division of the empire, the freedom-loving Netherlands ended up under the rule of Madrid. Parts of the Netherlands seceded from Spain in 1581, but it was not until 1648 that the Netherlands gained independence.

8. Orange Stripes

Netherlands (since 1596)

The earlier version with the orange stripe

The anti-Spanish uprising was led by William of Orange. This name has nothing to do with the colour orange or with the citrus fruit. It was because William came from the French principality of Orange. Nevertheless, orange became the characteristic colour for William and his troops.

The king liked to wear an orange cloak, a white hat and a blue collar, and these colours formed the basis of the first Dutch flag. Apparently, it was the first tricolor in the world that became a national flag. Some say that the flag of the Netherlands inspired the French revolutionaries to create their own tricolor. If this is true, then the Dutch tricolor is the most influential flag in history.

The use of orange on the flag turned out to be impractical – the orange paint faded over time. And so over a period of about thirty years, the orange was gradually replaced by red. Paintings of the time indicate that the transformation to red was complete by about 1660. Around the same time, this tricolor migrated to the flag of the Russian Empire.

However, the colour orange remained an important element of the symbolism of the Netherlands. Several times a year, during royal holidays, an additional orange ribbon is attached to the red-white-blue flag. And sports teams often wear orange kit, which is what confused my friend.

Ironically, the colour orange, which disappeared from the Dutch flag, remained on many other flags that are related to the Netherlands. For example, New York was originally called New Amsterdam, and its flag is blue, white and orange. In the centre of the flag is the seal of New York City, which has some Dutch attributes on it including a windmill, and the date 1625 – the year of the first settlement.

New York City

Luxembourg (since 1845)

The flag of neighbouring Luxembourg is similar to the flag of the Netherlands, although its blue and red stripes are a lighter shade than those on the Dutch flag. Luxembourg became independent in 1867; but its flag of red, white and light blue was not officially adopted until 1993.

Periodically, the country has discussions of the kind we have seen in other countries: some say that the flag of Luxembourg is too similar to the Dutch one, and should be changed. The most recent debate was in 2006, but the proposal was not supported and was dropped.

The largest country with traces of Dutch orange in its heraldry is the South African Republic. In the seventeenth century the southern part of the continent of Africa began to be colonised by the Dutch East India Company, and the Cape Colony was established. Later, during the Napoleonic Wars, these strategically important territories were conquered by the British, after which the Boers (the descendants of the Dutch settlers) retreated deeper into the continent and founded two new Boer countries: the Orange Free State and the Transvaal.

The flags of both countries had a clear Dutch heritage.

Orange Free State

Transvaal Republic

8. Orange Stripes

123

These republics were short-lived by historical standards – they existed for about a century. In 1910, as a result of the two Boer Wars, both republics together with the Cape and Natal were united to form the new state of the Union of South Africa.

At first, the flag of the new state was typical of British colonies, with the Union Jack on the canton and the coat of arms on a white disc. It was not popular: the Boers saw it as a British flag, and the British saw it as a watered-down Union Jack.

In 1928, after several years of bitter disputes, the country adopted a new flag. Because it was a compromise for both the British and the Boers, it turned out to be perhaps one of the strangest national flags in the world.

Let's take a closer look at this vexillological compromise.

South African Red Ensign (before 1928)

South Africa (1928–94) – with flag on a flag on a flag

Naval ensign – with flag on a flag on a flag on a flag

The flag consists of three stripes – blue, white and orange – which was the flag of the Netherlands two centuries previously. In the centre are three more flags: those of Great Britain and the two Boer republics. These three flags, and their location, were the result of a complex political compromise.

Note that the British flag in this arrangement is upside down (as can be seen by looking at the red diagonal lines). The flag of the Orange Free State is turned on its side. But the flag on the right – the Transvaal one – is the right way up. The idea was to give each of the three flags equal status, and so, for example, the Union Jack, which is nearest the flagpole (and therefore in a more important position on the flag), is represented with the hoist on the right. It's hard to explain!

And this flag became the only national flag in the world with a triple nesting – a flag on a flag on a flag. Moreover, in 1952 the country's naval forces adopted a new ensign having this very flag (with a triple nest) on its canton, so that created a banner with a quadruple nest.

After the Second World War, from 1948 onwards, the Union of South Africa passed a number of strict laws that severely limited the civil rights of the black population. This was known as the apartheid era. In March 1961, the South African prime minister gave formal notice that the country was changing from a constitutional monarchy to a republic but, because of apartheid, permission was not granted for the new republic to be part of the British Commonwealth. In May that year, the Union of South Africa ceased to exist and the Republic of South Africa was created; it was not in the British Commonwealth and was subjected to all sorts of sanctions from the international community.

The apartheid policy continued until 1994, when Nelson Mandela came to power after spending twenty-seven years in prison. Much later, in 2019, the South African court ruled that the triple-nested flag was a symbol of apartheid and banned its use in much the same way that the fascist swastika, the Soviet hammer and sickle, and the Russian symbol Z are banned in many countries.

Republic of South Africa (since 1994)

After such radical changes in the country, it is not surprising that the question of creating a new flag arose. So in 1994 a new flag with a very original design was adopted. The red, white and blue colours are derived from the British and Dutch flags; the black, green and yellow are borrowed from the symbols of the African National Congress – the main party of the country, which came to power during Mandela's presidency and has ruled ever since. At the time it was the only national flag to have six colours in its main design. The shade of red on this flag is called chilli red, and is also a kind of compromise, being somewhere between red and orange.

The flag was created by the South African vexillologist Frederick Brownell. A few years previously he had worked on the design of the flag of Namibia, which separated from South Africa in 1990. Notice how the sun with twelve rays on the flag of Namibia is surprisingly similar to the sun on the flag of Taiwan, which we will discuss later.

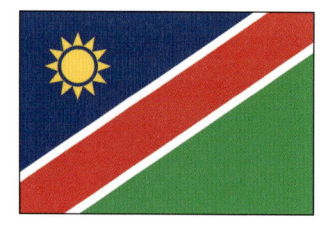

Namibia (since 1990)

Taiwan

Another country with a trace of the Netherlands on its flag is Ireland. To understand this you need to go back to 1526 when the English king Henry VIII fell in love with Anne Boleyn and demanded that the Pope give him a divorce from his first wife, Catherine of Aragon. When the Pope refused to agree to this demand, Henry severed his relations with Rome and the Catholic Church. A few years later the king's passion for Anne faded and she was beheaded – but a Protestant church, independent of the Pope, had already been established in England. While the English were being successfully converted into Protestants, the Irish remained mostly Catholic.

In the mid-1840s, a potato blight in Ireland caused a terrible famine, which killed almost a million people. This was made worse by the Corn Laws, which blocked the import of cheap corn, until their repeal in 1846. At the same time, there was a growing political movement committed to independence. A small group of French women sympathic to Irish nationalism presented a green–white–orange tricolor to the leader of the Irish rebellion. It is natural to assume that the Irish tricolor was inspired by the French flag.

The flag symbolised the hope for peace (white) between Catholics (green) and Protestants (orange). Support for the starving Irish also came from other countries. The most unexpected source was the United States, where the Native Americans learned about the Great Famine.

They collected $170 – a large amount in 1847 – and sent it as aid to Ireland. More than 170 years later, in 2020, when the Covid-19 epidemic broke out in the world and swept through the Navajo Nation, grateful Irish people collected more than $2.5 million to return the favour and help the Navajo.

In 1921 Ireland was divided into two parts – several Irish provinces in the north remained part of Great Britain, becoming Northern Ireland. The other provinces first became self-governing, and then, a year later, became the independent Republic of Ireland, though the green-white-orange tricolor wasn't officially recognised until 1937.

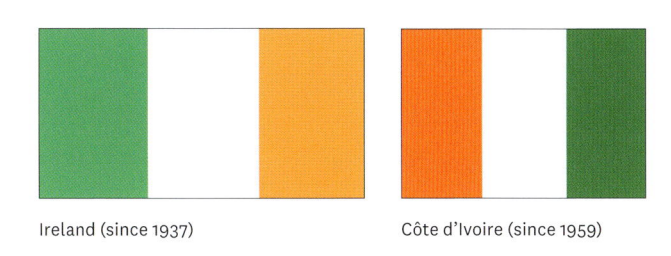

Ireland (since 1937)

Côte d'Ivoire (since 1959)

The flag of the African state Côte d'Ivoire is very similar to that of Ireland. If you ignore the proportions and shades, its flag is the exact reverse of the Irish one. At the athletics World Indoor Championships in 2018 a sprinter from Côte d'Ivoire took advantage of this. Having won the race, but realising she did not have the customary winner's flag, she borrowed an Irish flag from a fan in the crowd to celebrate her victory. And in 2013 Belfast unionists mistakenly burned the Ivorian tricolor instead of the Irish one on their annual 12 July bonfire.

However, Côte d'Ivoire might have ended up with an even less original flag. In 1960, when the country declared independence from France and designed its own banner, it was decided to use the layout of the French tricolor in orange, white and green. At the last moment, one of the members of the commission dealing with the approval of the flag suggested that the orange be replaced with red (a symbol of struggle and blood ... well, there you go again). Fortunately, the suggestion was declined.

The orange colour here symbolises the lands of the African savannah and has nothing to do with Protestantism. But it is interesting that since half of the population of Côte d'Ivoire professes Islam and the other half is Christian, the flag could carry the same symbolism as the Irish one: reconciliation between the two religions.

Niger (since 1959)

Zambia (since 1964)

In the same year, 1960, another West African country, Niger, gained independence from France. The orange colour on its flag represents the desert and the orange disc in the centre is the rising sun of the young country. Another interesting feature is that the flag is almost square – it has an unusual 6:7 aspect ratio.

The third African country that has an orange stripe on its flag is Zambia. Personally I find this flag one of the most original and aesthetically pleasing – especially after 1996 when the green colour of the flag was made grassier. And the composition of the banner – its main elements are located not on the canton but in the lower right corner – is a bold deviation from heraldic templates.

The orange colour here symbolises the country's resources of copper (which gives it an affinity with the flag of Cyprus). After Zambia became independent from Great Britain in 1964 its president set out on a policy of 'Zambian humanism', which included nationalising its copper companies. But despite its huge reserves of copper ores, Zambia has become one of the poorest countries in the world. So it seems that this whole venture of nationalisation has not been very humane after all.

As we have already seen, the flags of different countries are often similar. But no other coincidence amazes me as much as the similarity between the flags of Niger and India. I know that the flags have different shades and ratios, and the round element in the centre is different, but I still find the similarity striking.

India (since 1947)

Flag adopted by the Indian National Congress in 1931

Gandhi flag

From 1773 until 1858, India was ruled by the British East India Company. It was the Indian Mutiny in 1857 that led to the end of the Company's rule. The mutiny began with a rebellion of Hindu and Muslim sepoys (soldiers) in a town north-east of Delhi. The men objected to having to bite off the open ends of rifle cartridges, which, it was rumoured, were smeared with animal fat. If the grease really was made of beef or pork, then the British managed to offend both Hindus, who consider the cow sacred, and Muslims, who consider the pig an unclean animal. The rebellion spread, but was brutally suppressed. After that, India passed from private ownership to being ruled directly by the British government.

In the twentieth century Mahatma Gandhi, who preached the principles of nonviolent disobedience, led Indian resistance against the British. In 1921, he proposed that a flag be designed that had a spinning wheel in the centre, symbolising his hope that Indians would become self-reliant by producing their own clothes. (To emphasise his point, Gandhi often appeared at public events with a spinning wheel in his hands.) This initial design had two stripes, in the colours associated with the two main religions of India: red for the Hindus and green for the Muslims. Later Gandhi added a white stripe in the centre, to represent the other religions in India.

In 1931 the Indian National Congress officially recognised the flag, but replaced the red stripe with one of orange (actually, deep saffron). The final modification of the flag occurred a few days before the declaration of independence in 1947. The Constitutional Assembly decided to replace the spinning wheel with the Ashoka Chakra – a Buddhist symbol in the shape of a wheel, symbolising law and movement.

Of course, the Ashoka Chakra was not as politically neutral as a spinning wheel, but by that time it was already clear that the Indian territories inhabited mainly by Muslims would be allocated by the British to the separate state of Pakistan.

8. Orange Stripes

However, given that other drafts of the flag depicted Ganesha (a god with the head of an elephant) and Kali (a blue-skinned goddess with four arms), the option chosen was relatively secular.

Mahatma Gandhi did not agree with the new design of the flag. He saw it as another deviation from the ideas of peace and harmony among peoples that he believed in so fervently. A few months later, he was shot dead by a Hindu extremist who did not want peace with Muslims (the assassin was caught and executed despite the pleas of Gandhi's relatives for clemency).

Today India has among the strictest laws governing the handling of the national flag. Only one company is authorised to make and supply the Indian flag for the entire country of a population of one and a half billion. The Flag Code of India stipulates the fabric of the flag (a hand-spun cloth called *khadi*; or, since 2021, polyester), the density of fabric (exactly 150 threads per square centimetre), and the sizes of the cloth (there are nine sizes allowed).

The Flag Code also specifies the material that holds the flag to the pole – this must be made from a material called khadi-duck. It is believed that only a few dozen masters in the whole country can spin this fabric correctly. Flying a flag made of any other material than khadi is punishable by law with imprisonment up to three years, as well as a fine.

In August 1947, British India was divided into two independent dominions: India and Pakistan. The partition was made along religious lines, despite all Gandhi's efforts towards harmony.

Pakistan (since 1947)

Alas, in the clashes between Hindus and Muslims more than half a million people died, and it is estimated that about sixteen million were forced to move to their majority religious area. It was one of the largest displacements in history.

The national flag of Pakistan became a green field with a white crescent and a star on it, and a white stripe to the left. As in India, the green colour symbolises Islam and the white stands for all other religions. However, unlike Gandhi's flag, the colour of the country's dominant religion dominates the flag.

Shortly before the declaration of independence of Pakistan, the British Viceroy of India suggested that the Pakistanis include a Union Jack on their flag, but they refused, on the grounds that a Christian cross would not be acceptable on the flag of a Muslim country.

Initially, the borders of Pakistan were unusual in that the country consisted of two separate parts – one to the west of India and one to the east of India. These were called West Pakistan and East Pakistan, respectively. In the east of the country was the world's only third-order enclave: that of Dahala Khagrabari. It represented the territory of India surrounded by the territory of Pakistan, surrounded by the territory of India, surrounded again by the territory of Pakistan.

In 1971 East Pakistan separated from West Pakistan and became known as Bangladesh. The previous year, a tropical cyclone in East Pakistan killed about half a million people, but relief efforts from West Pakistan were minimal. This added to the discontent among the East Pakistanis. A bloody war broke out, which resulted in the creation of Bangladesh.

Bangladesh (since 1972)

Flag used for Bangladesh during the Liberation War (1971–2)

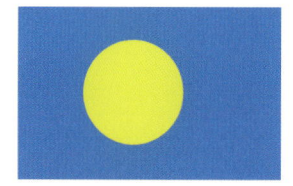

Palau (since 1981)

The Bangladeshi flag consists of a red disc on a green background. Although the dominant religion of the country is Islam, green here represents not religion, but also the 'generosity of the Bangladeshi land'

8. Orange Stripes

and the 'eternal youth' of its people. Initially, there was an orange map of the country on the red disc, but after a year the map was removed and the disc was shifted slightly to the left, so that, when the flag is flying, the disc appears to be in the centre.

Perfectionists may find this asymmetry with the disc offset to the hoist slightly annoying. You can see the same composition on the flag of the Pacific state of Palau. Meanwhile, if the red disc of Bangladesh symbolises the sun, the yellow disc of Palau represents the moon. Perhaps one day people will realise that flags are seen more often as graphic elements rather than fabrics fluttering in the wind, so they will shift the discs to the centre, as Japan did in 1999.

Off the coast of India is another country with orange and green motifs on its flag: Sri Lanka. This island country (then called Ceylon) gained independence from the British in 1948, the year after India and Pakistan.

The state symbols of India and Sri Lanka have much in common. The coat of arms of Sri Lanka shows the same Buddhist wheel as the Indian flag. The flag itself depicts a snub-nosed lion with a sword, which local kings have used in their heraldry since ancient times. The lion is surrounded by four leaves of a bo tree, which is a sacred plant in Buddhist culture (sacred fig, or *Ficus religiosa*). I think it's interesting that the shape of the island of Sri Lanka is similar to the shape of these leaves.

Sri Lanka (since 1972)

The colours on this flag also symbolise nationalities. The maroon background represents the dominant Sinhalese population, and the green and orange stripes represent the Muslim and Tamil (Hindu) ethnic groups, respectively.

Oh, if only peace between nations could be achieved by placing their colours on a single flag! But from the start of Sri Lanka's existence, there were bloody conflicts between the Sinhalese and the Tamils. The climax occurred in 1981 when, during interethnic clashes, a Sinhalese mob (including some drunken police officers) burned down the Jaffna Public Library. Almost 100,000 culturally important books and manuscripts were destroyed, in what was one of the largest incidents of book burnings ever. That incident was one of the catalysts for a long civil war between the government of Sri Lanka and the Tamil rebel movement, the Tamil Tigers, which ended only in 2009 with the defeat of the latter.

Fortunately, not all countries of the South Asian region have such a bloody history. The small Himalayan Kingdom of Bhutan has never taken part in any military conflict – neither international nor internal. Moreover, the Bhutanese government officially measures the gross national happiness index of its population and actively promotes this concept at the UN.

Bhutan means 'the kingdom of the dragon' in the local language. Actually, it is the Chinese dragon that is depicted on the country's flag – an ancient mythological creature that, unlike the dragon in European culture, is the embodiment of kindness. Had St George met a Chinese dragon during his travels, he would most likely not have killed it, but rather have gently stroked its soft horns.

Bhutan

Bhutan is interesting for its isolationist policy. For example, television was not allowed there until 1999. Also unusual is the fact that male genitalia are painted on the walls of many houses. The tradition of these drawings dates back to the fifteenth century, when a sex-mad Tibetan monk came to Bhutan and put about the legend that painting phalluses on walls and flying hanging phalluses from the rooftops would drive away evil spirits and subdue demonesses.

Sometimes I can't help wondering about the reaction of the international community should this kingdom place an image of a phallus on its flag instead of the dragon, to drive away any evil spirits from its happy country.

09. Grim Reaper
Flags

In 1871 French neo-Jacobins, socialists and anarchists, singing 'La Marseillaise', seized power in Paris and ruled the country for seventy-two days. The Paris Commune, as we mentioned in Chapter 1, made its official flag a cloth of solid red.

This was a crucial point in communist historiography because Marxists later called it the first example of the proletariat taking power into its hands. Since then the ideas of communism have permeated into all the nooks and crannies of the world, soaking many national flags with communist red.

The most famous communist banner was the flag of the Union of Soviet Socialist Republics, the USSR. From 1922 until the collapse of the Soviet Union in December 1991 the Red Flag fluttered over 'one-sixth of the Earth's land surface', as the Kremlin proudly put it.

Soviet leaders thought big and hatched plans to build communism in all countries of the world, despite resistance. Every element of the state symbols of the Soviet empire related to the idea of world expansion.

USSR (1955–91)

State emblem of the USSR. The sickle hilt was represented incorrectly for the first 14 years.

The five-pointed star – the main distinguishing feature of the fighters for communism – symbolised the five continents to be triumphantly encompassed by Marxist ideas. For some reason they decided to have mercy on the sixth continent of Antarctica. Or maybe they were just unwilling to deal with the symbol of the Jewish people?

Another famous communist symbol is the hammer and sickle, which symbolises the unity of industrial workers and agricultural workers. The hammer and sickle was prominent on both the state emblem of the Soviet Union and the Soviet flag. The motto of the USSR, written on the state emblem, was: 'Workers of the world, unite!' There was a popular joke in the USSR about Karl Marx, who came back to life and declared on Soviet radio: 'Workers of the world, please excuse me!'

The hammer and sickle was introduced into Soviet heraldry in 1923. The artist who won the competition to create the design asked someone to bring him a real peasant sickle as a model. Apparently, they brought him an old tool: its handle was fixed upside down, and thicker towards the blade, which was not customary. So this sickle with a defective handle was depicted on the Soviet banner and stayed there for 14 years.

Wrong presentation of the tool symbolising peasants ... It is difficult to find a more expressive heraldic metaphor for Stalin's man-made famine in which about five million people died of hunger across the USSR.

Crossing of tools is quite common in heraldry. Before the hammer and sickle were used in the emblem of the USSR, the crossed plough and hammer were used in heraldry. And on the flag of socialist East Germany the hammer was crossed with a pair of compasses, representing the intelligentsia.

German Democratic Republic

The Soviet Union consisted of fifteen socialist republics, which gained independence with its collapse in 1991. Until then, their flags were very similar: a red cloth with gold letters on the canton representing the abbreviated name of the republic. The flag of Ukraine, for example, contained the letters Y.C.C.P. (with full stops after each letter until 1937, and without the full stops since 1937); the flag of Belarus had Б.С.С.Р. However, thanks to the UN this monotony has ended.

Armenian SSR	Azerbaijan SSR	Byelorussian SSR
Estonian SSR	Georgian SSR	Kazakh SSR
Kyrgyz SSR	Latvian SSR	Lithuanian SSR
Moldavian SSR	Tajik SSR	Turkmen SSR
Ukrainian SSR	Uzbek SSR	Russian SFSR

When the UN was created in 1945, the West and the USSR tried to increase the number of member countries loyal to themselves. Thus, several countries that were not completely independent became members of the UN General Assembly. For example, New Zealand and India became members, although neither had yet gained independence from Great Britain, as did the Philippines, which was a US protectorate.

9. Grim Reaper Flags

Stalin sought to ensure that, in addition to the USSR itself, Ukraine and Belarus would join the UN. Formal attributes of independence were therefore created in these republics – for example, their own ministries of foreign affairs. Although it was clear that the republics were not in fact independent, Stalin did achieve his goal and the two republics joined the UN.

The fact that the Ukrainian and Belarusian flags were similar to each other and to the flag of the USSR introduced a certain heraldic confusion at the UN. So the Soviet leadership decided to make the flag of each Soviet republic more distinctive

The flags of the Soviet republics, especially if placed side by side, look strange. It would be natural to suppose that they should all obey certain standards – at least, for the size of the hammer and sickle, or the width of the stripes. Perhaps the Soviet tailors sewing these flags were not sober and introduced inconsistencies.

Among the countries that were not part of the USSR, the flag of the Republic of the Congo looked the most Soviet for a time.

French Congo (1959–60); Republic of the Congo (1960–70) and since 1991

People's Republic of the Congo (1970–91)

While under French colonial rule, the country was known as the French Congo. Granted autonomy in 1959, it replaced the French tricolor with a distinctive flag in green, yellow and red, in a unique diagonal pattern. When the country became independent in 1960, it kept this flag until a coup forced a change of government (to a Marxist-Leninist one), a change of name (to the People's Republic of the Congo) and a change of flag (to a red banner adorned with a star, and crossed hammer and hoe).

In 1991, after the collapse of the Soviet Union and of the People's Republic of the Congo, the country's name reverted to the Republic of the Congo and the new government immediately restored the original flag.

Republic of Mozambique (since 1983) 　　Angola (since 1975)

Proposed flag of Angola (2003)

Today we see proletarian symbols on the flags of two other African countries: Mozambique and Angola. Both nations received independence from Portugal in 1975 after the Carnation Revolution took place in Lisbon.

Having become an independent state, Mozambique set on a path of communism. The president, Samora Machel, established a one-party system, began to fight against religion and introduced a planned economy. Samora ruled his country for eleven years until he died in a plane crash on the border with South Africa. Later, his wife Graça married the South African president Nelson Mandela, becoming the only woman in history to have been First Lady in two countries (unless we count Eleanor of Aquitaine, the mother of Richard the Lionheart, who divorced the king of France and married the king of England).

The flag of Mozambique still has a look of the Soviet style. It has a socialist star on the left; on the star is an open book, which is criss-crossed with a hoe and a Kalashnikov rifle with a bayonet attached. This makes Mozambique the only country with a modern firearm on its flag.

The Mozambican opposition occasionally tries to change the flag and remove the star with the rifle, but so far to no avail.

The flag of Angola also looks somewhat belligerent. It has a star, a machete and half a cogwheel. The machete is an African analogue of the sickle symbolising agricultural labourers, and the cogwheel represents industrial workers.

Like Mozambique, Angola first followed a socialist path, but then began to introduce market reforms. And thus the question of replacing the flag arose. In 2003 a parliamentary commission proposed a new flag with blue and white stripes and a sun reminiscent of ancient cave paintings in the country. However, the proposal was rejected.

The red-blue-white stripes of the rejected flag of Angola are reminiscent of the flag of another communist country: North Korea.

For most of its history Korea pursued a policy of isolation, and in 1910 it was annexed by Japan. After the Second World War, Korea was divided into two parts – the communist North and the capitalist South. In 1950 a war broke out between them, killing more than a million people and completely destroying the infrastructure. As a result, a border between the two countries – the Military Demarcation Line – was established, which runs near the 38th parallel.

Korea (since 1883), now South Korea

North Korea (since 1948)

Korean unification flag

On this border between North and South Korea is one of the highest flagpoles in the world. A huge North Korean flag flutters on it, and loudspeakers are installed which thundered with propagandistic radio towards South Korea for many years. At some point the South Koreans responded by turning on their own propaganda weapon – K-pop music. In the end, slightly freaked out by the cacophony, both sides stopped their broadcasts by mutual agreement.

The flag of North Korea was adopted in 1948, which is the 37th year according to the country's system of numbering years. (Its *Juche* calendar starts with the birth of the first communist leader Kim Il Sung in 1912, which became *Juche 1*). According to the official North Korean version, Comrade Kim himself designed the flag, although in fact he initially wanted to keep the Korean flag that was used before the country was divided. The Soviets did not agree with this, considering the Korean flag and its ancient Buddhist symbols to be superstition. So the design for a new flag was drawn up in Moscow and sent to Pyongyang – with a five-pointed star and a dominant red colour.

It is easy to understand why the Soviets wanted to change the Korean flag. After all, the USSR was a strictly atheist country, consistently uprooting religious symbols wherever they were found.

The current official flag of South Korea features the yin and yang. Around these are four sets of black bars called trigrams, each of which represents different things in seven categories. One trigram, for example, represents the sun (a celestial body), autumn (a season), south (a cardinal direction), justice (a virtue), daughter (family member), and fire (a natural element), together meaning fruition. I ask you to pay attention to the first trigram and its meaning: 'south'. We'll come back to it shortly.

The main colour of the South Korean flag is white, which represents peace and is also the colour of traditional Korean clothing.

There is another interesting phenomenon in Korean vexillology – the Korean unification flag. This banner was created for the 11th Asian Games in 1990, in which North and South Korea agreed to participate jointly. In the event, they played as separate teams, but the unification flag remained. It was first used officially in the World Table Tennis Championships the following year, and has been used at several international events since then.

On the flag, we see the outline of the Korean Peninsula in blue. Having read the chapter on the UN flag you should not be surprised by this design. Nevertheless, this seemingly neutral flag creates its own difficulties. Periodically Koreans depict small islands on the flag, which are disputed with neighbouring Japan and China. Of course, this causes protests every time.

There is another country in the world whose flag depicts the yin and yang: Mongolia. Until 1992, the flag also had a five-pointed star on it. But first things first.

Mongolia (since 1992)

Mongolia (1945–92)

The story of Mongolia is usually told from the thirteenth century, when the great and bloody Genghis Khan created an empire stretching from Korea to Poland. This empire is considered the largest in the history of mankind. Today, Mongolia is also one of the largest countries in the world, although its population is only about 3.4 million people.

Mongolia had its first communist government in 1921, just a few years before it became the Soviet Union's first satellite in 1924, and was a province of China from the seventeenth century. It is now customary to distinguish between the autonomous region of China and the independent state - the country of Mongolia.

Independent socialist Mongolia chose as its official flag a red banner with the Mongolian Soyombo symbol on it. The Soyombo is a Buddhist symbol featuring the yin and yang, and other traditional elements. After the Second World War, the flag was changed to one with three stripes, and a communist five-pointed star was placed over the Soyombo, making it look like a Christmas tree.

How Mongolians managed to keep the Soyombo on their flag – albeit with a star – remains a mystery to me. After all, the USSR, which de facto ruled the country at that time, tried to destroy all religious symbols. In the late 1930s, Stalin extended his Great Repression into Mongolia, persecuting the Buddhist clergy and exterminating about 18,000 lamas. The population of Mongolia was reduced by 5 per cent.

The destruction of the Manjusri monastery is a classic example of Soviet zeal in destroying all Buddhist cultural heritage. The monastery was in a beautiful place in the Mongolian mountains, and Buddhist monks meditated in special niches carved in the rocks. But all twenty of the monastery's temples were destroyed by the Mongolian communists, and its lamas were arrested and later shot. The Soviet Union even sent bombers to destroy this beauty!

As expected, after the collapse of the USSR, Mongolia quickly said goodbye to communism and removed the star from its flag. Now it has only the Soyombo on it.

After the collapse of the USSR the main remaining red communist banner is that of China.

People's Republic of China (since 1949)

The flag of China before 1912 (Qing dynasty)

China (1912–28)

Republic of China (since 1928). Now the flag of Taiwan

Until the twentieth century, the flag of China featured a kindly Chinese dragon, making it very similar to the flag of Bhutan. The main colour was yellow, representing the imperial Qing dynasty (at that time in China, only members of the emperor's family were allowed to wear yellow clothes). There is a red circle in the upper left corner of the flag. You might think that this is the sun, and the Chinese dragon is looking up at it, about to sneeze. In fact, this is not the sun, but a red pearl – a symbol of wealth and good luck.

In 1912 there was a revolution in China, ending more than 2,000 years of imperial rule. A wave of uprisings swept across the country, the Chinese began to cut their pigtails in protest against the Manchu dynasty. (The Manchus had forced Chinese men to wear their hair in a specific style known as a queue – what we might call a pigtail – under pain of death.)

So China became a republic, and the dragon on the flag was replaced by five horizontal stripes, symbolising the five major nationalities of China. The white stripe was the symbol of the Hui people: Chinese Muslims – in particular, the Uighurs – whom China is accused of oppressing today.

In 1928 Chiang Kai-shek became leader of the Republic of China, and the flag featuring a white sun with twelve rays became the main banner of the country. The number twelve here symbolises twelve months, as well as twelve Chinese *shi* hours (one *shi* equals two modern hours). So the image of the sun with twelve rays is sending out a message about working 'round the clock, all year round'.

After the Second World War, the communists came to power in China under the leadership of Mao Zedong, and Chiang Kai-shek and his government were forced to retreat to the island of Taiwan. The flag with the white sun moved along with them, and is now more commonly referred to as the flag of Taiwan.

In the next twenty years Mao launched a series of grandiose experiments on his country. In the desire to catch up and overtake capitalist countries, the party embarked on a programme known as the Great Leap Forward. This included the Four Pests campaign, in which rats, flies, mosquitoes and sparrows were considered as pests to be exterminated. Millions of sparrows were killed, which, far from protecting the crops, led to total crop failure because actually these birds eat the locusts that destroy the crops.

Estimates vary, but the Great Leap Forward led to a great famine which caused the death of between twenty and forty-five million Chinese. It became the biggest social disaster in human history.

The large yellow star on the flag symbolises the Communist Party of China. Four smaller stars, each 'looking' at it, denote the four classes of Chinese society: the working class, the peasantry, the petty bourgeoisie and the national bourgeoisie (the classification is taken from Mao's speech in 1949).

On the red flag of neighbouring Vietnam, we also see a yellow communist star, though it is slightly larger and placed in the centre.

Socialist Republic of Vietnam (since 1955)

Socialist Republic of Vietnam (1945–55)

Republic of Vietnam (1948–75)

Before the Second World War, Vietnam, along with Laos and Cambodia, was part of a French colony called French Indochina. Then the Japanese temporarily captured this territory, and after the war the French returned.

The struggle against the French colonialists was led by the Vietnamese communists. Considering that the USSR provided decisive support in this struggle, it is not surprising that the red banner with a five-pointed star became the flag of socialist Vietnam. Until 1955, this star had a nice rounded shape.

The war against the French went down in history as the First Indochina War. Afterwards, Vietnam, like Korea, was divided into two: North (communist) and South. Soon after, the Second Indochina War (also known as the Vietnam War) broke out, with the USSR and China on the side of the North and the United States on the side of the South. This war was so hard for the United States and its Western allies that US President Nixon even considered using nuclear weapons against the northerners. In the end, the Western forces retreated, and in 1975 the two parts of Vietnam were united into a single socialist country.

The flag of South Vietnam was yellow with three horizontal red stripes. The three red stripes represent the symbol ☰, which means 'South' and is a reference to the word 'Nam' ('South') in the word 'Vietnam'. So one may say that the name 'South Vietnam', had a similar tautology as 'East Timor'.

Vietnam's neighbour, Laos, was also once a part of French Indochina. After the Second World War, it gained independence from France and became a kingdom, but after the defeat of the United States in the Vietnam War, the Lao king was overthrown, and the country joined the path of communism. It did not stay communist, however.

9. Grim Reaper Flags

Laos (since 1975)

Kingdom of Laos (1947–1975)

Before its socialist period, white elephants were the main characters on the flags of Laos, in a graphic reference to the country's poetic name – the Land of a Million Elephants and a White Parasol. Today, because of massive deforestation, elephants in Laos are on the verge of extinction. As of 2022 a more accurate name for the country would be The Land of Eight Hundred Elephants. Of course, eight-hundred elephants are more numerous than a mere fifty Dominican parrots, but still…

After the victory of the communists, the flag was changed to the current one: two red stripes and a blue stripe with a white disc in the centre. The red stripes symbolise the two peoples of Laos: those who live in Laos itself, and those who live in what is now north-eastern Thailand. These two nations are separated by the Mekong River, represented by the blue stripe on the flag. The white disc on the flag represents the moon, as well as the hope for the future reunification of the two peoples. Thus, it turns out that the banner of Laos is another flag that is filled with potential conflict with a neighbour.

As for the white disc on the banner… perhaps it is a bird's eye view of the same white umbrella. But that's just my personal guess.

The disc on the flag of Laos looks especially interesting if you have come across such figures on the flags of other countries. It usually symbolises a cut-out coat of arms, as a symbol of the revolution. This approach was used by the participants in the revolutions in Hungary, Romania and East Germany, who opposed the totalitarian communist regimes.

Flag of the Hungarian Revolution of 1956

After the fall of the Berlin Wall, many Germans cut out the emblem of East Germany (1991)

Flag of the anti-Ceaușescu protesters during the Romanian Revolution (1989)

The flag of Thailand is similar to the flag of Laos, both in design and in its history. Thailand, previously known as Siam, is the only country in South-East Asia that has been independent throughout its history, mainly because it served as a buffer zone between colonies. For exactly one hundred years, the Thai flag also featured a white elephant in royal regalia, until in 1917 the country adopted the current flag of five horizontal stripes: red, white, blue, white and red.

Thailand (since 1917)

Thailand (1893–1917)

9. Grim Reaper Flags

147

Siam/Thailand (17th–19th centuries)

Unlike its neighbours, Thailand never tried to introduce communism, though it did have a solid red banner from the seventeenth to the nineteenth century.

Neighbouring Myanmar placed a large five-pointed star on its flag, as Vietnam did.

Myanmar (1948–74)

1974–2010. Even more stars

Since 2010. One star is enough

Until 1948, Myanmar (then called Burma) was a British colony. The liberation movement of the country was led by General Aung San, who was killed by the conspirators a few months before the country declared independence.

The first flag of Myanmar had a design somewhat similar to the Taiwanese flag, with a red background and a blue canton. The canton has one large star and five smaller ones (reminiscent of the stars on the Chinese flag, which was adopted a year later). And in 1974, an even more sophisticated image appeared on the blue canton – a cogwheel and an ear of paddy rice. As with the flag of Angola, the cogwheel here symbolises the industrial workers, and the rice symbolises the peasantry.

A distinctive feature of Myanmar is its special form of religion: Buddhism, permeated with astrology and numerology. The vast majority of Myanmarians, including the country's leadership, check all decisions of even slightest importance against the astrological calendar. The transfer of the capital from the city of Yangon to the city of Naypyidaw took place on 6 November 2005 at 6:37 a.m. – on the date and at the exact time prescribed by court numerologists.

When General Ne Win seized power in 1962, he based many of his decisions on the advice of astrologers and numerologists. For example, allegedly at the prompting of Ne Win's astrologer, on 6 December 1970, the government made the country change from driving on the left to driving on the right. And in 1988, Ne Win unexpectedly decided to withdraw all banknotes in denominations of 25, 35 and 75 kyats. Instead, banknotes of 45 and 90 kyats were introduced, as they were divisible by the lucky number nine. This led to the 8888 Uprising, which takes its name from the date it started: 8 August 1988.

One of the leaders of that uprising was Aung San Suu Kyi, the daughter of the murdered General Aung San. She was put under house arrest, and in the following year, 1991, she was awarded the Nobel Peace Prize. Aung San Suu Kyi lived under house arrent for a total of fifteen years in a twenty-one-year period, until she was released in 2010. She was one of the political leaders of the country from 2016 until 2021, when there was another military coup. She has been in detention ever since, facing twenty-six years in prison.

There is one more socialist country in the world that has a star on its flag. Unlike the countries described above, it is still communist, even after the collapse of the USSR. It's Cuba.

Cuba (since 1902)

The five-pointed star on a red background gives the Cuban flag a very socialist look. But it was adopted back in 1902, when communist symbols did not really exist. And Cuba itself, having just gained independence from Spain, was building a market economy with the support of the United States. The colours of the flag were inspired by the French Revolution, and the star reflected Cuba's desire to become another state of its mighty neighbour.

Cuba turned to communism after Fidel Castro seized power in the country in 1959. Actually, Castro did not plunge into Marxism–Leninism immediately. At first, he made attempts to improve relations with the United States, but could not forgive the Americans for humiliating him on his first official visit there, when President Eisenhower pointedly went to play golf instead of meeting him.

The USSR took advantage of the split between Cuba and the United States, and began to support the island financially and politically in every possible way. The worsening of relations between the two superpowers over Cuba culminated in 1962 with the Cuban Missile Crisis.

Another country whose flag can be mistaken for a socialist banner is Suriname, a former Dutch colony in South America. Today Suriname is the only country besides the Netherlands where the majority of the population speaks Dutch. If we remove the green and white stripes from the flag, we have the Vietnamese banner. However, its origin also has nothing to do with socialism.

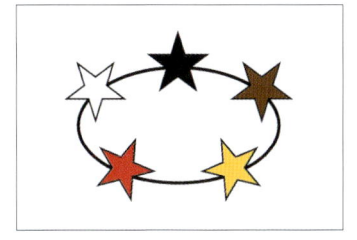

Suriname (since 1975)   (1959–75)

Before the country gained independence from the Netherlands in 1975, it had five stars on its flag, symbolising the five ethnic groups of the country: Africans, Indians, Chinese, Americans and Europeans (which makes it somewhat akin to the emblem of the Olympic Games). The colour of each star was clearly correlated with the colour of the skin of the corresponding ethnic group, for which the flag was criticised. Today, there is only one star on the Surinamese flag, and its five points symbolise those five ethnic groups.

Now that we've talked enough about five-pointed stars, let's move on to six-pointed ones.

10. Six-pointed Stars

On 14 May 1948, the Israeli Declaration of Independence was proclaimed. The next day five Arab countries immediately declared war on Israel and attacked the new country from different sides. Later that year, five months into the war, Israel adopted its new flag. It features the Star of David with two blue stripes on a white background.

Israel (since 1948)

By the time Israel was created, the six-pointed star had become the main symbol of the Jews. But the Israeli flag could easily have been quite different. Theodor Herzl, who played one of the key roles in the creation of Israel, suggested a flag with a Star of David and also seven golden six-pointed stars in a circle to symbolise the seven golden hours of the working day. His idea was to show that the state was open to the ideas of socialism, which were considered progressive at the time.

The state's leaders had a reservation about putting the Star of David on the flag. They were worried that Jews in other countries using the Star of David might be accused of disloyalty to their country of residence. In the end, these doubts were cast aside and Israel's flag is the one we see now.

The Star of David is associated not only with the Jewish people, but also with the persecution they suffered for many centuries. The most well-known and terrifying example is when the German fascists forced Jews to wear yellow Stars of David on their clothing. However, Hitler was not the first to do this. During the Middle Ages, Jews were sometimes forced to wear the yellow Star of David, to identify them as religious or ethnic outsiders. Such measures were necessary, according to one of the papal decrees in the thirteenth century, so that Christian men would not 'have relations with' Jewish women, and vice versa.

The blue colour on the Israeli flag has a special meaning in Judaism, as white and blue stripes are present on the design of the *tallit*, which is a fringed shawl that Jews wear during prayer. In ancient times, the blue dye was made from specific snails – probably the *Murex* marine snail. This dye is mentioned many times in the Torah. Although the secret of its manufacture was lost many centuries ago, a handful of scientists have finally managed to recreate the process.

The dyes from these snails varied in hue from blue to purple. Perhaps, if certain other snails had been used, the Israeli flag would have been purple, not blue.

Israeli law does not define the precise shade of blue on the flag. But by an amazing coincidence the colour most commonly seen on the internet on the flag of Israel is the same as a shade called International Klein Blue. This is the colour developed by the French artist Yves Klein, with which he painted the naked bodies of models and made them roll over a white canvas, creating paintings worth millions of dollars.

There are countless conspiracy theories surrounding Jews, and the flag is no exception. In an interview with *Playboy* magazine, the Palestinian leader Yasser Arafat claimed that the two blue stripes on the flag symbolise the Nile and the Euphrates, and show that Israel intends to seize the land between the two rivers.

The flag of Israel first flew into outer space in 2003. Israel's first astronaut Ilan Ramon raised the white and blue flag aboard the space shuttle *Columbia*, which crashed on its way back to Earth.

At the time of the creation of Israel, another country had the Star of David on its flag: Nigeria. But how did the Jewish symbol end up on the flag of a distant African country? There is a rather confusing story here.

Nigeria (since 1960)

1914–53, with a Tudor Crown

1953–60, with a St Edward crown

In the nineteenth century the territories of modern Nigeria were British colonies. For some time they were divided into Northern Nigeria and Southern Nigeria, but in 1914 the British, under the governor-general of Nigeria, Sir Frederick Lugard, united the two parts into one vast state. The northern and southern parts of the country are still quite different. The southern lands are predominantly populated by Christians (which is logical, because there was greater access to the sea and thus more contact with Europe), and the northern lands by Muslims.

In creating the flag of the newly formed colony, the British were not original: they placed the Union Jack on the canton. On the right side of the flag was the Star of David with the Tudor Crown inside it; this was replaced by St Edward's Crown when Elizabeth II came to the throne.

The Star of David was included in the flag on the recommendation of Lugard, who had seen this sign on the lid of a beautiful goblet. (He called it Solomon's Seal.) This goblet had been captured by British troops from the Hausa, the largest ethnic group in Nigeria. Lugard seemed to be quite straightforward: he liked the symbol, and just placed it on the flag without additional research.

But that goblet, apparently, was once captured by the Hausa themselves from another, less numerous Igbo people. The six-pointed star had been used by the Igbo for many centuries, ever since Jewish merchants came to the area in the early thirteenth century. Today, among the Igbo there are between 3,000 and 30,000 Nigerians professing Judaism.

Just appreciate this vexillological history! Many centuries ago, Jews influenced the Igbo. Then the Hausa tribe took those goblets with the six-pointed star from the Igbo tribe as a trophy. Then the British governor-general naively admired them and made the six-pointed star a symbol of one of the largest British colonies.

In 1959, a year before independence, the Nigerian government held a contest to design a new flag. The contest was won by Michael Taiwo Akinkunmi, a young Nigerian student in London who learned about the competition in a library. In Akinkunmi's version the flag had a red sun in the centre, strongly reminiscent of the Vergina sun which we will meet a few chapters later in North Macedonia. However, the sun was removed from the flag, leaving a laconic white-and-green variant.

Akinkunmi's original proposal for the flag of independent Nigeria (1959)

There is another state in Africa with a six-pointed star on its flag: Equatorial Guinea. Here are six stars representing the country's mainland and the five principal islands. This drawing has nothing to do with the Jews, but the yellow six-pointed stars do have something in common with the design of the flag of Israel by Theodor Herzl.

Equatorial Guinea (since 1968)

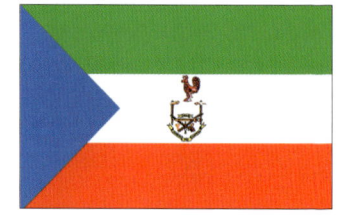

Flag of Francisco Nguema (1973–9)

The name Equatorial Guinea is confusing, because the country is not on the equator.

Under the stars on the flag of Equatorial Guinea is a silk cotton tree and the national motto below it in Spanish, which translates as: 'Unity, Peace, Justice'. Meanwhile, life in this small African country can hardly boast of justice. Equatorial Guinea is a major oil exporter, but its income is distributed very unevenly.

Previously, Equatorial Guinea was a colony of Spain and was called Spanish Guinea. Today it is the only country in Africa where Spanish is the official language. In 1968, the country gained independence, and Francisco Macías Nguema came to power.

It is believed that in the years of his reign Nguema killed about a quarter of the country's population. The executions were sometimes very bizarre. For example, at Christmas in 1979, the president had 150 of his opponents gunned down in a football stadium by soldiers dressed as Santa Claus.

During the final years of his reign, Nguema began to show signs of mental illness. Relations with other countries deteriorated; terror gained momentum. Perhaps one of the signs of dementia was the new flag of the country adopted in 1973. It showed a red and black chicken with one white leg, a sword and several tools including a pickaxe and a hoe.

In the end, the dictator was overthrown by his nephew, and Nguema was sentenced to death. But then a problem arose: the Equatorial Guineans believed that Nguema had supernatural powers. None of the local soldiers agreed to take part in his execution, and a platoon of foreign mercenaries – Moroccan soldiers – had to be invited for that purpose.

At the time of writing, in 2023, Teodoro Obiang Nguema Mbasogo is still the country's president, making him the longest-serving non-royal president in the world. The quality of his government can be judged by the fact that 75 per cent of the country's population lives below the poverty line, and one in five children does not live to the age of five. However, not everything is so bad. For example, the president's son, also named Teodoro, is doing well. He has the honorary position of vice president and minister of agriculture and forestry. He is also famous for his love of buying luxury sports cars and expensive real estate around the world. For example, over the years police have repeated seized his luxury cars, including Bugattis, Ferraris and a Maserati. The vice-president does not even try to conceal his hobbies: he actively posts all his luxury on Instagram.

But let's get back to the Star of David and the six-pointed star. From a geometric point of view, it is a hexagram. This figure can be found in various parts of the world – among Muslims, Christians, Buddhists and even in the writings of Aristotle. It is difficult to say which culture was the first to use this symbol. Perhaps it originated independently in different parts of the world.

Often hexagrams are presented as two overlapping triangles, which in turn symbolise the merging of two principles – for example, male and female (and then we have an analogue of yin and yang).

The Muslim counterpart of the Star of David is the Seal of Solomon. King Solomon's life is described both in the Torah and in the Quran. According to these scriptures, Solomon wore a signet ring with a special design, which gave him some kind of super strength. Today, the Seal of Solomon is found on the flags of some Arab countries, but more often in the form of a five-pointed star than a six-pointed one. For example, we see it on the flag of Ethiopia, which is one of the most influential in the world. Many African countries, having gained independence, chose Ethiopian colours for their flags. This is because Ethiopia is one of two countries in Africa that has never been a foreign colony (the other is Liberia).

From the thirteenth century until 1974, Ethiopia was ruled by a royal dynasty who claimed to be descended from King Solomon. The five-pointed star on the flag is this same seal. The connection with the biblical king can also be traced in earlier versions of the Ethiopian flag, which had the image of a lion. This formidable red-eyed beast is not just an abstract beast, but has his own name: the Lion of Judah. Judah is another character in the Torah, and the lion is his symbol. King Solomon, whose kinship has always been the pride and joy of Ethiopia's rulers, also comes from this family.

Ethiopian flag with the Lion of Judah (1913–36 and 1941–74)

After the revolution, the Lion of Judah lost his crown and was given a spear instead of the cross

Traditional flag of Ethiopia; the Lion could not take it anymore, so has gone away

With Solomon's Seal (since 1996)

The lion flag flew above Ethiopia until 1936, when Italy occupied the country for five years. When Italian forces, under the fascist dictator Benito Mussolini, invaded Ethiopia, the League of Nations tried to impose economic sanctions against the Italians. However, these were toothless and had no effect – even though Mussolini had used chemical weapons. Later, Mussolini remarked to Hitler that if mineral sanctions for Ethiopia had been introduced, Italy would have had to retreat from Ethiopia within a week.

Having been in exile during the Italian occupation, the emperor of Ethiopia, Haile Selassie, returned in 1941, and the country regained the lion flag. He was overthrown by a military coup in 1974. The revolution was bound to affect the lion – first the crown was removed from his head and the Christian cross was replaced with a spear; and then he was completely banished from sight.

Haile Selassie I left an unexpected mark on world culture, giving rise to the religious movement Rastafarianism. The word is derived from the word Ras, which was his royal title, plus his own name before he became emperor: Tafari Makonnen. There are up to a million Rastafari around the world (including about 1 per cent of the population of Jamaica); Bob Marley is probably the most famous Rastafari there has been.

Rastafari believe that Haile Selassie was the embodiment of God on earth; they are also famous for their love of cannabis. Marcus Garvey, who we will look at in the next chapter, is considered a prophet in this religion.

We can see Solomon's Seal on the flag of another North African country: Morocco. Unlike Ethiopia, Morocco has Islam as its state religion. Therefore, the star is represented in green (the colour of Islam), and its five points symbolise the Five Pillars of Islam. The main colour on the flag has been red for almost a thousand years. During one particular dynasty in the twelfth and thirteenth centuries, there was a chessboard on the flag. During a later dynasty, the flag was solid red for 250 years.

Morocco (since 1915)

(1147–1269)

(1666–1915)

In the first half of the twentieth century Morocco was divided between France and Spain, and the Spaniards owned the south-western part of the country, almost completely covered by the sands of the Sahara desert. Morocco gained independence from the French in 1956, but it was only in 1975 that the Spanish left the Western Sahara. To force Spain to hand over this area, the Moroccan king organised a protest on an incredible scale: a peaceful march of 350,000 of his subjects to the contested territory.

Today, the Sahrawi Arab Democratic Republic (SADR) – also known as the Western Sahara – is a partially recognised state, recognised by forty-five UN states, and there is still conflict about its sovereignty. In 2010 Morocco laid out a huge Moroccan flag there, weighing 20 tonnes and measuring 60,000 square metres, which was authenticated by *Guinness World Records* as the largest flag in the world. However, the award was removed because this is disputed territory.

11. Horizontal Stripes of Eastern Europe

Eastern European countries have many common motifs in their history. Before the First World War, the main forces here were the Ottoman, Austro-Hungarian and Russian empires. In recent history, Russia has dominated in the region, and many countries ended up behind the Berlin Wall – that is, in the Communist Bloc.

Eastern European flags too have a common element: horizontal stripes. Of course, there are horizontal stripes on flags elsewhere, but in Eastern Europe they are found in abundance.

In terms of territory, Ukraine is the largest state in Europe (except for Denmark with its huge Greenland). Ukraine's capital was the centre of the powerful state of Kievan Rus from the late ninth to the twelfth centuries, but then, for most of its history, was ruled by empires – the Tatar-Mongol, the Polish, the Austro-Hungarian and the Russian ones. In 1918, after the First World War and the Bolshevik revolution in Russia, Ukraine briefly gained independence. The blue and yellow bicolour became the flag of the new state. Blue and yellow have been the traditional colours of Ukrainian heraldry since the twelfth century.

Ukraine (since 1992)

11. Horizontal Stripes of Eastern Europe

Unfortunately, Ukraine was not independent for long. After a couple of years, the Bolsheviks seized power in the country and joined it to the Soviet Union. In Soviet times, flying the blue and yellow flag was banned and could result in two years' imprisonment. In 1991, the USSR collapsed and Ukraine regained its independence; the blue and yellow bicolour became the Ukrainian flag the following year.

Today there are only four countries in the world whose flag consists of only two horizontal stripes. Moreover, the Ukrainian flag is unique among them, as the other three flags – Poland, Monaco and Indonesia – are similar to each other and have red and white stripes.

The Ukrainian flag is said to represent a typical Ukrainian landscape – blue skies above fields of golden wheat. But some people believe that the placement of the stripes is wrong. They say that the yellow stripe should be above the blue one, and if Ukraine turned its flag over, then life in the country would immediately improve! Some people insist that this was the order adopted in Ukraine before the coming of the communists. Some say that the flag depicts not the blue sky over the field, but the golden sunny sky over the blue water of the Dnieper. And some even refer to feng shui.

When Russia launched a war against Ukraine in 2014 and then radically intensified it in 2022, the Ukrainian flag acquired special significance. Every time the Ukrainian army liberates a city or village, the Ukrainian flag is hoisted above the local administrative buildings, as a sign of victory. The residents greet Ukrainian soldiers with the blue and yellow banners which they have kept secretly throughout the Russian occupation. Seeing these scenes, of course, evokes in me, like millions of other Ukrainians, a completely new attitude towards our flag, unfamiliar in times of peace.

As a sign of support for Ukraine in this war, the Pantone Color Institute has given new names to the shades of blue and yellow used on the Ukrainian flag: Freedom Blue and Energising Yellow. Thus, Ukraine has become one of several countries in the world whose flag has specifically named shades of colour.

Belarus (since 1995). Remake of the Soviet Belarusian flag from 1951

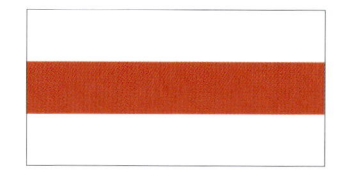

Belarus (1991–5). An inversion of the Austrian flag

To the north of Ukraine is Belarus, which is taking part in the war on the side of Russia. It is the only post-Soviet republic that has kept the flag of the Soviet era.

Independent Belarus did not always have the Soviet-style flag. In 1991, after leaving the USSR, the Belarusians adopted a white–red–white tricolor (like the flag of Austria, but vice versa). A few years later, Alexander Lukashenko became president and held a referendum on the adoption of a new flag. The new flag adopted is a slight adaptation of the Soviet-era flag – the only differences being that the communist symbols of the red star and the hammer and sickle were removed, and the colours in the decorative pattern by the hoist were reversed.

The white–red–white flag of Belarus is now used by the Belarusian opposition. Most likely, when democratic forces win in the country, this banner will receive official status again.

Armenia (since 1990)

After secession from the USSR, Armenia adopted the horizontal stripes of red, blue and orange as its flag. This flag is mentioned in the anthem of Armenia, and there is an interesting story associated with it. The Armenians based their anthem on the poem 'Song of an Italian Girl' by the Armenian poet Mikael Nalbandian. It describes the struggle of the

11. Horizontal Stripes of Eastern Europe

Italian people against the Austrian occupation. In the Armenian anthem, 'Italy' was understood as 'Armenia', 'Austria' was replaced by 'enemies', and the line about the tricolor was left intact, because both the Italian and Armenian flags are tricolors.

There is also an interesting story about the coat of arms of Armenia. It depicts Mount Ararat, which, according to the Bible, is where Noah's Ark was stranded after the Great Flood. Previously, the mountain was part of Armenia, but in 1921 the Soviet government transferred this territory to Turkey. On one occasion, the Soviet foreign minister was asked by his Turkish counterpart why Mount Ararat is on the flag of Soviet Armenia, when Ararat is not part of Armenia. Gromyko's witty reply was to ask why the Turkish flag has a crescent moon, when the moon does not belong to the Turks.

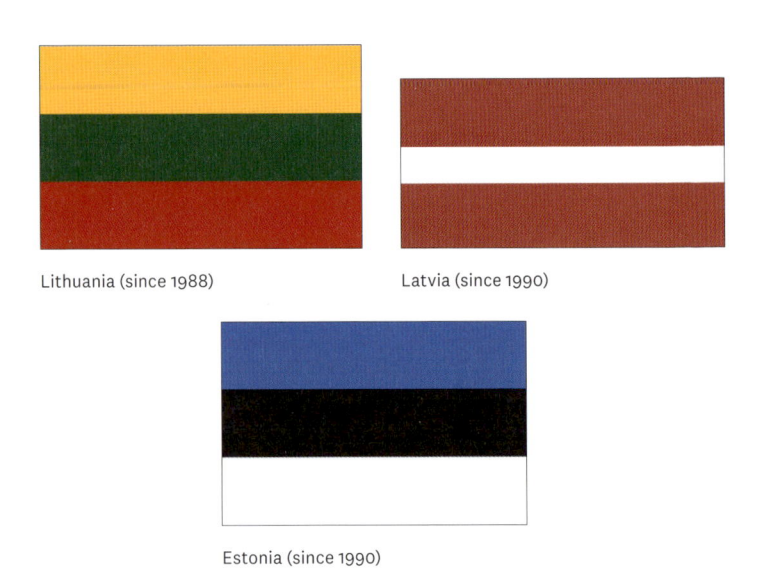

Lithuania (since 1988)

Latvia (since 1990)

Estonia (since 1990)

Lithuania, Latvia and Estonia also have three horizontal stripes on their flags. The history of these flags is similar to the Ukrainian one – in 1918, these three Baltic countries declared independence and adopted new flags. Then, as a result of a conspiracy between Stalin and Hitler, they became part of the USSR, and after the collapse of the Soviet Union they restored the flags adopted before the Soviet occupation.

The flag of Lithuania is painted in colours that are usually called pan-African (although the Lithuanian flag appeared long before this concept arose). The flag of Estonia has blue, black and white stripes, symbolising sky, earth and snowy peaks. And the flag of Latvia has two red (more precisely, carmine) stripes and a narrow white stripe in the middle.

Of these three, Latvia's flag has the longest history and is considered one of the oldest in the world, as it was used by the Livonian Order as far back as the thirteenth century. According to legend, in one battle, the leader of the Latvians was mortally wounded, and his white shirt soaked in blood was used as a military banner. Let me remind you that the modern flag of Austria has a similar origin.

The flag of Russia is also a horizontal tricolor. Its origins lie in the seventeenth century, when (as one story goes) Peter the Great hired craftsmen from the Netherlands to build the first ship for the Russian navy. As the Russians did not have a naval flag, they decided simply to use a flag similar to the Dutch red-white-blue one, with the slight difference that the Russian flag had the stripes as white-blue-red. And that is how red, blue and white stripes got into Russian heraldry.

Flag of Russia before the October revolution of 1917

Russia (1858-96)

In the nineteenth century, the Russian tsars began to use another tricolor – black, yellow and white – thus introducing some confusion into the national heraldry. For a while, Russia had two flags, but in the end, the white-blue-red was recognised as the official flag. This flag was used when the last tsar of Russia, Nicholas II, was crowned. Participants at the coronation were given ribbons and commemorative medals in white, blue and red, and ordinary Muscovites were given white, blue and red commemorative mugs.

During the distribution of these gifts in Moscow, there was a monstrous stampede, in which about 1,400 people were killed. The incident made a strong impression on Russian public opinion, especially as Nicholas II attended all the celebrations as planned, despite the tragedy. Many said that this was a bad omen for the country. And they were right. In 1917, there was a revolution in Russia, and the country spent most of the twentieth century under the Soviet banner.

During the Second World War, the white-blue-red tricolor was used by the Russians who fought on the side of Hitler, and in the late 1980s, democratic forces opposing the communist regime began to use it. And in 1990, during the World Chess Championship match between Garry Kasparov and Anatoly Karpov, because both players were from the Soviet Union, Kasparov played under the white-blue-red flag, and Karpov played under the red Soviet one.

After the collapse of the USSR, Russia regained its pre-revolutionary white-blue-red flag. It is said that when it was first hoisted over the Kremlin, it hung upside down for some time by mistake.

Today, with Russia waging a war of conquest against Ukraine, its flag has become associated with totalitarianism and aggression. A new anti-war flag used by the Russian opposition has a second white stripe in place of the red one. The red stripe is associated with both communism and blood, so its removal is symbolic. Gradually, the white-blue-white flag has begun to enter Russian anti-war culture. Of course, the current Russian authorities consider this white-blue-white flag extremist, and you can get sentenced to prison in Russia for its display (as well as for flying the Ukrainian flag, by the way).

Not only ex-Soviet Union republics of Eastern Europe have horizontal stripes on their flags. We have already mentioned how Hungary had to adopt horizontal stripes because of the Italians. Now let's deal with Poland, the Czech Republic and Slovakia, whose destinies and flags are closely intertwined.

Slovakia (since 1992)

Czech Republic (since 1993)

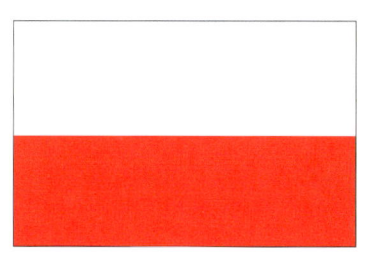

Poland (since 1980)

The flag of Slovakia is usually included with flags of pan-Slavic colours. Its history began in 1848, when a wave of revolutions swept across Europe. Then the Slovaks fought against the Hungarians, and the Russian Empire provided them with assistance. After that, the Slovaks began to use a banner with the same colours as the Russian one.

The flags of Poland and the Czech Republic both contain white and red stripes – and this is no coincidence. According to legend, the history of these two countries comes from the brothers Czech and Lech. From ancient times, the colours red and white were used in the heraldry of both countries, which eventually led to a vexillological embarrassment. When the Czechs and Slovaks were merged into Czechoslovakia after the First World War, the flag of the new country became a white and red bicolour, exactly the same as the flag of neighbouring Poland, which became independent at about the same time.

Well, we could live with similar flags of, say, Indonesia and Monaco ... but when two neighbours have the same flags, it's really confusing! Fortunately, two years later, in 1920, Czechoslovakia changed its flag by adding a blue triangle.

When the Czechs and Slovaks united, they created their national anthem in an original way – by combining a verse from a Czech opera and a verse from a Slovak song. After they divorced in 1993, each country simply took its verse from the Czechoslovak anthem and made it into their own anthem. But the question of the flag after the collapse of Czechoslovakia was not so easy to solve. First, the Czechs and Slovaks agreed that neither successor state would use the state symbols of Czechoslovakia. But then the Czech Republic went against this agreement and made the Czechoslovak flag its national banner anyway.

Slovakian coat of arms – with mountains Tatra, Fatra and Matra. Matra is located in Hungary

Hungarian coat of arms – with mountains Tatra, Fatra and Matra. Tatra and Fatra are located in Slovakia

Armenian coat of arms with Mount Ararat, which is located in Turkey

Another interesting heraldic interweaving can be found on the coat of arms of Slovakia. It depicts three mountains with sonorous names: Tatra, Fatra and Matra. The Tatras and Fatras are in Slovakia, but the Matra range is in Hungary. And these same three mountains are depicted on the coat of arms of Hungary! The image of a mountain that is actually in the territory of a neighbour ... well, we have seen this heraldic situation on the coat of arms of Armenia.

Another country whose flag is derived from the Russian one is Bulgaria. The white–green–red Bulgarian flag first appeared after the Russo-Turkish war ended in 1878. Most likely, the Bulgarians took the flag of Russia, and changed the blue colour to green. Here we have a beautiful kinship with the birth of the Italian flag – after all, Italy also took the blue–white–red flag of its neighbour France as a basis, and changed the blue to green.

Bulgaria (1879–1947, and since 1990)

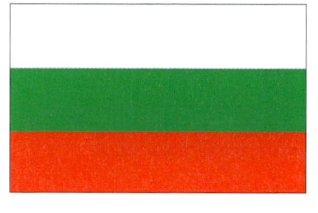

Slovenia (since 1991)

Croatia (since 1990)

In the previous chapter, I mentioned that I am struck by the similarity between the flags of Niger and India. But there is another amazing pair of flags: those of Slovakia and Slovenia. Both have white–blue–red stripes, as well as the country's coat of arms to the left. And both coats of arms depict three mountains. As if these two countries are not tired enough of being confused because of having similar names! (And to puzzle everyone completely, the Slovaks call their country Slovenská republika.)

Ten years after independence, this confusion annoyed some Slovenes to the extent that there was an official initiative to change the flag to a more distinctive one. A competition was held in 2003, which received some rather unusual submissions, but the matter was not taken any further. Probably, having read this far, you won't be surprised by such vexillological conservatism.

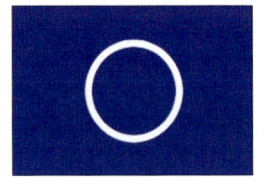

Winning alternative design for the Slovenian flag

Second prize

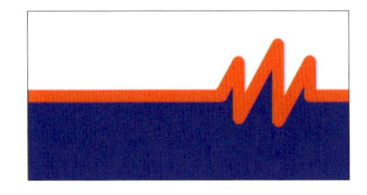

Honorary prize

The similarity of their flag with the Russian one makes Slovenes somewhat uneasy. For example, when Russia began bombing Kyiv in 2022, most foreign diplomats immediately left the Ukrainian capital. A few months later, when the Russian troops retreated from the area around Kyiv, the Slovenian diplomats returned to their embassy. They say that the Ukrainian police asked them not to fly the Slovenian flag, because it can easily be mistaken for the Russian one.

The Slovenes first started to fly a flag with white, blue and red stripes during the Spring of Nations in 1848 while struggling against Austria-Hungary. The flag of Slovenia is also commonly referred to as a pan-Slavic flag. However, unlike the flags of Serbia and Slovakia, sharing the Russian stripes is probably a coincidence.

Also in 1848, the prototype of the modern flag appeared in the Kingdom of Croatia. It also consisted of three pan-Slavic stripes, but in addition has its distinctive coat of arms of red and white checks. One story has it that this appeared on the flag after the Croatian king won new territories for his country playing chess – though, alas, this story is a beautiful fiction. Fans of chess might be upset to learn that these chequered squares have nothing to do with chess but are based on local long-standing heraldic traditions. Above the chessboard are five smaller shields from Croatia's different regions. Pay attention to the coat of arms of Dalmatia, which is the middle one: it has three leopards, similar to the lions on the coat of arms of the English kings. (The leopard in heraldry is traditionally depicted the same as a lion, but in a walking position with its head turned to full face.) And so, in Dalmatia's case, the beasts are not walking past but facing us – which is why they are referred to as leopards.

Two of these five shields have six-pointed stars. They are not related to the Star of David, but are a representation of a celestial body often called the 'morning star', because it is the last to disappear before the sun rises. Interestingly, this name is an astronomical error. It's not actually a star, but the planet Venus, which is considered the third brightest celestial body after the sun and the moon.

So, thanks to vexillology, we deepen our knowledge in astronomy as well. It is a very practical area of knowledge!

12. Pan-African
Colours

We have now met historical figures who influenced the colours of the flags of several countries: for example, Francisco de Miranda, who gave yellow, blue and red to Latin America; and William of Orange, who gave orange to the Protestants. Now it's time to introduce you to Marcus Garvey, who had a significant impact on the flags of African countries.

Garvey was born in Jamaica at the end of the nineteenth century and moved to the United States in his late twenties. He devoted his life to the struggle for the rights of black people on a global scale. He called for the separate self-development of African Americans within the United States. To this end, he created the Universal Negro Improvement Association (UNIA), first in Jamaica and then, in 1914, in the United States. Its banner was a red–black–green tricolor.

Garvey's struggle for black rights was ahead of its time. But although he did contribute to the recognition of the rights of black people, history has either criticised or forgotten him. For one thing, he advocated racial segregation and met with the Ku Klux Klan. For another, he believed that ultimately all black people should return to their homeland in Africa.

In 1922, Garvey was arrested for financial fraud, and sent to prison. On his release, he was deported to Jamaica, before he moved to London in 1935. In 1940, the London newspapers published his obituary while he was still alive. This made such an impression on him that he had a heart attack and actually died six months later – which is an example of a self-fulfilling prophecy. After Garvey's death a cult developed around his personality, and he was even considered a prophet of Rastafarianism. In 1965, his body was solemnly reburied in Jamaica's capital, Kingston. Martin Luther King even once visited his grave.

Thus, the colours of Marcus Garvey's UNIA tricolor – red, black and green – became associated with the struggle for the rights of black people and, as a result, penetrated the flags of some African countries. Since

Garvey's activities took place in the English-speaking world, these were mostly former British colonies.

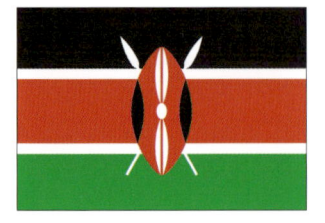

Kenya (since 1963)

Take Kenya, for example, which became free from British rule in 1963. Its struggle for independence had been led by the Kenya African National Union (KANU), which ruled the country for nearly forty years after gaining independence. The banner of this organisation consisted of the three colours of Marcus Garvey's Universal Negro Improvement Association and became the basis for the Kenyan national flag.

Wide stripes are separated by narrow white ones, which vexillologists call fimbriation. There is a striking image in the centre of the flag – a Maasai shield with two crossed spears. The Maasai are a nomadic ethnic group that live in this part of Africa; their shields are traditionally made of buffalo hide sewn onto a wooden frame, and decorated with geometric patterns like the one on the flag.

Malawi (1964–2010 and since 2012)   (between 2010–2)

The flag of Malawi, which gained independence from Great Britain six months after Kenya, has a similar story. The liberation movement in Malawi, as in Kenya, had used the UNIA colours in its symbolism, which then migrated to the national flag. The upper stripe of the flag depicts the sun with thirty-one rays. This number symbolises that Malawi was the thirty-first country in Africa to gain independence. What a diversity of numerical symbolism there is on the flags of the world!

For about thirty years, Malawi was led by Hastings Banda. He had a bachelor's degree in philosophy from the United States and a medical degree in the UK, which might seem an excellent foundation for a progressive ruler. However, Banda turned into a dictator who made his country the poorest in Africa, yet his own business empire accounted for at least 10 per cent of the country's GDP.

In 2010, the Malawi Cabinet unexpectedly redesigned the flag. They swapped the stripes to match the order on the Garvey flag, shifted the sun to the centre and made it white. This metamorphosis was supposed to symbolise the progress that Malawi had allegedly achieved. The Malawians did not seem to appreciate this change (perhaps they preferred to think that all the progress of Malawi was still ahead of them), and the old flag was returned under the next president.

South Sudan (since 2011)

The youngest state in the world, South Sudan, which gained its independence from Sudan in 2011 after a series of bloody civil wars, has a similar flag. The fight against Sudan was led by the Sudan People's Liberation Movement, which also had its banner in Garvey's colours. When South Sudan became independent, the leader of this liberation movement, Salva Kiir, became president of the country (in public he always wears a cowboy hat, which was given to him by George W. Bush), and the colours of the army banner formed the basis of the country's flag. Its black, red and green stripes are arranged in the same sequence as on the flag of Kenya, and also have thin separating white stripes symbolising peace. Unfortunately, the white stripes did not help: in 2013 a civil war broke out between the two largest ethnic groups in the young country.

We also see Garvey's colours in Libya. The Libyan flag evolved from a black flag with an Islamic crescent, which itself was apparently inspired by the flag of the Ottoman Empire (a white crescent on a red background).

Libya (since 2011)

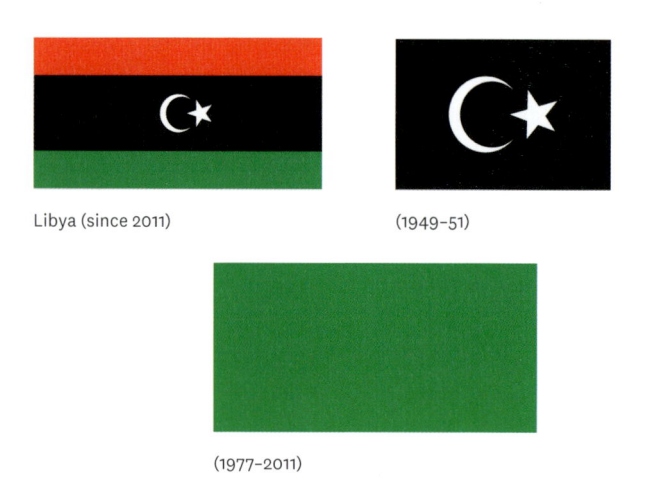

(1949–51)

(1977–2011)

In 1969, there was a coup in Libya, and one of the most odious politicians in world history came to power: the Bedouin Muammar Gaddafi. He held power for more than forty years and evoked extremes of passion that were felt in almost every corner of the world. Colonel Gaddafi was an adherent of pan-Arabism and dreamed of uniting all Arab countries into a single state. Here are some of the alliances that Libya forged with its neighbours: in 1970 with Egypt, in 1974 with Tunisia and Algeria, in 1980 with Syria, and in 1983 with Morocco. None of them lasted long, but almost every time they were accompanied by the adoption of new flags in pan-Arab colours, which we will come to later.

Gaddafi's politics centred on his Third International Theory, which he outlined in his *Green Book*. It was a marvellous mixture of European anarchist ideas and Islamic teachings (it was called the third because, according to Gaddafi, it was an alternative to capitalist and socialist ideologies). In 1977, commemorating the *Green Book*, the country adopted a new flag that was solid green.

In 2011, there was a revolution in the country and Gaddafi fell into the hands of angry rebels, who brutally killed him, and put his corpse on display in a vegetable refrigerator. After the overthrow of the colonel, the country returned to the flag adopted before Gaddafi.

But back to Marcus Garvey. His contribution to vexillology was not only in colours, but also in a feature – the black star. After all, it was in honour of Garvey's shipping company the Black Star Line that Ghana placed the black star on its flag, after gaining independence from Britain in 1957.

Because of its large reserves of gold, this region was called the Gold

Coast. In fact, the middle yellow stripe on the flag symbolises gold. The name 'Ghana' means 'strong warrior king' and was the title given to the kings of a medieval African empire (which, paradoxically, was outside the territory of modern Ghana). Kofi Kwame Nkrumah became the country's first president.

Ghana (since 1957)

First flag of the Union of African States with Guinea (1958 and 1961)

Second flag of the Union of African States (1961-3) - after Mali joined.

Ghana (1964-6)

Nkrumah, like Garvey, dreamed of the gradual unification of African countries into a single entity. To this end, in 1958, the unification of Ghana with Guinea was announced, and in 1961 Mali joined them. Each time, a black star was added to the flag. I wonder how the flag designers would have managed if several more countries had joined this union.

As we know from history, voluntary attempts to unite countries are often a hopeless undertaking. This union was no exception and disintegrated rather quickly. So Ghana returned to its original flag with one star, but at the same time substituted a white stripe for the yellow one (was the country out of gold?). But two years later, there was another military coup and the yellow stripe got back on to the cloth again.

In 1979, there was an attempted coup led by Lieutenant Jerry Rawlings. The coup failed; Rawlings was captured and put on trial. He was sentenced to death by firing squad, but a group of junior army officers helped him escape from prison. Moreover, he even managed to come to power after that. And then something rather atypical for Africa occurred. In 1992, he won the presidential election, becoming the first head of a military regime in Africa to be democratically elected as president. Judging by the pace of Ghana's economic growth, Rawlings proved to be an outstanding leader.

The flag of Ghana, in turn, had a direct influence on the flags of Guinea-Bissau and Cape Verde. There we see the same colours and the same black star of Marcus Garvey.

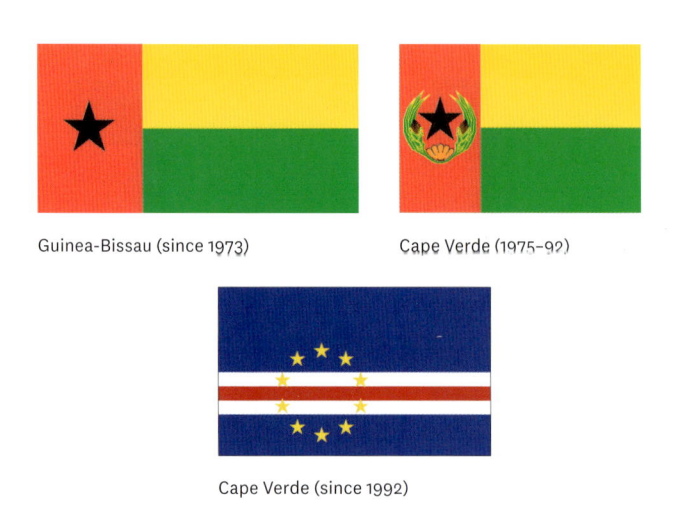

Guinea-Bissau (since 1973)

Cape Verde (1975-92)

Cape Verde (since 1992)

Both flags are based on that of the African Party for the Independence of Guinea and Cape Verde (PAIGC), which fought for the independence of these two countries from Portugal. The two countries suffered a similar fate to Angola and Mozambique. All four countries gained independence after the Portuguese Carnation Revolution and zealously started on a path of communism.

PAIGC representatives came to power simultaneously in both Guinea-Bissau and Cape Verde. The initial plan was that the two countries would unite, but this was thwarted by a military coup in Guinea-Bissau. Interestingly, the PAIGC is still the leading political power in Guinea-Bissau and has kept the letter 'C' for Cape Verde in its name.

In 1992, Cape Verde adopted a flag with a fundamentally new design, thus finally turning the page of its shared history with Guinea-Bissau. Ten yellow stars are arranged in a circle representing the main islands of this small Atlantic nation. This is strongly reminiscent of the EU flag.

It is a strange that there is no green on the flag, because Cape Verde in Portuguese means 'Green Cape'.

São Tomé and Príncipe (since 1975)

We also see two black stars on the flag of another former Portuguese colony: São Tomé and Príncipe. As you might guess, they symbolise two islands: São Tomé and Príncipe.

There is some confusion in vexillology about which colours to call pan-African. In addition to the black, red and green set of Marcus Garvey, the green, yellow and red colours from the Ethiopian flag are also often considered to be pan-African.

We have already discussed some of the countries with a trace of Ethiopia on the flag. Now let's deal with the others.

Cameroon is the second country after Ghana to have Ethiopian colours on its flag. During its history, it has been under the rule of the Portuguese (in Portuguese, the word 'Cameroon' means 'river of shrimps'), the Dutch and Germans, and after the First World War it was divided between France and Great Britain. This division in many ways still determines the fate of this country.

Cameroon (since 1975)   (1961–75)

12. Pan-African Colours

Cameroon (1957–61)

French Cameroon was the first to gain independence, in 1960. The French Cameroonians made their flag a vertical tricolor, like the French one, in pan-African colours. The following year, a referendum was held in British Cameroon, and people were asked to choose whether they would like to join Cameroon or Nigeria. Cameroon won, and so the ex-British Cameroon united with the ex-French.

To respect the rights of the English-speaking minority, a federal form of government was adopted. This was expressed on the flag by the addition of two stars. But after fifteen years, Cameroon, despite the protests of the English-speaking population, became a unitary state: and instead of two stars in the leftmost stripe, one star defiantly occupied the centre. There are still separatist sentiments in the English-speaking part of Cameroon, with periodic armed conflicts.

Guinea (since 1958)

Another country with a red–yellow–green tricolor is Guinea (not to be confused with Equatorial Guinea or Guinea-Bissau). Ahmed Sékou Touré became the first president of Guinea after it gained independence from France in 1958. Comrade Touré was an ally and friend of the president of Ghana, Comrade Nkrumah, which is believed to have influenced the colours of the Guinean flag. You have probably already guessed that Touré was a communist, and he brought communist ideology to stratospheric heights. The government of Guinea sought to control absolutely everything, including, for example, the number of traders in the bazaar. In 1977, there was a series of protests and riots that became known as the Market Women's Revolt, after which the state gradually began to abandon left-wing ideas.

Despite its colossal mineral reserves, Guinea today is one of the poorest countries in the world. Once it also had a rich wildlife, but in the last century gorillas, leopards and elephants have all but disappeared. It might have been the case that the last place in Guinea where elephants could be seen in the country was on its coat of arms, but in 1984 the elephant was removed from there too.

If you flip the flag of Guinea, you get the flag of neighbouring Mali. At first, the country was called French Sudan. Had this name not been changed, there would have been not only three Guineas in Africa, but also three Sudans.

Mali (since 1961)

Mali flag with the figure of a black man (1959– 61)

Shortly before gaining independence in 1960, a very distinctive flag was adopted in Mali, with a black stylised human figure (known as the *kanaga*) in the centre. But the next year the little man was removed, because the dominant religion in Mali is Islam, which prohibits any image of the human form.

Senegal (since 1960)

12. Pan-African Colours

Shortly before gaining independence, Mali received autonomy from France and united with Senegal. Later, when Senegal seceded, it took the flag of Mali as a basis, but placed a green star in the central stripe. Since then, the flag has never been changed, although in 2004 the government tried (but failed) to replace the star with a baobab.

The third country that originally planned to join the union of Mali and Senegal was the former French colony of Upper Volta.

Burkina Faso (since 1984)

Upper Volta flag

Upper Volta made its flag a black, white and red tricolor – a rather uncommon combination for the region, coinciding with the flag of the German Empire. In a military coup in 1983, Thomas Sankara came to power. He got the nickname 'Africa's Che Guevara' for his charisma and leftist views. During the four years that Sankara was in power, he carried out many important reforms in his poor country: he reduced child mortality, banned female circumcision and polygamy, and actively fought corruption. One of his decisions was to rename Upper Volta as Burkina Faso, which means 'land of honest people'.

With the new name, the country also adopted a new flag: a red-green bicolour with a yellow star in the centre, which was supposed to be a beacon for those honest people on their way towards communism. Sankara himself was definitely an honest man. He was called the poorest president in the world. He did not use the air-conditioning in his office, he travelled economy class and forced all officials to do so too, and when he was overthrown and killed after four years in power, his personal possessions consisted of an old Peugeot car, four bicycles and three guitars.

Neighbouring Benin also had a different name for its first years, until 1975. After gaining autonomy and then independence from France, the country was called Dahomey. Its flag had one vertical green stripe and two horizontal stripes of yellow and red. (Almost all variants of the vertical tricolors had already been used by that time, so they had to invent a new arrangement.)

Kingdom of Dahomey (1818–59)

The last flag of the Kingdom of Dahomey. An elephant's tusks instead of the elephant itself

Benin (1959–75, and since 1990)

With a communist red star (1975–90)

During the first years of independence there were military coups every year in the young country, until Brigadier General Mathieu Kérékou seized power. This man played a special role in the history of his country. During the first years of his presidency, he actively implanted the ideas of Marxism–Leninism. To commemorate this fact he even renamed the country 'Benin', and in 1975 adopted a new flag with a red socialist star on a green background. (That same year, Kérékou caught his wife committing adultery with his interior minister and had him shot on the spot.)

However, when the USSR burst at the seams, Kérékou retreated from left-wing ideas and restored the previous flag. We should pay tribute to the flexibility of his world view, because throughout his career he changed not only his economic views, but also his religion: he was initially a Roman Catholic; then, under the influence of the Libyan dictator Gaddafi, converted to Islam; and finally became a Protestant.

There is another flag in the history of Benin that has a vexillological puzzle that I have not yet been able to solve. In the first half of the

12. Pan-African Colours

nineteenth century, Dahomey had a very unusual flag: an elephant with a crown on its head. Moreover, the crown was not an abstract crown, but well known to us from other flags – the crown of St Edward. How did this crown end up on the flag of a distant African country that was never a British colony? Perhaps this has something to do with the fact that Dahomey had flourished due to the slave trade, and British traders were the main customers. Actually, the decline of Dahomey and the subsequent colonisation by France occurred after the British banned the slave trade. It is interesting that the last flag of the kingdom was a flag that no longer featured an elephant, but only its tusks. There is some rather sad symbolism in this.

Togo (since 1960)

To the west of Benin is Togo, whose flag is somewhat reminiscent of the flag of Liberia, which was inspired, let me remind you, by the flag of the United States. If you look closely at Togo's flag, you will notice that it has some elusive artistic beauty. It was created by the Togolese artist Paul Ahyi, who used the rule of the golden ratio while designing the flag.

The Ethiopian colours are also on the flag of Zimbabwe, which was considered one of the most developed African countries just after independence. At that time, it was called Southern Rhodesia (Northern Rhodesia became Zambia).

In the 1960s, Great Britain gradually began to grant independence to its colonies, but acted on the principle of no independence before majority rule (NIMBAR), by which colonies gained independence only after power was transferred from the white colonial minority to the majority. In Southern Rhodesia, this did not happen, and the white minority in power declared independence unilaterally. This government, which was not recognised by most countries in the world, pursued a policy of segregation in the country, similar to apartheid in South Africa.

Rhodesia (1968–79)

Zimbabwe Rhodesia (1979)

Zimbabwe – with pan-African colours (since 1980)

The flag of the unrecognised country had a design similar to the flag of Nigeria, except that the coat of arms was located on the white central stripe. In the centre of the emblem was the Great Zimbabwe Bird, based on a stone carving found in the ruins of the ancient city of Great Zimbabwe. This bird persisted on the flag in 1979, when the country was renamed Zimbabwe Rhodesia as a result of a compromise between the white minority and the black majority. It was even on the flag of 1980, when power finally passed to the ethnic majority.

On the current flag, the bird is placed on a red star, symbolising the commitment of the country's leadership to socialist ideals. The seven stripes of the flag are taken from the party banner of an organisation that fought against the white government. Canaan Banana became the first president of Zimbabwe. In 1982, he passed a law banning people from making jokes about his name (apparently, they made him go bananas). The next president was Robert Mugabe, who ruled the country for over thirty years and brought it to extreme poverty. What was once one of the continent's most prosperous countries plunged into economic stagnation, and local hyperinflation meant that Zimbabweans had to carry stacks of money in a wheelbarrow to buy just one loaf of bread.

Now let's move on to another group of flags that can be united by a common history and colour scheme: the pan-Arab flags.

13. Pan-Arabic Colours

In 1916, at the height of the First World War, a nationalist uprising of Arabs against the Ottoman Empire began on the Arabian Peninsula. The leader of the Arab Revolt, as it was called, was a representative of the Hashemites named Sharif Hussein ibn Ali. Britain and France provided support to the Arabs in these riots, because it was beneficial for them to divert the Ottoman troops from the front line of the war. British diplomats made it clear to Hussein that Britain would support Arab independence if Hussein's forces revolted against the Turks.

The help of the British was expressed not only in diplomatic and military support, but also in their contribution to Arab heraldry. British diplomat Sir Mark Sykes designed the flag, which was immediately popular with the Arab rebels. The flag consisted of black, green and white stripes, with a red triangle by the flagstaff. Each of these four colours represents one Arab dynasty. The red referred to the Hashemite dynasty – Hussein's own lineage. Perhaps it is precisely because of the important role of Hussein in those events that the red element on the flag stands apart.

Flag of the Arab Revolt (1917)

13. Pan-Arabic Colours

However, it turned out that Hussein and the Europeans had different ideas about what had been agreed. Information leaked to Soviet newspapers revealed that Great Britain and France had divided the Arab region into spheres of influence, in a secret treaty known as the Sykes–Picot agreement (the same Sykes who designed the flag). Hussein felt betrayed, having acquired only part of the Arabian Peninsula instead of the entire Arab region.

Hussein had four wives and eight children. The sons, together with their father, took an active part in the Arab Revolt, and then ruled several countries in the Middle East. One son, Ali, became king of the Hejaz state, which later became part of Saudi Arabia. Another one, Abdullah, became Emir of Transjordan and later king of Jordan when it became independent. The next son, Faisal, was king of Syria, and then became the king of Iraq. Because of all these family redistributions, the flags of the countries under the brothers' rule were very similar – all in the same colours of the flag of the Arab Revolt with a seven-pointed star as a symbol of the seven oft-repeated verses of the Quran.

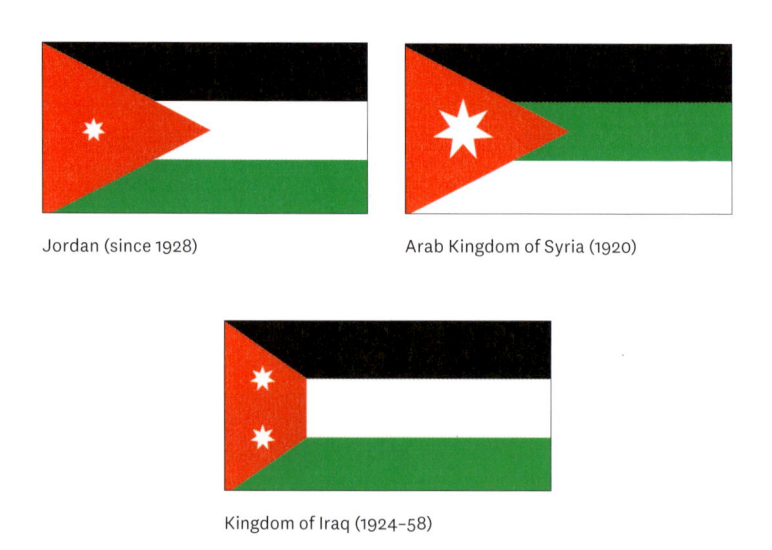

Jordan (since 1928)

Arab Kingdom of Syria (1920)

Kingdom of Iraq (1924–58)

In 1958, Jordan and Iraq made an attempt to unite (the rulers of the two countries were cousins), and the Hashemite Arab Federation was formed. However, it lasted only five months, because of a military coup in Iraq.

In general, the creation of interstate unions has become one of the main topics of international relations in this region. Almost every Arab country at one stage or another has tried to unite with one of its neighbours. For this reason, we see Arabic colours on almost all of the flags.

The largest country by population with the pan-Arab colours of red, white, black and green in the history of its flag is Egypt. Indeed, Egypt is an example of a country whose history can be studied through changes in its flag. Egypt was originally part of the Ottoman Empire, but after a revolt in 1882 was occupied by the British. The flag of the country was very unusual – a red flag with three crescents and stars. Three moons on the flag is the same unusual astronomical arrangement as the two suns that we saw on the Panamanian flag project. The design had double symbolism. It symbolised the activities of Egypt in three continents (Africa, Europe, Asia). And, because it was inspired by the flag of the Ottoman Empire, the three moons could signify the superiority of the Egyptians over the Turks. Why not? Georgia had five Christian crosses on its flag!

Flag of the Khedivate of Egypt (1881-1914) and the Sultanate of Egypt (1914-22)

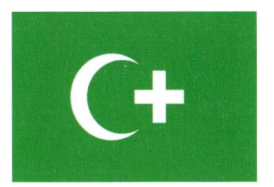

Flag used during the anti-British Revolution of 1919

Kingdom of Egypt (1922–53) and co-official flag of the Republic of Egypt (1953–8)

After the First World War, massive demonstrations began in Egypt for independence from the British. The movement united Muslims and Christians, and its flag was a green cloth with an Islamic crescent and a Christian cross. (If you are a computer coding person, the flag may remind you of the programming language C++.) Having the symbols of two religions on one flag is unique. Unfortunately, when Egypt did gain independence in 1922, this bold symbolism was not preserved, and instead of a cross beside the crescent, three stars were placed inside the crescent. The stars are said to symbolise the people who lived in the country – Muslims, Christians and Jews – or possibly Egypt, Nubia and Sudan.

In 1952, a group of officers led by Colonel Gamal Nasser overthrew King Farouk, and Egypt became a republic for the first time in its long history. From then on, the Egyptian flags entered their bird period. At first, the flag was decorated with the Eagle of Saladin with a crescent and three stars on its belly. In 1972, Egypt attempted to unite with its neighbours (this time with Libya and Syria) and formed the Federation of Arab Republics and replaced the two stars on the flag with the Quraysh hawk – an emblem of Arab nationalism. Although the federation lasted only five years, Egypt kept the flag until 1984, when it again replaced the hawk with the Eagle of Saladin.

Republic of Egypt (1952–58) – with the falcon of Horus

United Arab Republic (1958–71)

Federation of Arab Republics (1972–84) – with the Quraysh hawk

Egypt (since 1984) – with the eagle of Saladin

We have already mentioned Saladin in the chapter on the Union Jack, when we talked about the Third Crusade. Saladin ruled Egypt and Syria in the twelfth century, and it was he who defeated Richard the Lionheart and other European kings in Palestine. It is not surprising that he was held in special esteem among the Arab revolutionaries – after all, he personified the struggle against the hated British and French. However, we must give Saladin his due: he was apparently a great ruler. He was fond of philosophy and poetry and showed unprecedented humanity for those cruel times. For example, when Saladin captured Jerusalem, he preserved the Church of the Holy Sepulchre and allowed Christian pilgrims to visit the holy sites.

You see how interestingly it turned out! The confrontation that took place almost a thousand years ago between the Egyptians and the British is reflected on the modern flags of Great Britain and Egypt.

The only Egyptian flag without a bird was adopted in 1958 when Egypt and Syria formed the United Arab Republic. The flag of this union was the same pan-Arab tricolor, but with two green stars in the centre, symbolising Egypt and Syria.

This flag had an amazing fate. The alliance between Egypt and Syria lasted only three years. However, after Syria left this union, Egypt called itself the United Arab Republic for another ten years and kept the two-star flag.

Moreover, today the flag with two green stars is the official flag of Syria. Let's see how it happened.

Syria (1946–58 and 1961–3)

United Arab Republic (1958–61) and Syrian Arab Republic (since 1980)

Union with Egypt and Iraq (1963–72)

Syria (1972–80) – as part of the Federation of Arab Republics, 1972–7

13. Pan-Arabic Colours

As in Egypt, Syria's ordeals to unite with its neighbours, as well as its military coups, can be tracked by its flags. After gaining independence from France, the Syrians adopted a green–white–black tricolor with three red stars – the same pan-Arab colours, but in a different order.

Then there was an alliance with Egypt and a flag with two stars. A couple of years later, a military coup took place in Syria, and the previous flag was returned. And then there was another coup, and the red–white–black flag was again approved in the country, but this time with three stars in honour of the planned union with Egypt and Iraq. (Iraq then adopted the same flag.)

The alliance with Iraq and Egypt did not come to pass, but in 1973 Syria was about to enter into an alliance with Egypt and Libya and adopted the flag with the Quraysh hawk. Finally, in 1980, when it became clear that yet another union venture had failed, the Syrians returned to the flag with two green stars to demonstrate their commitment to the Arab union.

You are probably somewhat overwhelmed by this star shower, but I never promised you an easy walk in the Middle East!

At the time of writing, there is still civil war in Syria. Part of the territory is controlled by former ophthalmologist Bashar al-Assad, who became president after his father. The other part of Syria is controlled by the opposition, which uses the good old flag with three stars, adopted immediately after independence.

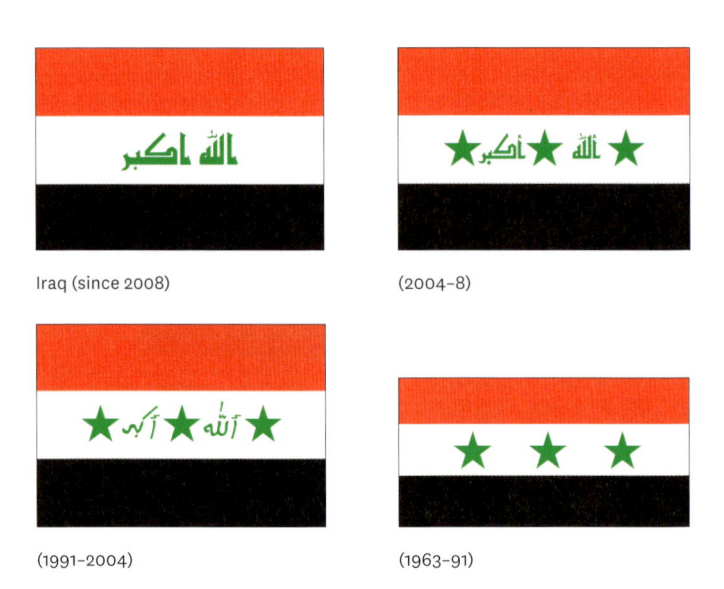

Iraq (since 2008)

(2004–8)

(1991–2004)

(1963–91)

194

Republic of Iraq (1959–63)

Iraq under British administration (1921–32) and Kingdom of Iraq (1932–58)

Proposed flag during American occupation (2004)

Unlike Syria and Egypt, Iraq gained its independence before the Second World War, in 1932. The red triangle was replaced with a distinctive feature – a trapezoid with two seven-pointed white stars, symbolising the Tigris and Euphrates rivers. After a military coup in 1958, Iraq became a republic, and adopted a new flag of a rather unusual design for the region: three vertical stripes and the yellow sun that represented the Kurdish minority. When a new government, aspiring for unity with Syria and Egypt, adopted a three-star flag, it became a bad omen for Kurds.

It quickly became clear that this union was not viable, but a flag with three stars persisted in Iraq for almost thirty years. The next person to change the flag was Saddam Hussein, who carried out a palace coup in 1979 and removed his cousin from power, though didn't in fact change the flag until twelve years later.

Saddam Hussein is perhaps one of the most famous sadists of the twentieth century. Before seizing power, he was head of the Iraqi government's internal security. His rule was marked by an estimated 250,000 killings, and he personally enjoyed torturing those being interrogated. It is believed that Saddam had 107 interrogation methods in his arsenal, which included extinguishing cigarettes against a person's eyes and dipping people into acid pools. There were many examples of the Iraqi dictator's brutality. Possibly the worst was the use of chemical weapons against the Kurds in 1988, which killed or maimed 15,000 civilians. (The Nazis had created this nerve agent; but Hitler did not use it.) Saddam's uncle, who had a great influence on his nephew, was a big admirer of Hitler. He even wrote a pamphlet called *Three Whom God Should Not Have Created: Persians, Jews, and Flies.*

Towards the end of his reign, Saddam Hussein became demonstrably religious. For example, in the late 1990s, he put on public display the 'Blood Quran', a handwritten version of the Quran allegedly inked with the blood of Saddam Hussein. Hussein's piety was also reflected in the flag of Iraq: in 1991, a *takbir* (an inscription in Arabic meaning 'Allah Is Great') was placed between three stars, written in Saddam's handwriting. After the Americans overthrew Hussein in 2003, the design of the flag was changed again. First, the *takbir* was rewritten in a standard font, and in 2008, the three stars were removed.

Interestingly, in 2004 the Americans suggested that Iraq adopt a flag of a fundamentally new design and in colours that were completely atypical for the region. The crescent symbolised Islam; the yellow colour symbolised the Kurds; and the two blue stripes were the Tigris and Euphrates rivers. But the Iraqis found the new design too radical, and it was never adopted.

Another geometric variation of the banner of the Arab Revolt is the flag of the United Arab Emirates (UAE). Here we see not a trapezoid or triangle along the flagstaff, but a vertical stripe.

United Arab Emirates (since 1971)

The UAE is a federation of seven emirates. Bahrain and Qatar had been part of the preceding union of coastal states, but then became separate independent states. The flag of the Emirates was chosen as part of a competition advertised in an Arabic newspaper. The winner was nineteen-year-old Abdullah Mohammed Al Maainah, who went on to become the UAE ambassador to Chile. According to his memoirs, he did not know that his design had won until the day that the flag was hoisted over

Mushrif Palace in Abu Dhabi. There was no wind that day, so Al Maainah had to wait for a breeze before he could be certain that it was his design on the flag.

Before gaining independence, the UAE was under the external control of the UK and was called Trucial Oman. This name is somewhat confusing, because modern Oman is a different country, next to the UAE.

A couple of centuries ago, Oman was a fairly large state, which included territories from Tanzania to Pakistan, but today it is a relatively small country of five million people. The national emblem is on the canton of the flag – a *khanjar* (a curved Omani dagger) fastened over two crossed swords.

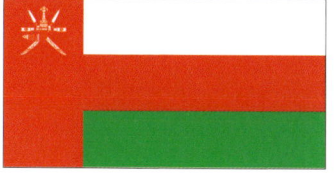

Oman (since 1995)

Sultanate of Muscat and Oman (before 1970, except 1868–71)

To the south-west, Oman borders Yemen, which has the most uncomplicated flag in the region: stripes of red, white and black, like the inverted flag of the German Empire. The Arabic word Yemen comes from the word *yaman* – which literally means 'right side', which is regarded as auspicious, and hence happy. Today, many adjectives can be applied to Yemen, but alas 'happy' is not one of them. After the First World War, North Yemen first gained independence from the Ottoman Empire, and almost forty years later the British granted independence to South Yemen. Bitter wars began between North and South Yemen until in 1990 they united into a single republic. Unfortunately, this did not make the country any happier, and a devastating civil war continues there.

Yemen (since 1990)

Another state with pan-Arab colours on the flag is Sudan, which until 1956 was under the joint administration of Egypt and the UK. On gaining independence, the Sudanese adopted the blue–yellow–green tricolor as their flag, coinciding with the inverted flag of Gabon.

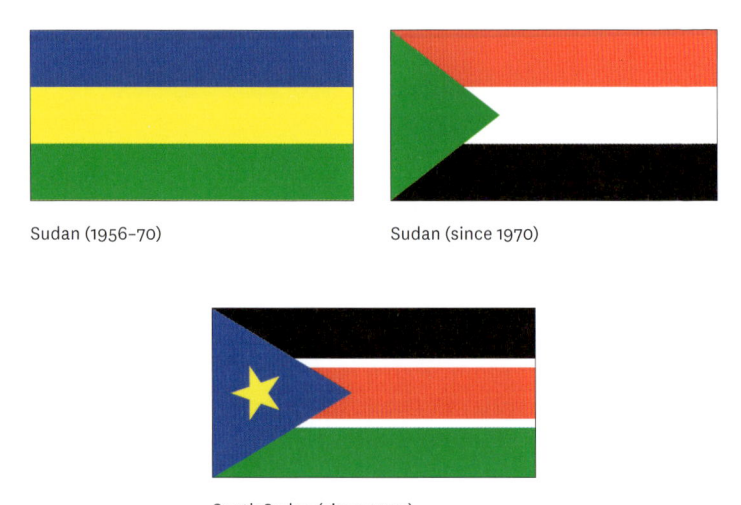

Sudan (1956–70)

Sudan (since 1970)

South Sudan (since 2005)

The borders of Sudan were formed during the colonial period and did not take into account ethnic and religious differences among the population. That is why these three colours, unusual for this region, were chosen for the first Sudanese flag – they seemed most politically neutral. But, unfortunately, the flag did not help. Sudan spent almost its entire history in a state of civil war, which ended with the formation of South Sudan as a separate state in 2011. The flag of South Sudan, remember, is made in pan-African colours, whereas the flag of Sudan has pan-Arab colours. The colours of the flags of Sudan and South Sudan provide a vivid illustration of why there has been no peace there for so long.

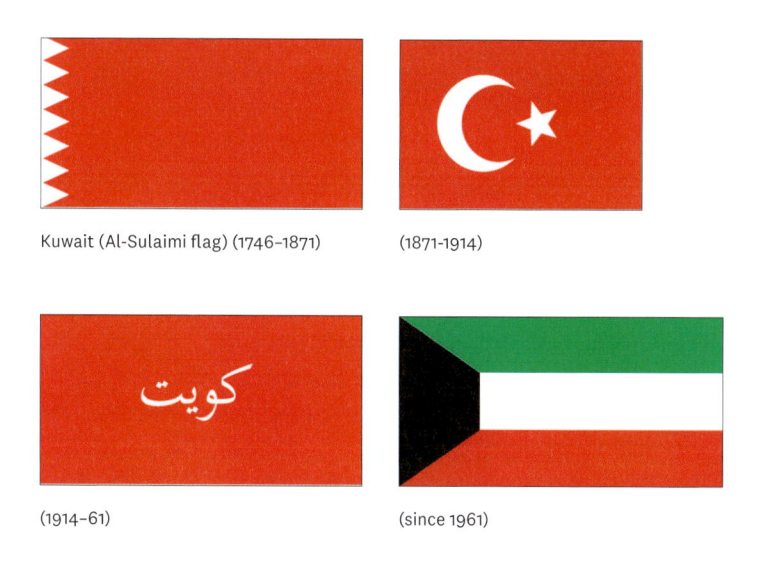

Kuwait (Al-Sulaimi flag) (1746–1871)

(1871–1914)

(1914–61)

(since 1961)

The flag of Kuwait is also painted in pan-Arab colours. On it is a trapezoid, which we have already met on the flag of Iraq, but here it is black. The official interpretation of these colours refers to the verses of a fourteenth-century Arab poet: 'White are our deeds, black are our battles, green are our lands, red are our swords.' However, given that Kuwait is one of the richest countries in terms of 'black gold' reserves, this trapezoid can also be seen to represent its oil fields. And, if you switch on your imagination, you can see a three-dimensional room with a black wall on the left.

Kuwait itself was formed as a fort at an important junction on the Persian Gulf (in fact, the name Kuwait means 'fort'). Like other Arab countries, Kuwait took part in the Arab Revolt against the Ottomans. In 1914, Kuwaiti troops used the Ottoman flag out of habit, and were mistakenly fired upon by the British. This incident was the impetus for Kuwait to adopt a new flag with the word 'Kuwait' written on a red background.

Centuries earlier, even before the Ottomans, Kuwait adopted a flag called Al-Sulaimi. We are interested in it because it became the progenitor for the flags of two smaller countries in this region – Bahrain and Qatar.

Qatar (since 1971)

Bahrain (since 2002)

The commonality of the flags of Bahrain and Qatar and Kuwait's Al-Sulaimi flag is because for a long time they were ruled by one royal dynasty. A distinctive feature of these flags is the toothing dividing the white and red parts. Moreover, in the nineteenth century, all three countries had a solid red rectangle as their official flag! And this means that during that century there were six countries in the world that had the same flag: France (during the Paris Commune), Thailand, Morocco, Oman, Qatar and Bahrain. Isn't that amazing? Both Bahrain and Qatar gained their independence from the British in 1971 and have been living rich petrodollar lives ever since. Especially Qatar, which leads by a wide margin in terms of GDP per capita.

The flag of Bahrain contains a broad white serrated band with five teeth, which symbolise the five pillars of Islam (we have already seen these five pillars on the flag of Morocco, as a five-pointed star). The flag of Qatar has nine white teeth. This is a reminder that Qatar could have become the ninth member of Trucial Oman, which would later be renamed the United Arab Emirates. Qatar never became part of that federation, but the nine teeth remain on the flag.

The Qatari flag is interesting for two features. First, it is the only one flag in the world whose length is far more than twice its height (the aspect ratio is an amazing 11:28). Secondly, it is maroon – a colour not seen on any other flag. This shade has an interesting origin. Historically, Qatar has been a major producer of purple-red dyes from shellfish. It is logical that these shades were used in the first Qatari flags. Over time, the heat of the desert climate faded the colours – to maroon. So the Qataris decided not to argue with nature and made maroon their official colour.

Another country in this region that does not have pan-Arab colours on its flag is Lebanon. Before 1975, when the civil war between Christians and Muslims broke out there, it was a prosperous and wealthy country, nicknamed the Switzerland of the Middle East.

Lebanon (since 1943)

The Lebanese flag has two horizontal red stripes, with a white stripe in the middle (called the Spanish belt). And on that white stripe is a Lebanese cedar. This tree is the symbol of Lebanon, and is mentioned seventy-two times in the Bible.

Saudi Arabia (since 1973)

The flag of the largest country (by area) in the Middle East – Saudi Arabia – also does not have pan-Arab colours. This is because the Saudis fought against the Hussein family (the leaders of the Arab Revolt). Saudi Arabia is one of three countries named after the ruling dynasty (the Saudis). The other two are Jordan (the Hashemite Kingdom of Jordan) and Liechtenstein.

The inscription on the Saudi flag is the Islamic creed, or *shahada*: 'There is no god but Allah; Muhammad is the messenger of Allah.' Under this Muslim holy text is a sabre, as if hinting at the fate of those who doubt this dictum.

The fact that the Saudis placed a sacred text on their flag has caused many practical problems. Firstly, the law strictly prescribes that the flag must be sewn in such as way that the phrase on the reverse side also reads from right to left. Secondly, the Saudi flag must never be used inappropriately. For example, at the 2020 FIFA World Cup, when FIFA

13. Pan-Arabic Colours

planned to include a football with the flags of all the participants (which included Saudi Arabia), the Saudis protested that someone's feet could kick the sacred creed.

Perhaps the fact that the image of this flag is on this page implies some responsibility on you as well. You had better treat this book with respect!

After Saudi Arabia, it is logical to switch to the flag of Afghanistan, which also depicts the *shahada*. This flag was adopted in 2021 when the Taliban took over.

Afghanistan (1880–1901)

(1901–19)

(1928)

(2002–21- modifications in 2004 and 2013)

Islamic Emirate of Afghanistan (2021)

With its challenging history, filled with military and palace coups, Afghanistan has had about nineteen flags since the beginning of the twentieth century alone – more than any other country during this period. At the start of the twentieth century, its flag was unusual: just a black cloth. Then a mosque and wheat were added to it, but the flag remained black and white.

In 1928, the Afghan king travelled to Europe. There he saw the German tricolor and decided that fresh colour would fit his flag and his country, so green and red were added to the Afghan flag. The black colour in the new flag symbolised the dark ages of the past; green, the future; and red, the blood shed by the Afghans in the struggle for independence. A month later, the king changed the horizontal stripes to vertical ones.

As is often the case when a country has a revolution and changes its flag, two versions of the Afghan flag can now be seen around the world: the white Taliban flag with a black *shahada*, and the black–red–green tricolor. The latter is used by the Afghans who do not recognise the new government in Kabul, and also by some Afghan athletes in international competitions.

14. Crescent on the Flags

Of the 195 countries in the world, about a third have religious imagery on their flags. Although the most represented religion on flags is Christianity (on the flags of thirty-one countries), Islam (represented on twenty-two flags) has a richer collection of heraldic symbols. For Christians, everything is simple: the main and almost the only symbol is the cross. Muslims have more choice: Islamic symbols on the flag can be the colour green, the numbers five and seven, the Arabic inscriptions *takbir* and *shahada*. But the most common is the crescent, of course. As one vexillological joke goes, many countries have a moon on their flag, but only a few have a flag on the moon.

Let's start with the flag of the Ottoman Empire, which is also the flag of Turkey, because the Islamic crescent became mainstream thanks to the Ottomans. This is logical, given that most modern Muslim countries were part of that great empire in one form or another.

Turkey (since 1844)

It is believed that the crescent appeared in Ottoman symbolism because of a dream. Osman I was the first ruler of the state that would later become the Ottoman Empire, and in fact gave his name to the empire. In his dream, Osman saw the moon sink onto his chest; a tree grew from his navel, and its shade covered the whole world. This dream was 600 years before Sigmund Freud, but nevertheless there were wise men to interpret Osman's dream: the Ottomans must conquer the whole world.

An alternative, more prosaic explanation is that the Ottomans borrowed the image of the crescent from the coins of Christian Byzantium. And the Byzantines probably took the symbol from pagan beliefs.

After its defeat in the First World War, the Ottoman Empire collapsed, and Turkey succeeded it. The Turks made the Ottoman flag their banner and have not changed it since. Meanwhile in other areas they felt pretty comfortable changing traditions. Mustafa Kemal Atatürk came to power in the 1920s in Turkey and carried out a series of Westernising reforms. He created the prerequisites in Turkey for a successful market economy, and created a secular pro-Western state.

Atatürk was well known for his elegant, fashionable clothing, and in 1923 he issued a decree on dress that meant Turkish women were no longer obliged to wear a headscarf. In the same decree, he ordered prostitutes to wear a veil. This had the intended effect, and the veil instantly went out of fashion. Meanwhile, to strengthen its position, Atatürk's government executed a woman who refused to accept the new fashion.

In 2021, I visited Baku, the capital of Azerbaijan. The country was celebrating victory over Armenia in the war for Nagorno-Karabakh. The national flags of Azerbaijan were hung all around the city together with the flag of Turkey as its main military ally. The two flags are quite similar, for historical reasons.

Azerbaijan (since 2017)

Azerbaijan Democratic Republic (May to November 1918)

As in Turkey, the central place on the flag of Azerbaijan is occupied by a crescent and a star. But, unlike the Turkish one, the Azerbaijani star has eight points, not five, which is said to symbolise the eight traditional Turkic peoples – or the eight letters in the word 'Azerbaijan' in Arabic.

In 1918, before Azerbaijan joined the USSR, the Azerbaijani flag was almost indistinguishable from the Ottoman flag, but later two stripes were added to it: blue (the symbol of the Turkic people) and green (the symbol of Islam).

The colours and symbols of the Azerbaijani flag echo the flag of neighbouring Uzbekistan. There we also see a crescent moon, and three stripes: a Turkic blue stripe, a white stripe and a green Islamic stripe.

Uzbekistan (since 1991)

Algeria (since 1962)

Tunisia (since 1835)

Near the Uzbek crescent are twelve stars, representing the zodiac. They serve as a reminder that astronomy was developed on the territory of Uzbekistan in the Middle Ages. We have already met the signs of the zodiac on the flag of Ecuador.

The crescent with a star in the centre is also on the bicoloured flag of Algeria, whose territories were part of the Ottoman Empire between the sixteenth and nineteenth centuries.

In 1830 Algeria was invaded by France. This was prompted by an incident when the Algerian ruler, angry with the French government's debt to Algerian wheat suppliers, hit the French consul three times with his fly whisk (or fan, depending on the version you read). After the invasion, Algeria was a French colony until 1962, except for a short occupation by Nazi Germany.

Surprisingly, the person who is generally credited as having sewn the first version of the Algerian flag, in 1934, was French. She was called

14. Crescent on the Flags

Émilie Busquant, she was a feminist and anarchist, an ardent opponent of French colonialism, and she was married to an Algerian nationalist leader.

Tunisia, next to Algeria, has a similar history: several centuries of Ottoman rule were replaced by French colonisation. The French took Tunisia half a century after Algeria, but in this case Tunisia became a protectorate of France by treaty rather than conquest. It seems that the Tunisian diplomats were more restrained with their fly whisks.

The original version of the Tunisian flag was officially adopted as early as 1835. It is obvious that the design is influenced by the flag of the Ottomans (despite the red possibly symbolising the blood of the Tunisians shed in the fight against the Ottomans). The main difference between the Tunisian flag and the Turkish one is a white sun disc, containing a red crescent and a star. You could say that, from an astronomical point of view, the flag of Tunisia depicts a solar eclipse.

Mauritania (since 2017)

Previous flag without red, blue or white (1959–2017)

To the south-west of Algeria is another former French colony – Mauritania. After gaining independence, the country also placed an Islamic crescent with a star on its flag. Unlike the flags of the neighbours, here the horns of the crescent are directed upwards rather than to the side. This arrangement always seemed strange to me until I went on holiday to a tropical country and was surprised to discover that in those latitudes the crescent in the sky really does look up, and not to the side.

Until recently, the flags of Mauritania and Jamaica were the only two in the world without red, blue or white. But in 2017, the president of Mauritania, Mohamed Ould Abdel-Aziz, held a referendum to abolish the senate and also to add red stripes to the flag at the top and bottom – as a symbol of blood and struggle, of course. The Mauritanian opposition complained that the real reason for the referendum was the president's desire to stay for a third term. (I wonder if they knew about Duvalier's trick in Haiti, mentioned in the first chapter.) The referendum was successful: the flag was changed, but Abdel-Aziz did not seek re-election in 2019.

When Mauritania changed its flag (and in general flags don't change that often), I wondered how quickly Apple, Google, Whatsapp and other platforms would update this design in their emoji library. For most of the platforms. it took them from two to four years to update the flag design! Well, we vexillologists consider this delay unacceptably long.

If we travel south from Mauritania and to the other side of Africa, we find ourselves in a small island country – the Comoros. Its name comes from the Arabic word meaning 'moon', and the islands are nicknamed 'islands of the moon'. So it is not surprising that there is a crescent moon on the flag.

Comoros (since 2001)

(1996–2001)

(1992–6)

(1978–92)

(1975–8)

(1963–75)

14. Crescent on the Flags

209

Comoros has a turbulent political history. In 1975, a month after gaining independence from France, the first military coup took place. The socialists came to power, and red became the main colour of the flag for two years. However, neither the communists nor the red colour on the flag lasted long, and green was returned to the banner. Then the main changes to the flag were the location of the crescent, which began diagonally, then turned upside down, then was moved to face upwards, and finally looked sideways. Eventually, in 2001, Comoros adopted a new constitution and a radically new flag design, with fresh, bold colours.

The only thing that has remained unchanged on the flag is the crescent and four stars, which symbolised the four main islands. One of these islands is Mayotte. Despite the protests of the Comorian leadership, it is still under the control of France. The discrepancy between the number of stars on the flag and the number of islands is the vexillological twist that we have already met in Tuvalu (although for a different reason).

There is another island Islamic state in the world that has a green colour and a white crescent on its flag: the Republic of Maldives. The Maldives gained independence from the British in 1965 and since then have never changed their flag – a sure sign of a calm political life.

Maldives (since 1965)

If you are looking for a country whose flag is impossible to confuse with any other, it is Brunei. This small Islamic country gained its independence in 1984 – much later than other British colonies in the region. The reason for this was the oil deposits discovered in the country in 1928, so the UK delayed its departure.

Initially, the British planned to make Brunei part of Malaysia. Until the 1930s Brunei was a poor nation. The Sultan's palace was falling apart, and the Sultan himself wore shabby clothes. But, of course, everything changed after oil was discovered. The Sultan of Brunei has become one of the richest people in the world. For example, he owns more than 600 Rolls-Royces, 450 Ferraris and more than 380 Bentleys. Meanwhile, unlike in Equatorial Guinea, some of the petrodollars do end up in the pockets of his subjects: the average Brunei family has three cars.

Brunei (since 1959)

Protectorate of Brunei (1906–59)

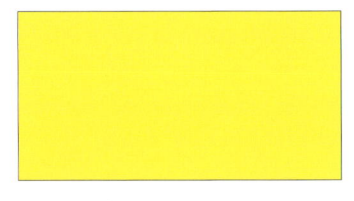

(1368–1906)

For almost all its history, Brunei has been a sultanate, as it is today, with Islam as the state religion. The yellow colour was traditionally considered a symbol of the power of the Sultan. Before the arrival of the British, the flag of the Brunei Empire was a solid yellow cloth. Then diagonal stripes of white and black were added, symbolising the Sultan's two chief ministers. The white stripe represents the first minister; his seniority is shown by the fact that his stripe is 12 per cent wider than the black stripe of the second minister.

In 1959, the national crest was placed in the centre of the Brunei flag. In the middle is a crescent moon with its horns facing upwards. At the top is a parasol, which is a symbol of royalty. There are two inscriptions on the crest: 'Always render service with God's guidance' and 'Brunei, abode of peace'. The two hands at the sides represent the government's concern for the welfare of the people.

There are also countries whose flag has a crescent moon that does not symbolise Islam. We have already mentioned two of them: Palau and Croatia. Now let's talk about another one: Nepal.

Nepal (since 1962)   (1930–62)

Nepal is a very distinctive country located in the Himalayas. Its uniqueness is also reflected in its flag. Let's start with the obvious: Nepal's flag is the only non-rectangular national flag in the world (Switzerland and Vatican City have square flags, but a square is a special type of rectangle). This unusual flag consists of two pennants whose triangular shape symbolises the southern and northern peaks of Mount Everest. There is a crescent moon on the upper pennant, and the sun on the lower one (we met the moon and the sun together on the Tunisian flag). With these celestial bodies, the Nepalese indicate the permanence of their country, and the hope it will last for as long a time as the sun and moon. (Talking about time, Nepal has an unusual time zone: it is plus five hours and forty-five minutes from Greenwich Mean Time.)

Until 1962, the sun and the moon on the flag had human faces, which made them look like ghosts from a cartoon. Historically, they symbolised two opposing dynasties in Nepal – the royal dynasty of the Shahs, and the Ranas, who historically held the post of prime minister.

The flag of Nepal is a sad illustration of a Shakespearean-type tragedy that occurred in 2001. During a gathering at the royal palace in Kathmandu, the crown prince opened fire and killed nine members of his family, including the king and queen, and wounded four others. The prince then put a bullet in his own head and died three days later (during which time he was the official king of Nepal).

There are various theories as to why he did this, one being that his family opposed his proposed marriage to a woman from the Rana dynasty.

After the massacre, the brother of the murdered king came to the throne. He and his son were very unpopular, and conspiracy theories spread that he had been behind the shootings. Demonstrations swept through the country, which eventually led to the fall of the monarchy and the formation of a democratic republic in 2007.

Well, we somehow figured out the moon, now let's move on to another celestial body, which is also often found on flags – the sun.

15. The Sun on the Flags

During the Second World War, Japan's leaders pumped up their soldiers, telling them that Japan was superior to other nations in every way. One of the advantages was the Japanese flag – the *hinomaru* (meaning 'circle of the sun') – which was said to overshadow all others.

The Second World War put Japanese militarism in its place. Nevertheless, the *hinomaru* does stand out for its beauty and simplicity.

There is a paradox associated with the Japanese flag. On the one hand, it is possibly the oldest national flag. The first documented use of a sun flag for Japan is in 1184, though there are oral traditions going back centuries – possibly to as early as 645. On the other hand, it was not formally adopted until 1999. Let's dig a little deeper into history to understand why this was.

One of the main reasons why a country needs a flag is to identify itself on the international stage. But for most of its history, Japan tried to stay isolated from the outside world, so did not really need a flag. Everything changed at the end of the nineteenth century, when the Japanese stunned the world by winning wars, first against China and then against Russia. Since then, the flag has acquired a sacred status in the country.

Japan (since 1999) – the *hinomaru*

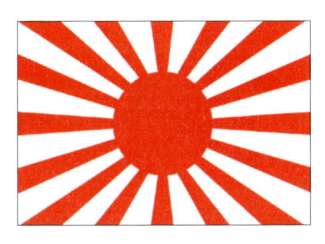

Imperial Japanese Army (1870–1945) – the 'rising sun' flag

15. The Sun on the Flags

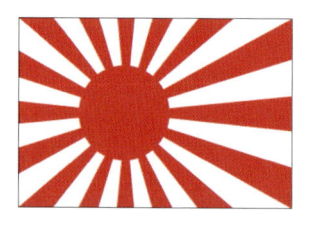

Naval ensign of Japan between 1889 and 1945, and since 1954

The *hinomaru* was used as the national flag during the Second World War, until the United States dropped two atomic bombs on the country, leading Japan to surrender. Then it was barely seen, as the Americans placed severe restrictions on its use during the US occupation. Even when the Japanese regained power in their own country and the restrictions were abolished, the *hinomaru* was still rarely used because of its associations with the country's shameful militaristic past.

There was a similar situation in Germany. After the Second World War, it was not customary for Germans to fly their flag or show their patriotism in any way. But the difference is that Germany changed its flag after the war, restoring the old one. But the Japanese, after a little discussion on this topic, decided not to change the *hinomaru*. As they say, unlike the German one, their flag was adopted long before the war.

Actually, in the Second World War, Japan did not use the *hinomaru* much, preferring the 'rising sun' flag, which has red rays coming out of the red disc. Although this flag was originally a symbol of good luck, it became the country's war flag in 1870, used by the Japanese army and navy, and thus became a symbol of Japanese militarism. This flag (with minor changes) is now used by Japan's navy, but its use by Japanese fans at sports events is a bone of contention with the country's neighbours, China and South Korea.

In 1999, the Law Regarding the National Flag and National Anthem was passed, specifying the *hinomaru* as the national flag. This was prompted by the suicide of a head teacher, whose teachers and school board disagreed about whether to start the school day by singing the anthem and raising the flag. However, the flag remains a sore point in Japanese society. And even though the *hinomaru* has official status, the Japanese media periodically write about teachers being fined or even fired for refusing to follow the flag law.

Unlike many countries, Japan does not have a ban on burning the Japanese flag, but it does prohibit burning the flags of other countries. We have already encountered such unusual legislation in Denmark.

Interestingly, the Japanese flag is the only one that is represented twice in emojis in our smartphones. This is how the world pays tribute to Japan for giving us the emoji.

Japan is often referred to as the Land of the Rising Sun (it's quite natural, given the fact that the Japanese islands are located in the Pacific Ocean to the east of Asia's east coast). It is this image – the rising of the sun – that we see on the *hinomaru*. Originally, the red sun disc on the flag was very slightly offset to the left (1 per cent), but in 1999 it was moved to the exact centre – possibly to the envy of Bangladesh and Palau with their slightly off-centre discs.

As for Palau, it not only has a flag in common with Japan, but also shares part of its history, because Palau was occupied by the Japanese from the First World War to the Second World War. Despite some similarities between the flags of Japan and Palau, the key difference is that the flag of Japan has the sun, whereas the flag of Palau has the moon.

Another country that Japan occupied during the Second World War is the Philippines. Its flag also features the sun.

The Philippines gained its independence from Spain in 1898. It was very quick off the mark with its new flag, which was formally unfurled during the proclamation of independence. The flag contains so many symbols that it would be enough for a dozen countries.

The sun, in the white triangle, has eight main rays, symbolising the eight provinces that rose in revolt against Spanish rule. The three stars on the flag symbolise the three main island groups, and the white triangle stands for liberty, equality and fraternity.

The flag's length is exactly twice its width, and there is also a lot of geometry on it. The white triangle is an equilateral triangle: each side is the same length and is half the length of the flag. Each of the eight rays of the sun actually consists of one major ray and a minor ray on each side. The angle between the minor rays is half the angle between the major rays, and each major ray is twice the width of each minor ray. Despite the flag's many elements, it is symmetrical about the central horizontal line.

Philippines (since 1998)

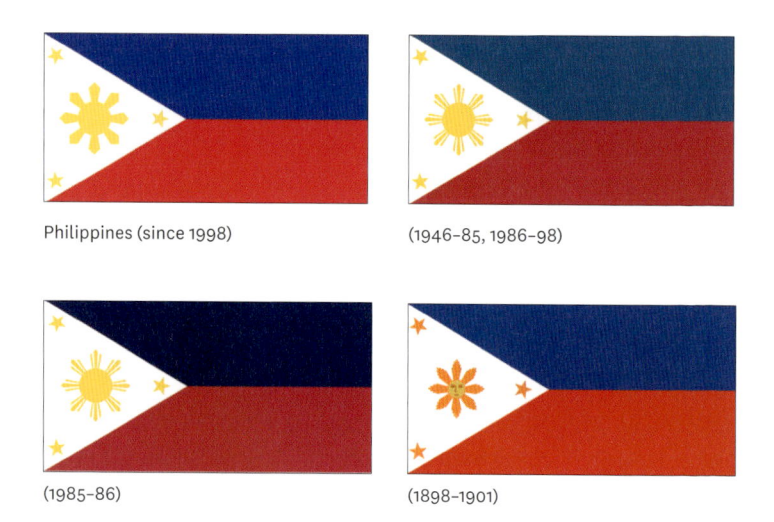

(1946–85, 1986–98)

(1985–86)

(1898–1901)

Incidentally, I like to think that the 'human flag' power move in calisthenics – where the gymnast grasps a vertical pole and stretches out horizontally – comes from this arrangement on a flag.

But the most amazing feature of the Philippine flag is how much it borrowed from the heraldry of other countries. The composition was inspired by the Cuban banner. On the 1898 version of the Philippine flag, the sun had a face on it – like the sun on the flag of Río de la Plata, which later evolved into the flag of Argentina. And after the Second World War, the Filipinos, grateful to the United States for help in the fight against Japan, changed the shade of blue to that used in the US flag.

The blue colour on the Philippine flag is an exciting story in itself. During the twentieth century it was changed six times – more often than the blue on the Greek flag. The dark blue shade lasted until 1985, when President Ferdinand Marcos changed it to pale sky blue, like that on the flag of Cuba.

Marcos was in power for more than twenty years. He was elected president in 1965 and, once in power, engaged in raking in money at a fast pace and in vast amounts. Estimates of the amount of money that Marcos stole during his presidency range from $5 billion to $13 billion. (The Philippines commission set up to investigate and recover the Marcos family's wealth has now retrieved about $5 billion.) To some extent, Marcos' greed can be understood: he needed to provide for his wife, whose extravagance was legendary – she is reported as having almost 3,000 pairs of shoes alone. Eight hundred pairs are on display in the country's Shoe Museum.

In 1986, a year after Marcos changed the blue on the Philippine flag, his cheating, his falsifying of documents, his greed and his human rights abuses caught up with him. After a snap election he was removed from power. The presidential couple hastily fled to the United States. A US customs officer who checked their luggage mentioned that they must have been dragging half of the country's budget with them. In their luggage were found twenty-four bars of gold (with the touching inscription: 'To my husband on our twent-fourth wedding anniversary') and $15 million in cash.

Marcos' successor returned the dark blue to the flag, reversing the change that Marcos had made just a year earlier, but again, it did not last long. In 1998, the blue stripe was changed once more, from dark navy blue to a lighter royal blue.

And here's another unique feature of the Philippine flag. If the blue panel is above the red, the country is at peace. If the red panel is above the blue – which can be achieved by turning the flag upside down – the country is at war.

However, the symmetry of the flag is constantly under threat. For example, there have been requests to add a ninth ray to the sun (one reason being to represent a ninth province that also took part in the revolt against the Spaniards). There have been demands to add a fourth star. And in 1995 the president suggested adding a golden crescent next to the sun, to represent the Muslims in the country.

Iran is another major state with the sun's footprints on its flag. Since the fifteenth century, the rulers of Iran (until 1935 the country's name was Persia) used the lion and sun emblem on their flags – though the emblem itself, a symbol of power and royalty, dates back to the twelfth century. Interestingly, the crescent moon is also found in Persian heraldry, but because the moon was already used as a symbol of the Ottoman Empire, the Persians favoured the sun. Another possible reason for choosing the sun rather than the moon was that Persia traditionally used the solar calendar, compiled by Omar Khayyam, whereas most Arab countries used the lunar calendar.

Iran (since 1980)

(1906–80)

(1852–1906)

Throughout its history, the Persian flag has evolved constantly. At some point, a sword appeared in the right paw of the lion, and the sun 'lost its face' (which echoes the evolution of the sun on the flags of the Philippines and Nepal).

In 1979, there was an Islamic revolution, led by Ayatollah Khomeini, which overthrew the shah. Incidentally, the first major order for the Mercedes off-roader, the G-wagen, fell through because of this revolution. The Shah of Iran had put in an order for 200,000 vehicles, for the Iranian army, but he was overthrown before they were delivered, and there was no money to pay for them.

One of Khomeini's first decisions was to change the national flag. The horizontal stripes were retained, but a *takbir* ('Allah is great') was added to the green and red stripes, written twenty-two times, which referred to the date of the revolution: the twenty-second day of the eleventh month of the Iranian calendar.

The lion and sun symbol was removed from the flag and replaced by the new coat of arms. This stylised design can be seen as a tulip (a flower said to grow on the graves of soldiers who fell for Iran) or as part of a *shahada* ('There is no God but Allah'). In the centre of the emblem is a double-edged sword – so to some extent we can discern in the new emblem a continuity from a lion with a sword in its paw.

We see the influence of the Iranian flag on the flag of Tajikistan, a country associated with Iran by a common culture and history.

Tajikistan (since 1992)

In the centre of the flag are a crown and seven stars – the number seven is a symbol of perfection in Persian mythology. One explanation for the seven stars is that they symbolise seven outstanding Tajik poets. A Tajik legend has it that the heavens consist of seven beautiful gardens, surrounded by seven mountains, on each of which is a shining star. Or they could represent unity among the different social classes in the country. It's a pity… I think the explanation of seven poets is less *prosaic*.

Although Tajikistan is the smallest state in Central Asia (by land area), its leadership has always had a penchant for big PR. For example, in 2011, the world's tallest flagpole with the Tajik flag was erected in the country. And in 2015, the Tajik media outdid themselves by announcing that one of the small planets in the solar system had been named 'Tajikistan', commemorating the outstanding contribution of Tajik scientists to astrophysics. This story has spread so widely on the internet that I felt I had to mention it.

Two of the other 'stans' – Kazakhstan and Kyrgyzstan – have put the sun in the centre of their national flags.

Kazakhstan (since 1992)    Emblem of Kazakhstan

15. The Sun on the Flags

Kyrgyzstan (since 1992)

The main colour of the Kazakh flag is turquoise. Beneath the sun is a proudly soaring golden steppe eagle.

The coat of arms of Kazakhstan has the same turquoise and gold colours. In the centre is a *shanyrak* – the structural elements of a yurt, in the form of a lattice cross. We see the same pattern, though a more stylised version, on the flag of neighbouring Kyrgyzstan.

The sun also takes centre stage on the flag of the Balkan country of North Macedonia. Historically, Macedonia was a fairly large area located on the territory of three modern countries – Greece, Bulgaria and Serbia. From 1945, it was one of the six republics of Yugoslavia, known as the Socialist Republic of Macedonia, until it gained independence in 1991. The use of the name 'Macedonia' for the new country angered the Greeks, who viewed Macedonia as part of their own country's heritage. Athens imposed economic sanctions against Macedonia, and blocked its entry into NATO.

North Macedonia (since 1995)

Republic of Macedonia with Vergina sun (1992–5)

Socialist Republic of Macedonia
(1946-92)

Until a solution was found, the country was called the former Yugoslav Republic of Macedonia (FYROM). An agreement was finally reached in 2018 and in 2019 the country changed its name to North Macedonia.

A similar epic unfolded around the flag of the young country. In 1992, the yellow Vergina sun on a red background became the official banner of Macedonia. The Vergina sun is the symbol of ancient Macedonia, and was used all around Greece, as a symbol of the Greek parliament, as a sign on Greek coins, and also on the flag of the Greek region of Macedonia. No wonder the Greeks were outraged. Under pressure from Greece, the Macedonians were forced to change their flag in 1995.

So our solar chapter is crowned with the North Macedonian flag. And, to keep our sunny mood, we will now return to Africa.

16. Distinctive African Flags

By this point we have managed to consider most of the African flags. Many of them are in pan-African colours, but there are some special ones that we will look at in this chapter. Since most African countries have been independent for less than a century, the story of their flags is very concise.

We will start with the three former colonies of Belgium: the Democratic Republic of the Congo, Rwanda and Burundi.

The Democratic Republic of the Congo (DRC) has a unique history. Before independence, it was a colony named the Belgian Congo. But even earlier, these territories were considered the personal property of the Belgian king Leopold II. The Austrian emperor Franz Joseph regarded him as a 'thoroughly bad person' – and history does not disagree.

Leopold, who ruled the Belgians in the second half of the nineteenth century, had serious colonial ambitions. But what could he do if all the most 'delicious' territories had been snatched up by more efficient European countries? For some time, the Belgians tried to buy the rights to the Philippines from Spain, and when that didn't work, they decided to concentrate on the African continent. With this in mind, Leopold II created the International African Association – an allegedly altruistic organisation, which was tasked to civilise and develop the regions of Central Africa. This enabled him to secure for himself the rights to African territories, including the land of the Congo – a massive area that was seventy-seven times the size of Belgium.

The flag of this 'altruistic' organisation was a banner with a yellow star on a blue background. This flag then became the flag of the colony itself.

Democratic Republic of the Congo (since 2006)

Zaire (1971–97)

Flag of the International African Association (1877–85), the Congo Free State (1885–1908)and the Belgian Congo (1908–60)

The activities of Leopold in his new colony were hardly altruistic. He was responsible for widespread atrocities, causing the death of up to fifteen million people. There's a shocking photo from 1904, in which a Congolese man is looking at the severed hand and foot of his five-year-old daughter. His daughter (and his wife) were killed because he had not fulfilled his rubber quota for the day. The English writer Arthur Conan Doyle wrote that Leopold II's crimes in the Congo were 'the greatest to be ever known'.

The DRC gained independence from Belgium in 1960, and the banner that we see today became the country's flag. After a military coup five years later, the country's new ruler, Mobutu Sese Seko, gave the Congo a new name in 1971: Zaire. Its flag depicted a hand holding a burning torch. But in 1997, when Mobutu was overthrown, the former name of the state, the Democratic Republic of the Congo, was restored – and the old flag was restored, too.

The modern flag of Congo is a clear successor to the flag of the International African Association that Leopold II so hypocritically created. It is surprising that the Congolese chose to keep these Belgian marks on their flag.

The flag of neighbouring Rwanda also contains an image of a yellow celestial body (the sun) on a blue background. This country received its independence from the Belgians in 1962, two years after the DRC.

Rwanda (since 2001)

Republic of Rwanda (1961–2001)

The recurring theme throughout Rwanda's history was the confrontation between the two main peoples of this region – the Tutsi and the Hutu. The enmity culminated in 1994, when the President of Rwanda was killed in a plane crash (his plane was shot down in a missile attack), which provoked Hutu extremists into a brutal genocide against the Tutsi. Between half a million and a million Tutsis, as well as moderate Hutu, were killed. A large part of the population of the country took part in the violence.

For forty years, the Rwandan flag was a vertical tricolor in Ethiopian colours. Initially, it was just a tricolor, but Guinea had exactly the same flag, so after a few months the letter R was added. The R stood for (take your pick) Rwanda, revolution or referendum.

In 2001, in an attempt to turn the terrible page of genocidal history, Rwanda adopted a fundamentally new design with completely different colours. The blue colour symbolises happiness; the green symbolises hope of prosperity; and the yellow, economic development. And it must be said that economic development in the country has been in good order since then. Sometimes Rwanda is called the African Singapore. It ranks high in the rating of the fight against corruption, and has had consistently high GDP growth for decades. The author of the Rwandan economic miracle is its president, Paul Kagame, who is regarded as a benevolent dictator. Kagame says that he does not accept the classic version of Western democracy, because it is useless for a country where the major part of the population almost obliterated the smaller part.

At the same time, there are less attractive features of this dictatorship. In 2020, Paul Rusesabagina, a businessman who is critical of Kagame, was allegedly abducted from Dubai by the Rwandan intelligence services. Rusesabagina is a Hutu, who saved the lives of more than a thousand Tutsis during the genocide.

Before gaining independence, Rwanda was part of the Ruanda–Urundi colonial territory. They split and became independent states in 1962: Rwanda and Burundi.

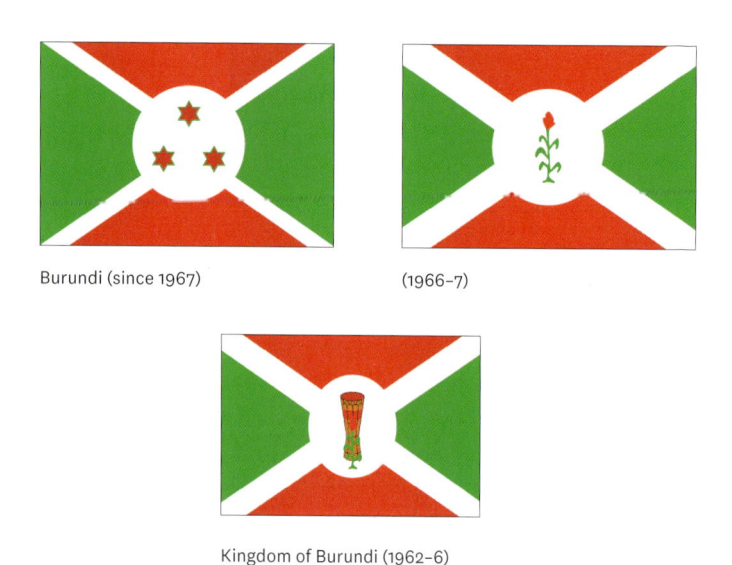

Burundi (since 1967)

(1966–7)

Kingdom of Burundi (1962–6)

For the first few years of its independence, Burundi was a kingdom. The centre of its flag was first occupied by a *karyenda* drum (which is said to have divine power), and a sorghum plant, one of the main agricultural products of Burundi. When the monarchy was overthrown and the kingdom became a republic, the drum, being a symbol of the monarchy, was removed, and sorghum alone remained on the flag.

But sorghum did not last long on the flag either. A year later, three six-pointed stars were placed on the flag, corresponding to the national motto 'Unity, work, progress' – or, alternatively, symbolising the Tutsi, Hutu and the Twa people. Unfortunately, as in Rwanda, Tutsi and Hutu did not manage to cohabit peacefully. A bitter civil war broke out between them, which escalated in 1994 when the president of Burundi, who was travelling in the same plane as the president of Rwanda, was killed. It is the only occasion in which the presidents of two countries have died in the same plane crash.

Now let's move on to the former African colonies that used to belong to Britain.

Next to Rwanda is Uganda. Despite the many military coups that shook the country after gaining independence, its flag has never been changed. In centre stage is a crested crane, selected by the British for use on the British Blue ensign, and which was then adopted as Uganda's national symbol. The bird has one leg raised, to symbolise that the country is moving forward.

Uganda (since 1962)

However, unfortunately, there is not much progress in Uganda. And this is mainly because of a man named Idi Amin, the country's third president.

Amin is among the most brutal dictators in history. Having come to power after a military coup, he drowned his country in blood, and also became the subject of jokes and political cartoons. He liked to buy various awards from the Second World War from collectors and wear them on a specially long jacket.

He also appropriated pompous fictitious titles: 'doctor of all sciences', 'conqueror of the British Empire' and even 'King of Scotland'. And in 1975, he suddenly declared war on the United States and the very next day proclaimed himself its winner.

In 1978, he started a war against Tanzania, but underestimated the strength of the Tanzanian troops, who overpowered the Ugandan army and captured the Ugandan capital. Amin fled the country in a private plane – first to Libya, then Iraq and finally Saudi Arabia. He took with him, among other things, the original flag and coat of arms that the British had presented to the Ugandans on their independence. Uganda sent an official request to Saudi Arabia asking for the return of the flag and coat of arms, but received no response.

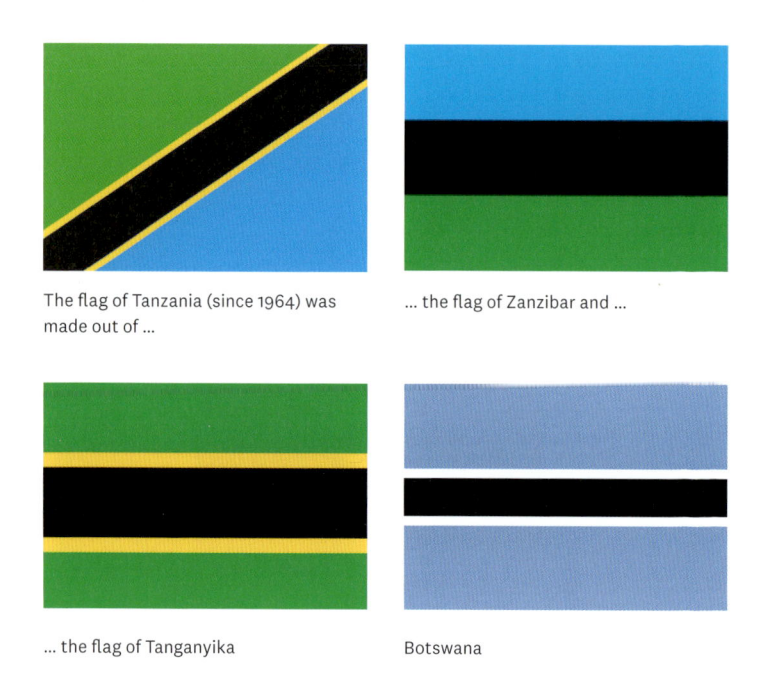

The flag of Tanzania (since 1964) was made out of ...

... the flag of Zanzibar and ...

... the flag of Tanganyika

Botswana

  The central place on the flag of Tanzania, which saved the Ugandans from the crazy Amin, is occupied by a black diagonal with yellow fimbriation. It was officially adopted in 1964, when the two former colonies of Tanganyika and Zanzibar united into a single country. The design was created by combining the flags of these countries. Actually, the word 'Tanzania' is a combination of these two names.

  The flag of Botswana also boasts a black stripe and fimbriation. Personally, I find it very beautiful and simple. The colour scheme is unconventional for the African continent. The blue colour of the flag symbolises water – specifically rain. Agriculture is such an important part of Botswana's economy that the country's motto, '*Pula*' ('Let there be rain'), is inscribed on the national coat of arms.

  The black stripe symbolises the indigenous black population; the white stripes represent national minorities. Together they symbolise friendship and harmony between races, and also resemble the stripes of a zebra, the national animal of Botswana which also appears on the coat of arms.

These stripes on the flag of Botswana are especially interesting if you know how the country gained independence. A key figure in the history of Botswana is Seretse Khama, who became its first president. Seretse was born to a royal family in a British protectorate, Bechuanaland, which later became Botswana. Just after the Second World War, he went to the UK for higher education, and in 1948 he married a white British woman. This interracial marriage caused a furore, in Seretse's own family and in the government of the Union of South Africa, where the apartheid laws prohibited interracial marriage.

The South Africans demanded that the British government not let Khama return to his homeland with his white wife. The British could not afford quarrels with South Africa because of the cheap gold mined there, and exiled Khama and his wife from Bechuanaland. It was not until 1956 that Khama and his wife could return, as private citizens. But he quickly made a political career there, ending up as the first president of independent Botswana. The country has grown into one of the most developed countries on the African continent, and this is in many respects because of Khama.

Interestingly, had the story turned out differently, Botswana might not have become independent but instead become part of the Union of South Africa instead, as the British had originally planned. But after South Africa and Britain quarrelled over apartheid, the plans changed.

There are two more countries in Africa that could have remained part of South Africa: Lesotho and Eswatini. Their flags look very individual too.

The flag of Lesotho features a *mokorotlo* – the traditional headdress of the Basotho people. The flag of Eswatini depicts a black and white shield and two spears (and a 'fighting stick'), similar to those that we saw on the flag of Kenya.

And similar to the flag of Lesotho is the tricolor of Sierra Leone. It also has three horizontal stripes of green, white and blue, but in a different order. 'Sierra Leone' translates from the Portuguese as 'Lioness Mountains' – and the Lion Mountains is a mountain range in the country. Alas, there are no longer many, (if any) lions in this African country. However, this did not prevent the Sierra Leoneans from putting three lions on their coat of arms.

The flag of the neighbouring country, the Gambia, is also a horizontal tricolor. It was adopted after the Gambia gained independence from Britain in 1965, and has not changed since – even for the seven years when it united with neighbouring Senegal into a confederation called Senegambia.

Lesotho (since 2006)

Eswatini (since 1968)

Sierra Leone (since 1961)

Gambia (since 1965)

With this strange word 'Senegambia' we finish the review of the flags of the African continent. And now we are ready for the final vexillological journey through the former British island colonies.

17. British
Island
Colonies

I mention the British Empire more often in this book than any other state. Whatever nook of the planet you peep into, you come across traces of the British colonists. Now there are only twenty-two countries in the world that were not at war with the British at some point.

In terms of heraldry, the British should be given credit. Although the flags of their territories looked rather monotonous, they were still different. The flag of a typical British colony (or protectorate or dominion) was blue, with the Union Jack on the canton and a unique emblem on the disc on the right. Usually, the emblems depicted the main export crops or elements of local nature. Some turned out to be really funny cultural twists, as we saw with the Star of David on the Nigerian flag.

We have already discussed the flags of most countries that were dependent on Britain. And in this chapter, we will make a short but fascinating journey through the remaining ones.

Let's take a look at the Caribbean first. The history of a typical Caribbean island goes like this. It was first discovered for the Western world by Christopher Columbus. Then the Europeans began to grow sugar cane and other crops there, using slaves imported from Africa. During the nineteenth century, almost all the Caribbean islands came under the rule of Britain, and in the twentieth century the most restless of them gained independence.

The flags of most local countries include blue, yellow, green and black. The symbolism of these colours is usually the same: the ocean, the sun, nature and the local population, respectively.

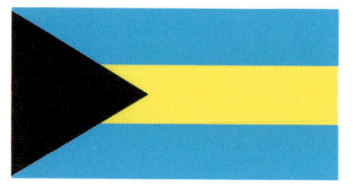

Bahamas (since 1973)

Crown Colony of the Bahama Islands (since 1869). In 1953 the St Edward's crown was substituted for the Tudor crown

The main distinguishing feature of the flag of the Bahamas is its beautiful aquamarine colour. The black triangle by the flagstaff is reminiscent of many other black flags in the history of the Bahamas: pirates' flags. At the beginning of the eighteenth century a 'pirate republic' was created on these islands. The locals used to hoist black flags with the skull and crossbones on their own ships and boarding passing ships. The skull and crossbones warned sailors that, if they resisted the pirates, they would suffer a painful execution. The most famous pirate who eventually settled in the Bahamas was the Englishman Captain Blackbeard, who became the inspiration for many pirates in works of fiction.

When the British did take control of these islands, they illustrated their victory over the pirates on the Bahamas flag. It depicts a British ship chasing two pirate vessels, and the inscription '*Expulsis piratis restituta commercia*' ('Pirates expelled, commerce restored'). Wouldn't that be an appropriate slogan for recording companies that shut down pirated file-hosting sites like Napster?

Blackbeard also left his mark in the history of neighbouring Barbados. The name 'Barbados', translated from Spanish and Portuguese, means 'bearded ones'. One explanation is that the first Portuguese man who landed on the island saw a *ficus* tree, whose roots resemble a beard.

Barbados (since 1966)

Colony of Barbados (1885–1966)

The flag of Barbados has three vertical stripes. Two ultramarine stripes at each side symbolise the ocean surrounding the country. In the centre, on a yellow stripe, is the head of a trident, often called a broken trident, which moved here from Barbados' colonial emblem, and is a symbol of Poseidon. The fact that the trident is broken symbolises the country's 'break' from being a British colony.

Note that Poseidon is a pagan god from Greek mythology. So here is another pagan trace on the flag of a Christian state. It's especially interesting to have the Christian cross of St George and the pagan Poseidon on the same flag, on the colonial flag. It's like having comic book heroes from the Marvel and DC universes in the same film!

The heraldry of Barbados is surprisingly similar to the heraldry of Ukraine. The two main colours of the Ukrainian flag are also blue and yellow, and the national emblem is the trident.

Jamaica is another relatively small Caribbean country that has had a great influence on world culture. Fort Port Royal was built there, in 1494, and gained fame as 'the most wicked and sinful city in the world'. Towards the end of the seventeenth century, there was a massive earthquake on the island, followed by a devastating tsunami. Most of the city was destroyed. The Church of Spain, whose ships had suffered most from the raids of Jamaican pirates, reported that God had punished the wicked city for its sins.

Jamaica (since 1962)

First proposed design for the Jamaican flag

(Before 1962)

17. British Island Colonies

The flag of Bob Marley's homeland of Jamaica has a special place in vexillology. It is the only national flag that does not contain a single shade of red, white or blue (if we count Qatari maroon as red, and Bahamian aquamarine as blue). On one heraldic forum, I found an amusing story about how, on the eve of their independence in 1962, the Jamaicans discussed the design of their flag with the British. The British said they didn't care what Jamaica's flag would be, as long as it used the colours of the Union Jack. After that, the stubborn Jamaicans did exactly the opposite. Fiction, of course, but beautiful!

It is interesting that initially the Jamaicans were going to make their flag in the same colours, but in the more banal arrangement of a tricolor. However, this was considered to be too similar to the flag of Tanganyika, a country which two years later became a part of Tanzania.

While still a colony, Jamaica had a rather explicit emblem on its flag: a girl with naked breasts. Jamaica did not change its emblem on gaining independence (a rare case), so today this girl looks at us just the same from the Jamaican coat of arms.

Antigua and Barbuda (since 1967)

Saint Vincent and the Grenadines (since 1985)

Saint Lucia (since 1967)

The flag of Antigua and Barbuda has a rather unusual design. The central place is occupied by the rising sun, with black-white-blue horizontal stripes forming the letter V, as a symbol of victory. As with Barbados, the name Barbuda is also derived from the Portuguese for 'bearded ones'.

We also see the V (for Vincent, this time) on the flag of the neighbouring country of Saint Vincent and the Grenadines. This flag is a tricolor in blue–yellow–green, with the central yellow panel being wider than the two side stripes. This makes it a Canadian pale, which we discussed in chapter 2. On the Canadian pale are three green diamonds in the shape of the letter V.

The author of this unusual flag is the Swiss designer Julien van der Wal, who had previously designed the flag of the Canton of Geneva. He took his inspiration from the fact that the islands are known as the 'Gems of the Antilles' or the 'Jewels of the Caribbean'. The diamonds (rhombuses) are slightly below the centre of the flag, indicating the location of the islands in the Antilles archipelago.

You can also see the letter V on the flag of tiny Saint Lucia, but here it is inverted (and is really a series of triangles). These triangles symbolise the two volcanic cones on the island. And this country with a population of only 180,000 people has the largest per-capita concentration of Nobel laureates in the world, with two Nobel prizewinners: one in economics, the other in literature. The black and white colours, next to each other on the flag, symbolise the peaceful coexistence of the different races in the country – as on the flag of Botswana.

Grenada (since 1974)

Saint Kitts and Nevis (since 1983)

Tiny Grenada, which has been both a French colony and a British colony in its history, also has an unusual flag. According to legend, an early French governor of Martinique, Jacques-Dyel du Parquet, bought this island from a French company in 1650 for a bunch of axes, several strings of glass beads and two bottles of brandy. Not a bad deal! The flag has the Ethiopian pan-African colours. There is a nutmeg on the left side of the flag, breaking all the rules of symmetry, to represent the island's main export and to remind us of the island's nickname: Spice Island.

17. British Island Colonies

The flag of Saint Kitts and Nevis is also made of pan-African colours (not the colours of Ethiopia, but of Marcus Garvey). The flag is crossed by a black diagonal symbolising the African roots of the locals. We saw the same diagonal and with the same symbolism on the flag of Trinidad and Tobago.

Now let's fast forward to the east, beyond Madagascar. Here we find the Seychelles and Mauritius – two island states with similar flags. They both have bright colours (which symbolise the main political parties) and an unusual composition. My compatriots and I can also see the Ukrainian flag lurking in both these flags.

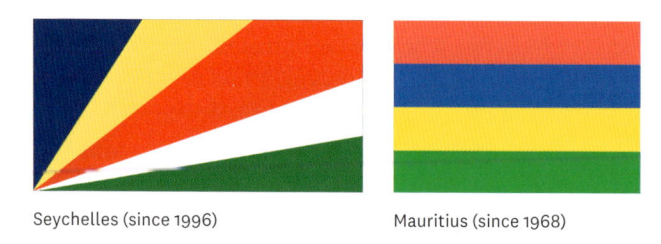

Seychelles (since 1996)

Mauritius (since 1968)

The island of Mauritius got its name from the Latin form of the name of Prince Maurice (Mauritius) van Nassau (later Prince of Orange), who laid the foundation for the independence of the Netherlands and gave orange colours to vexillology. It's a shame that orange didn't make it onto the flag of Mauritius.

Papua New Guinea (since 1971)

A little more to the east, and we come to Papua New Guinea.

Papua is derived from the Malay word for 'curly'. This name was given to the island by a Portuguese navigator, who noted the curly hair of the locals (as you can see, the sailors liked to exploit the theme of hair-covering when naming). The second part of the name – New Guinea – came from another Portuguese explorer, who noticed a resemblance between the locals and people he had seen along the coast of Guinea in Africa.

On the flag we see the constellation of the Southern Cross, and a silhouette of the local bird of paradise. The flag was designed by a fifteen-year-old curly-haired schoolgirl Susan Karike. Susan received little or no reward or recognition for her work. She died in 2017 in poverty. According to local media reports, there were three months between Susan's death and her funeral, as the prime minister's office had promised a state funeral, but this never happened.

Finally, let's move to the Pacific Ocean and look at the flags of the four remaining countries: the Solomon Islands, Samoa, Kiribati and Vanuatu.

Solomon Islands (since 1977)

Samoa (since 1949)

Vanuatu (since 1980)

The biblical king Solomon, whom we remembered while meditating on the flag of Ethiopia, left his footprints in this part of the world as well. After all, it was in his honour that the Spaniards named these islands – Solomon – because it seemed to them that this territory could provide them with the same riches as the biblical Golden Land of Solomon. The five stars on the canton symbolise the five provinces that made up the country at the time of independence. Although the number of provinces has increased since then, the number of stars on the flag has stayed the same.

We also see stars on the canton of the Samoa flag; like the Papua New Guinea flag, they are in the Southern Cross constellation. The Samoan Islands were once a single state, but as a result of their turbulent history,

17. British Island Colonies

the western part of the islands became an independent country (known as Western Samoa until 1997, when it became Samoa), and the eastern part (known as American Samoa) is now an unincorporated territory of the United States.

In December 2011, Samoa changed time itself. Because its economy is tied in with that of Australia, it moved the clock twenty-four hours forward, to be more in line with Australian time. So, 29 December was followed immediately by 31 December, missing out 30 December. Meanwhile, American Samoa remained in the US time zone. So, if you travel the mere thirty miles from Samoa to American Samoa, the time of day stays the same, but the date changes.

Let's move now to Kiribati – the only country in the world that lies in all four hemispheres. If you are attentive enough, it might strike you how similar Kiribati's flag is to the flag of Latvian SSR. On the latter, you can see a hammer and sickle soaring above the water. In the case of Kiribati it's the Sun and a frigate bird which represents power, freedom and Kiribati. By the way, the same bird is honoured on the flag of the island of Barbuda that is located almost on the opposite side of the Earth. This illustrates how huge the range map of this brave bird is.

Kiribati

Latvia

The flag is based on the colonial coat of arms when Kiribati was a colony of Great Britain. In fact, initially the College of Arms wanted to modify this design by reducing the area with water. The local people, however, insisted on the original design, where water fills half of the flag area... If you know this story, it might feel very symbolic – because now global warming and the sea water level is a huge problem for this tiny country. Even now its population has a density similar to Tokyo, and Kiribati is expected to be the first country to lose all its land territory to climate change...

As for the flag of Vanuatu, it has no stars at all. We see a boar's tusk on it, and a narrow yellow line (fimbriation) in the shape of the letter Y; the designer, a local artist, wanted it to resemble the shape of the islands relative to each other. Inside the tusk are two crossed leaves of the local *namele* tree, as a symbol of peace. On the branches, you can count thirty-nine leaves – the original number of members of parliament. And with their crossed shape, they resemble the element that we see on the flag and coat of arms of Kazakhstan and Kyrgyzstan.

Thus, on the flag of Vanuatu you can discern the letters X, Y and even Z, if you strain a little. This in itself can also be called symbolic, because it is on the flag of Vanuatu that you and I end this book.

Afterword

Well, dear readers, we have reached the end of the book. Country by country, we have covered the entire globe, from France to Vanuatu.

On these pages, I have loaded you with such a barrel of information that you would be lucky to remember just a bit of it. But it doesn't matter, because the purpose of the book is not to stuff you with information, but to entertain and inspire.

But you will return to this book more than once, at least mentally. The reason is that we constantly encounter flags all around us, and each of them will evoke chains of interesting stories in your memory.

Having read this book, you can safely call yourself a vexillologist (I confer an honorary virtual degree upon you). You may even begin to feel pity for those who do not know what you now know about flags.

I consider flags to be an excellent excuse to peek into every country in the world and get some idea about them. For me, flags have given me the feeling that I'm getting a better understanding of this world and all its amazing interconnections. I hope that you feel that too.

Index

Entries on illustrative matter are put in *italics*.

A
Abdel-Aziz, Mohamed Ould 208
Aborigines 36-7, *36*
ACS (American Colonisation Society) 112, 113
Afghanistan 202-3, *202*
Africa
   colonialism
      Belgium 225-6, 228
      Britain 124, 155-6, 176, 179-80, 186, 198, 229-30
      France 23, 119, 138, 182-4, 186, 207-8
      Italy 48
      Netherlands 123-4
      Portugal 180-1
   colour orange, symbolism of 127, 128
   influence of French flag 15, 20-2, 23
   pan-African colours
      definitions 102, 166, 175, 181
      Ethiopia as example 158, 181, 239
      flags 22, 176, 181-3, 186, *187*, 198, 225, 239
      Marcus Garvey and 175-6, 181
   post-colonial 51, 176-7, 179, 180, 184, 186, 229-30
   return of former slaves 112-13
   slave trade triangle 75
   stars, symbolism of 156
   weapons on flags 139, 176
Ahyi, Paul 186
Akinkunmi, Michael Taiwo 156
Albania 84, *85*, 85-6
Alexander the Great 88
Alfonso I 72
Algeria 178, 207-8, *207*
Amin, Idi 229-30
ANC (African National Congress) 125
Andorra 87, 90-1, *90*
Angkor Wat Temple 53
Angola 139-40, *139*, 149, 180
animals
   birds 70, 71, 187, *187*, 229, *229*, 242, *242*
   elephants 146, *146*, 147, *147*, 185
   horses 50, *50*, 97-8, *98*
   kangaroos 37
   whales 29, *29*
   see also eagles; lions
Antarctica 55, *55*
Antigua and Barbuda 238-9, *238*
apartheid 125, 186, 231
Arab Revolt 189-90, *189*, 199, 201
Arabs 153, 158, 178, 189-202, 219
Arafat, Yasser 154
Aragon 86, 87, *87*
Ararat, Mount 166, *170*
Argentina 98-100, *99*, 101, 103-4, 218
Aristotle 158
Armenia *137*, 165-6, *165*, 170, *170*
Ashoka Chakra 129
Assad, Bashar al- 194
Atatürk, Mustafa Kemal 206
Aung San, General 148
Aung San Suu Kyi 149
Australia 29, 30-1, *30*, 36-9, *36*, *37*, 47-8, 76, *76*, 242
Austria 16, 17, 50, *80*, 82, 167
Austro-Hungarian Empire 80, *80*, 82, 163, 172
Azerbaijan *137*, 206-7, *206*
Aztecs 7, 92

B
Bahamas 236, *236*, 238
Bahrain 199-200, *200*

Bainimarama, Frank 40
Banana, Canaan 187
Banda, Hastings 177
Bangladesh 131, *131*, 217
Barbados 236-7, *236*
Bartram, Graham 55
Bastille 11
Bavaria 66-7, *67*
Belarus 137, *137*, 138, 165, *165*
Belgium 17, 18, 62, 225
Belgrano, Manuel 98-9
Belize 66, 106-7, *106*
Benedict VII, Pope 69
Benedict XVI, Pope 70
Benin 184-6, *185*
Bermuda 35-6, *35*
Bhutan 133, *133*, 143
Bible 13, 27, 69, 154, 158, 166, 201
Bikini Atoll 116, *116*
Bismarck, Otto von 84
Blackbeard, Captain 236
BMW 67, *67*
Bokassa, Jean-Bédel 21-2
Bolivar, Simon 97, 98, 102
Bolivia 46, 53, 89, 98, 99, 100, 102-3, *102*, *103*
Boniface VIII, Pope 69
Bosnia and Herzegovina 54-5, *54*, 85
Boston Tea Party 109
Botswana 230-1, *231*, 239
Bourbons 13-14, *14*, *87*, 88
Brazil 72, 73-7, *74*, *76*, 98, 101, 117
Britain
    American independence and 109
    Arab revolt and 189-90
    coat of arms 26, 32
    colonies
        Africa 124, 128, 155-6, 176, 181-2, 191, 198, 229, 232
        Asia 148, 210-11
        Australia 30-1
        Caribbean 235-9
        granting independence to 186
        Latin America 106-7
        South Pacific 40-1, 242
        Union Jack and 11, 30-1, 40-1, 66, 235, 236, 238
        United States 109-10
    flag *see* Union Jack
    Northern Ireland and 127
    protectorates 49, 65
    republic 27-8, *28*
    slave trade and 75
    South African apartheid and 231

British Columbia 34-5, *35*
Brownell, Frederick 126
Brunei 211-12, *211*
Buddhism 129, 132, 141, 142, 149, 158
buildings 53, 68, 72, *86*, 87, *87*
Bulgaria 170, *171*, 222
Bunau-Varilla, Philippe 114-15, *114*
Burkina Faso 184, *184*
burning of flags 58, 216
Burundi 225, 228-9, *228*
Bush, George W. 177
Busquant, Émilie 207-8
Byzantium 79, 81, 85, 86, 206

C

Cakobau, Seru 40
Caligula 69
Cambodia 50, 52-3, *52*, 145
Cameroon 181-2, *181*, *182*
Canada 31-5, *33*
'Canadian pale' 34, 239
canton 20, 31, 59
Cape Verde 180-1, *180*
CAR (Central African Republic) 20-2, *21*
Caribbean 15, 71, 235-40
Carlos I (Portugal) 72
Carnation Revolution 53, 73, 139, 180
Castile 86, *87*
Castro, Fidel 150
Castro, Xiomara 106
Chad 22, *22*, 91
Charles I (England) 27
Charles I (Spain) aka Charles V (Holy Roman Empire) 88, 121
Charles III (England) 32
Charles III (Spain) 89, *89*
Chávez, Hugo 97-8
Chiang Kai-shek 143-4
Chile 19-20, *20*, 103
China 13, 119, 133, 141-4, *143*, 145, 149, 215, 216
Choctaw Nation 127
Christ 27, 64, 69, 72
Christianity
    Africa 155, 191-2
    Caribbean 70-1
    Europe 47
    Middle East 193, 200
    myths 25
    South Pacific 40, 64
    Scandinavia 57
    star, six-pointed 158
symbolism
    colour white 72, 127

247

cross 25, 27, 47, 62-3, 64, 70-1, 73, 131,
   191, 205
eagles 80-1, 86
numbers 69
olive branch 46, 47
paganism and 80-1, 86, 206, 237
Churchill, Winston 34, 45, 65
Clovis I (France) 13
cogwheel 139, 149
Colombia 45, 96, *96*, 97, 100, 114, 115
colours
   black, symbolism of
      African National Congress 125
      Arab dynasties 189
      battles 199
      black people 175, 181, 183, 231, 235,
         239, 240
      dark ages 203
      destruction of Bikini Atoll 117
      earth 167
      'obscurantism that needs to be
         overcome' 53
      'perseverance needed to reach the goal'
         107
      pirates 236
      ties to Africa 19, 240
   blue, symbolism of
      happiness 227
      Judaism 154
      peace 46, 49
      political parties 115
      silver 99
      sky 164
      the people 11
      Turks 207
      water 33, 95, 146, 154, 164, 196,
         230, 235
   gold 83-4
   green, symbolism of
      African National Congress 125
      Arab dynasties 189
      Catholics 126
      future 203
      'generosity of the Bangladeshi land
         and eternal youth of its people' 131-2
      hope 227
      Islam 21, 129, 130-1, 160, 205, 207
      nature 17, 199, 235
      political parties 73
   orange, symbolism of 47, 117, 122, 126, 127,
      128, 132, 175
   pan-African
      definitions 102, 166, 175, 181

      Ethiopia as example 158, 181, 239
      flags 22, 176, 181-3, 186, *187*, 198,
         225, 239
      Marcus Garvey and 175-6, 181
   pan-Arab 178, 189-99
   pan-Slavic 169, 172
   purple 71, 99, 105
   red, symbolism of
      Arab dynasties 189
      blood 20-1, 49, 95, 127, 168, 199, 203, 208
      communism 13, 31, 135, 138-46, 168,
         184-5, 187, 210
      Hinduism 129
      lava 61
      political parties 73, 115
      revolution 11-13, 17, 18, 19, 109, 150
      suffering 53
      sun 132, 156, 216-17, 223
      the people 11
   white, symbolism of
      Christianity 13, 72
      deeds 199
      ethnic groups 143, 231
      French monarchy 11, 31
      Judaism 154
      moon 146
      mountains 17, 167
      other religions 129, 131
      peace 115, 126, 177
      politics 211
      purity 13, 115
      silver 99
      white people 231, 239
   yellow, symbolism of
      African National Congress 125
      Chinese dynasty 143
      economic development 227
      gold 179
      Kurds 196
      moon 132
      power of the Sultan 211
      struggle for independence 53
      sun 23, 42, 95, 195, 223, 226, 235
      wheat fields 164
Columbus, Christopher 71, 235
Commonwealth of Nations 29, 30, 31, 40, 125
communism
   Africa 139, 180, 182-3, 184, 210
   Asia 140, 142, 143-6
   Commune and 135
   Europe 84, 163-4
   Latin America 107, 149, 150
   Soviet Union 135-6

symbolism
   colour red 13, 31, 141, 144, 145, 146, 168, 210
   hammer and compass 84, 136
   hammer and hoe 138
   hammer and sickle *80*, 83, 125, 135, 136, *137*, 13
   star, five-pointed 135, 141, 142, 144, 145, 149
Comoros 209-10, *209*, *210*
Comte, Auguste 75
Congo, Democratic Republic of the 7, 225-6, *226*
Congo, Republic of the 138, *138*
Constantine, Emperor 81
Constantinople 81
Cook, James 42, 63
Costa Rica 104-5, *104*
Côte d'Ivoire 127, *127*
Covid-19 9, 127
crescent 47, 63, 119, 130, 177, 191, 196, 205-11
Croatia 85, 171, *171*, 172-3, 212
Cromwell, Oliver 27-8
cross
   Britain 25-8
   Christian symbol 25, 27, 47, 62-3, 64, 66, 70-1, 73, 131, 191, 205
   Commonwealth 39
   Scandinavian 57-62
crowns 19, 32, 68, 69, 73, 82, 85, 90, 93, 155, 186, 221
Crusades 25-6, 58, 64, 192-3
Cuba 20, 100, 149-50, *150*, 218
Cyprus 46-8, *47*, *48*, 68, 99, 128
Czech Republic 168, *168*
Czechoslovakia 169

D
Dacko, David 22
Dahomey 184, *185*, 186
see also Benin
Dannebrog 57, 58, 59
'Defence of Fort M'Henry' (Francis Scott Key) 112
Denguiadé, Catherine 21
Denmark 57-8, *57*, 59, 60, 62, 65, 163, 216
desecration of flags 201-2
Dessalines, Jean-Jacques 19
discs 37, 75, 124, 128, 131-2, 146, 208, 216
Djibouti 51, *51*
Doe, Sergeant Samuel 113
Dominica 70, 71, 105
Dominican Republic 70-1, *70*

doves 46, 47
Doyle, Sir Arthur Conan 7, 226
dragons 25, 29, *29*, 133, *133*, 143, *143*
Driver, William 111-12
Duvalier, François 'Papa Doc' 19, 209

E
eagles
   Africa 21
   Asia 222
   Austro-Hungarian Empire 82-3
   Byzantium 79, 81
   Christianity 80-1, 87
   Europe 80-3, 84-7, 90, 91, 92
   France 12, 15
   Holy Roman Empire 81-2
   Islam 192
   Italy 15
   Latin America 7, 89, 93
   paganism and 7, 12, 80
   Rome (ancient) 80
   United States 46
East India Company (Dutch) 123
East India Company (English) 109-10, *109*, 129
East Timor 53, *53*
Ecuador 96, *96*, 97, 207
Edward I (England) 26
Edward III (England) 13
Egypt 178, 191-3, *191*, *192*, 194
Eisenhower, Dwight D. 150
El Salvador 100, 104-5, *104*
Eleanor of Aquitaine 139
Elizabeth I (England) 27
Elizabeth II (England) 32, 34
England 25-6, *26*, 27-8, 32, 58
ensigns 67, 89, 103, 125, 216, 229
Equatorial Guinea 156-7, *156*
Eritrea 46, 48-50, *49*, 54
Estonia *137*, 166-7, *166*
Eswatini 232, *232*
Ethiopia 20, 45, 49, 85, 158-9, *159*, 181, 186
EU 55, 180
Europe 11, 17, 54, 82, 84

F
Falange 90
fasces 96
fascism 96
Federal Republic of Central America 103-4, *103*, 105-6
Ferdinand II (Aragon) 86, 87, 88, 90
FIFA World Cup 9, 201-2
Fiji 29, 39-40, *40*

fimbriations 107, 176, 242
Finland 59, 60, *60*, 61, 66
First World War 83, 84, 85, 189, 206
'flags of convenience' 114
fleur-de-lys *12*, 13, 14, *14*, 32, *87*, 88, 90
Ford, Henry 76
France
    Andorra and 91
    Arab Revolt and 189-90
    colonies
        Africa 127-8, 138, 160, 181-2, 184, 207-8, 210
        Asia 145
        Canada 31-2
        Caribbean 18-19, 239
        French flag and 18-19, 20, 22
    Commune 13, *14*, 135, 200
    flag
        Dutch flag and 122
        history 11-15, *12*, *14*, *15*
        influence on others 15-16, 19, 20, 23, 61, 70, 95, 100, 105, 126-7, 170
    national emblem 96
    Revolution 11-12, 14, 15, 16, 17, 18, 62, 100, 150
    war with Mexico 92
Francis, Pope 69
Franco, Francisco *89*, 90
Franz II (Holy Roman Empire) 82
Franz Joseph (Austria) 225
freemasons 110
Freud, Sigmund 206

G
Gabon 23, *23*, 198
Gaddafi, Muammar 21, 178, 185
Gambia 232-3, *232*
Gandhi, Mahatma 7, 129, *129*, 130, 131
Garvey, Marcus 160, 175-6, 177, 178-9, 180, 181, 240
Genghis Khan 142
George III (England) 13
George VI (England) 65
Georgia 64, *64*, 72, *137*, 191
Germany
    colonies 181, 184, 207
    flags 81-2, 83-4, *83*, 184, 197, 203, 216
    GDR (German Democratic Republic) 84, 136, *136*, 146, *147*
    kingdom 81-2, 181, 184
        Federal Republic 83, *83*
    Nazi 83, *83*, 84, 91, 154, 207
    not flying flag after Second World War 216
    Schleswig-Holstein 58
Ghana 178-80, *179*
Giscard d'Estaing, Valéry 21
Goethe, Johann Wolfgang von 95
Golden Arrowhead 107
Gordian knot 88
Gran Colombia 96, *96*, 104, 114
Granada 87-8, *87*
Great Britain *see* Britain
Great Leap Forward 144
Greece 47, 48, 60, 66-8, 218, 222-3, 237
Green Book (Muammar Gaddafi) 178
Greenland 58, 163
Grenada 239, *239*
Gromyko, Andrei 166
Guatemala 104-6, *105*
Guinea 179, 182-3, *182*, 227
Guinea-Bissau 180, *180*
Güney, Ismet 47
Guyana 97, *106*, 107

H
Haile Selassie 159-60
Haiti 18-19, *18*, 70-1, *70*, 100, 209
hammer and compass 84, 136
hammer and hoe 138
hammer and sickle *80*, 83, 125, 135, 136, *137*, 138
Harald 'Bluetooth' Gormsson 57
jjΔΔx 28, 32
Hausa 155-6
Hawaii 42-3, *42*, 111
headdresses 69, *69*, 100, 104, 105, 232
    see also crowns
Heft, Robert 111
Henry I the Fowler (Germany) 81-2
Henry II (England) 25
Henry VIII (England) 126
Hercules 88
Herzl, Theodor 153, 156
Hinduism 129, 130, 132, 133
hinomaru 215, 216, 217
Hitler, Adolf 65, 83, 84, 166, 168, 196
hoe 138, *138*, 139, *139*, 157
Holy Roman Empire 81-2, 83, 89, 121
Honduras 104, 106, *106*
human figures 66, *106*, 107, 183, *183*, *236*, 237, *237*, 238
human sacrifice 7, 92
Hundred Years War 13
Hungary 17, *17*, 82, 146, *147*, 169, 170, *170*
Hussein, Saddam 195-6

Hussein ibn Ali, Sharif 189-90, 201
Hutu 227, 228

I
Iceland 61-2, *62*
Igbo 155-6
Incas 97, 99
indigenous peoples 20, 36, 38, 102, 231
India 7, 112, 128-30, *128*, *129*, 137, 171
Indonesia 53, 61, *109*, 110, 117-18, *118*, 119, 164
International African Association 225-6, *226*
internet domains 41, 42, 52, 85
Iran 219-20, *220*
Iraq 190, *193*, 194-6, *194*, *195*
Ireland 9, 28, 32, 126-7, *127*
Isabella (Castile) 86, 87, 88, 90
Islam
    Africa 21, 127, 155, 169, 177-8, 183, 191-2, 208
    Asia 119, 129-32, 143, 206-7, 210-11, 219, 220
    Europe 86
    radicalism 58
    St George and 25
    symbolism
        colour green 127, 129, 130-1, 132, 205, 207, 210
        crescent 21, 63, 119, 130, 177, 191, 196, 205, 208, 210, 219
        imagery prohibited 183
        inscriptions 201, 205, 220
        numbers 160, 200, 205
        stars 158, 200, 160
Israel 63, 67, 153-4, *153*, 156
Italy 9, 15, 16, *16*, 70, 96, 159, 170

J
Jamaica 159, 175, 208, 237-8, *237*
James I (England) 27
Japan 58, 117, 132, 140-1, 145, 215-17, *215*, *216*
Jerusalem 26, 64, *64*, 65, 193
Joan of Arc 13
John XII, Pope 82
John Paul I, Pope 69-70
Johnson, Prince 113
Jordan 190, *190*, 201
Juan VI (Portugal) 74
Juan Carlos (Spain) 90
Judaism 153-4, 155-6, 192

K
Kagame, Paul 227-8
Kalashnikov rifle 139
Karamanlis, Constantine 68
Karike, Susan 241

Karpov, Anatoly 168
Kasparov, Garry 168
Kazakhstan *137*, 221-2, *221*, 243
Kennedy, John F. 115
Kenya 176, *176*, 232
Kérékou, General Mathieu 185
Key, Francis Scott 112
Key, John 38
keys 69
KGB 118
khadi 130
Khama, Seretse 231
Khmer Rouge 52
Khomeini, Ayatollah 220
Kiir, Salva 177
Kim Il Sung 141
King, Martin Luther 175
Kiribati 7, 242, *242*
Klein, Yves 154
Korea, North 140-1, *140*
Korea, South 140-1, *140*, 216
Korea Unification Flag *140*
Ku Klux Klan 175
Kurds 195
Küstenmacher, Simon 61
Kuwait 199-200, *199*
Kyrgyzstan *137*, 221-2, *222*, 243

L
Laos 50, 90, 145-6, *146*
Latin America 19, 33, 75, 95, 96-8, 100
Latvia *137*, 166-7, *166*, 242, *242*
League of Nations 45, 64, 159
Lebanon 90, 200-1
Lee Kuan Yew 119
Leo X, Pope 13
León 87, *87*
Leonardo da Vinci 13
Leopold II (Belgium) 225-6
Leopold V (Austria) 26
Lesotho 68, 232, *232*
letters (alphabet) 66, 84, 106, 180, 206, 227, 238-9, 242-3
Liberia 113-14, *113*, 158, 186
Liberté, égalité, fraternité 11
Libya 90, 177-8, *178*, 192
Liechtenstein *18*, 19, 201
lions
    Asia 132, *132*
    Britain 26, 32, 35, 39, 172
    Christianity 81, 85
    Ethiopia 158-9, *159*
    Finland 60

Iran 219-20, *220*
Spain 87, *87*
Lithuania *137*, 166-7, *166*
Louis VII (France) 13
Louis XIV (France) 88
Lugard, Sir Frederick 155, 156
Lukashenko, Alexander 165
Luxembourg 123, *123*

M

Maainah, Abdullah Mohammed Al 196-7
Maasai 176
Macedonia 222-3, *223*
 see also North Macedonia
Machel, Samora 139
machete 139
Macron, Emmanuel 91
Madagascar 119, *119*
Majapahit Empire *109*, 110, 117
Makarios III 47, 48
Malawi 176-7, *176*
Malaysia 117, 117-18, *118*
Maldives 210-11, *210*
Mali 22, *22*, 179, 183-4, *183*
Malta 50, 65-6, *66*
Mandela, Nelson 125, 139
Mao Zedong 144
maps 46, *46*, 47, *47*, 54, *54*, 55, *55*, 132
Marcos, Ferdinand 218-19
Marley, Bob 159, 238
Marshall Islands 51-2, 116, *116*, 117
Mary, Virgin 13, 72
Marx, Karl 136
Maurice van Nassau 240
Mauritania *206*, 208-9, *208*, 211
Mauritius 240, *240*
McLaughlin, Donal 46
Mehmed II 81
Melzer, Fredrik 61
Merina kingdom 119, *119*
Mexico 7, 89, 92-3, *93*
Micronesia 51, *51*, 52
Miguel I (Portugal) 74-5
Miranda, Francisco de 95-6, *96*, 175
Mobutu Sese Seko 226
Moldova 91, *92*, 101, *137*
Monaco 61, 117, 164
Mongolia 141-2, *142*, 163
Monroe, James 112
Montenegro 84, *84*, 85
Moon, the 112, 146, 205, 212, 219
 see also crescent
Morales, Evo 102

Morocco 160-1, *160*, 178, 200
Mozambique 53, 139, *139*, 180
Mugabe, Robert 187
Muslims *see* Islam
Mussolini, Benito 1, 5, *16*, 70, 96, 159
Myanmar 113, 148-9, *148*

N

Nalbandian, Mikael 165-6
Namibia 126, *126*
Napoleon
 crowning himself Emperor 12, 15, 21
 expelling Hospitallers from Malta 65
 French flag and 12, 16, 21
 Italy and 15-16, 70
 Portugal and 72, 73, 74
 Wars 11, 18, 65, 82, 84, 123
Napoleon III 13, 16, 90
Nasser, Colonel Gamal 192
NATO 222, 223
Nauru *116*, 117
Navajo Nation 127
Navarre *87*, 88
Nazis *83*, 84, 91, 111, 196, 207
Ne Win, General 149
Nepal 212-13, *212*, 220
Netherlands
 Belgium and 18
 colonies 117, 123, 150-1, 181
 colour orange and 121-2, 123
 flag 19, 61, 121-2, *122*, 123, 124, 125, 126, 167
 independence from Spain 240
New York 45, 100, 122, *123*
New Zealand 29, 36, *37*, 38-9, 42, 137
Newfoundland and Labrador province 34, 35, *35*
Newport, Christopher 36
Nguema, Francisco Macías 157
Nguema Mbasogo, Teodoro Obiang 157
Nicaragua 71, 100, 104-5, *104*, 114-15
Nicholas II (Russia) 167-8
Niger 128, *128*, 171
Nigeria 154-6, *155*, 235
Niue 42, *42*, 52
Nixon, Richard 145
Nkrumah, Kwame 179, 182
North Macedonia 85, 222-3, *222*
Norway 57, 59, 60-1
numbers, symbolism of
 3 69
 5 72, 205
 7 205, 221
 12 144

13 110
31 176-7
Africa 176-7
China 144
Christianity 69, 72
freemasons 110
Islam 205
Persia 221

O

Obama, Barack 42
Old Glory 111, 112
olive branches 46, 47, 48, 49, 50, 101
Olympic Games 19, 37, 40
Oman 197, *197*, 200
Omar Khayyam 219
Orange Free State 123-5, *123*
Ordem e Progresso 74, 75
Osman I 205-6
Otto the Great (Germany) 82
Otto Wittelsbach (Greece) 66
Ottoman Empire
  collapse 197, 199, 206
  conquest of Constantinople 81
  crescent as symbol 205-6, 219
  flag 177, 191, 199, 205-8
  Greece and 65, 66
  rule over Eastern Europe 163
  rule over North Africa 191, 207-8
  Russo-Turkish War 63
  uprisings against 17, 66, 86, 189, 208

P

paganism 80-1, 84, 86, 91, 206, 237
PAIGC (African Party for the Independence of Guinea and Cape Verde) 180
Pakistan 129, 130, *130*
Palau 51, *131*, 132, 217
Panama 96, 114-16, *114*
Panama Canal 114-15
Papua 31
Papua New Guinea 240-1, *240*
Paraguay 19, 46, 91, 100-1, *100*
Paris
  Commune 13, *14*, 135, 200
  flag 11, *12*, *18*, 19
  Revolution 12
Parquet, Jacques-Dyel du 239
Paul I (Russia) 65
Pearson, Lester 32-4
Pedro I (Brazil) 74-5
Pedro II (Brazil) 75
Persia *see* Iran

Peru 101-2, *101*, *102*
Peter I the Great (Russia) 167
Peters, Winston 39
Philip II (France) 25
Philip IV (France) 69
Philip V (Spain) 88
Philippines 20, 137, 217-19, *218*, 220, 225
Pillars of Hercules *86*, 88, 89, 90
pirates 236, 237
Pius II, Pope 86
Pius VII, Pope 70
Pius XI, Pope 70
plants
  agricultural products 39, 88, 228
  cactuses 92, 93
  flowers 12, 13, 14, 32, 90
  leaves 31, 32, 33, 34, 38, 132, 242-3
  trees 157, 201
  see also olive branches
Pledge of Allegiance 111
Pocahontas 36
Pol Pot, General 52
Poland 61, 118, 163, 164, 168-9, *169*
Polo, Marco 119
Portugal 53, 71-5, *71*, *72*, 87, 139, 180, 181
Poseidon 237
Potosí 89, *89*
Pratt, Christopher 35
Puerto Rico 20, 111

Q

quartering 28, 31
Qatar 199-200, *200*, 238
Quran 158, 190, 196

R

Ramon, Ilan 154
Rastafarianism 159-60, 175
Rawlings, Lieutenant Jerry 179-80
Reconquista 87
Red Crescent 63
Red Cross 62-3, 65
Red Star of David 63
Rhodesia 186-7, *187*
  see also Zimbabwe
Richard the Lionheart 25-6, 58, 139, 192
Risorgimento 16, 70
Romania 17, *17*, 22, *23*, 91, *92*, 146, *147*
Rome (ancient) 12, 69, 79-81, *79*, 86, 91, 96
Roosevelt, Franklin 45
Roosevelt, Theodore 115
Rosas, Juan 99
Rusesabagina, Paul 228

Index **253**

Russia
  empire
    Byzantium and 81
    Eastern Europe and 163, 169
    Japan and 215
    Napoleonic Wars 65
    uprisings against 17, 60
  flag 19, 85, 122, 167-8, *167*, 169, 170, 172
  republic
    relationships with Belarus 165
    symbol Z 84, 125
    war against Ukraine 9, 81, 84, 164, 168, 172
  see also USSR
Russo-Turkish War 63, 170
Rwanda 225, 226-8, *227*, 229

S
Saakashvili, Mikheil 64
SADR (Sahrawi Arab Democratic Republic, aka Western Sahara) 160-1
Saint Kitts and Nevis 239-40, *239*
Saint Lucia *238*, 239
Saint Vincent and the Grenadines 34, *238*, 239
Saladin 26, 192-3
Salazar, Antonio de 73
Samoa 241-2, *241*
San Marino 53, 68, *68*
San Martin, General José de 101
Sankara, Thomas 184
Santa Anna, General Antonio López de 93
São Tomé and Príncipe 181, *181*
Saudi Arabia 67, 190, 201-2, *201*
Schleswig-Holstein 58
Scotland 26, 27, *27*, 28, 29, 32
Second World War 65, 67, 84, 85, 86, 117, 168, 215, 217
Sékou Touré, Ahmed 182
Senegal *183*, 184, 232-3
Serbia 84-5, *84*, 172, 222
Seychelles 240, *240*
shadada 201-2, *201*, *202*, 203, 205, 220
shanyrak 222
shapes 9, 17, 58, 62, *62*, 85, 200, 212
Shevchenko, Andriy 113
Sierra Leone 232, *232*
Sillsallaten 59
Singapore 117, *117*, 118, 212
Skanderbeg *85*, 86
slavery 19, 75, 112, 186, 235
Slovakia 168-70, *168*, *170*, 171, 172
Slovenia 85, 171-2, *171*, *172*
Smith, Whitney 107

socialism 22, 85, 86, 97, 139, 142, 146, 185, 187
Solomon, King 158, *159*, 160, 241
Solomon Islands 241, *241*
Somalia 50-1, *51*
Sons of Liberty 109, *109*
South Africa 123-6, *124*, *125*, 139, 231, 232
South Sudan 177, *177*, 198-9, *198*
Southern Cross (Crux) 30, *30*, 76, *76*, 241, *241*
Soviet Union *see* USSR
Soyombo 142
Spain
  Andorra and 91
  colonies 19, 92, 95-9, 101, 105, 121-2, 150, 157, 160, 217
  flag 53, 72, 86-90, *86*, *87*, *89*, 99, 101
  Franco *89*, 90
Sri Lanka 132-3, *132*
St Andrew 27, 28
St David 29, *29*
St George 25, 28, 29, 31, 39, 58, 66, 133
St John the Evangelist 81, 87
St Patrick 20
St Peter 69
Stalin, Josef 136, 138, 142, 166
Stanley, George 33
Star Wars 115
stars
  crescents and 21, 130, 191-2, 206, 207-8, 210
  five-pointed 135, 145, 148, 150, 158, 160
  Islam 21, 158, 190, 191-2
  Judaism 31, 63, 153-4, 158
  representing
    celestial bodies 30, 76, 173, 241
    Christianity 158
    ethnic groups 151, 182, 228
    member states 31, 40, 41, 51, 76, 97, 106, 110-11, 180, 193, 217, 241
    politics 103, 117
    zodiac 207
  seven-pointed 190, 195
  six-pointed 31, 63, 153-8, 173, 228
  symbolism
    communism 85, 86, 135, 139, 142, 144, 145, 149, 165, 184, 185, 187
    independence 113, 178-9, 180, 181, 184
    peace 115
    perfection 221
Stars and Stripes 112
stripes
  diagonal 138, *138*, *239*, 240
  horizontal
    Africa 20, 113, 184, 186, 227, 229-32
    Asia 143-7, 201, 220

    Eastern Europe 17, 163-9, 171
    Latin America 18-19, 97, 99-101, 106
    United States 110-12
  symbolism 43, 110, 145
  vertical
    Africa 20, 22, 182-4, 227
    Asia 195-6, 203
    Caribbean 19, 237
    Europe 12, 16, 17, 87, 90-1
    French Revolution and influence 12, 16, 17-18, 19
    Latin America 101
    Sons of Liberty 109
Sudan 177, 198-9, *198*
Sukarno 117-18
Sulaimi, Al- 199-200, *199*
Suleiman the Magnificent 65
sun
  Africa 126, 128, 208, 226
  Asia 126, 128, 176-7, 212, 215-22
  Caribbean 238
  Europe 222-3
  Incan empire 97, 99
  Latin America 97, 99-102
  moon and 208, 212
  South Pacific 242
  symbolism
    ethnic groups 195
    good luck 216
    independence 128, 176-7, 226
    months of the year 144
    power 242
    revolution 97, 99-102, 217, 219
  Vergina 156, 223
Suriname 150-1, *151*
swastika 83, *83*, 84, 125
Sweden 59, *59*, 60
Switzerland 9, 50, 62, 65, 212
Sykes, Sir Mark 189
Sykes-Picot agreement 190
Syria 178, 190, *190*, 192, 193-4, *193*

T

Taiwan *126, 143*, 144
Tajikistan *137*, 220-1, *221*
takbir 196, 205, 220
tallit 154
Tanganyika 230, *230*, 238
Tanzania 229, 230, *230*
Texas 20, 92
Thailand 61, 146, 147-8, *147, 148*, 200
Thomas, Harold 37
Togo 186, *186*

Tombalbaye, François 22
Tonga 63-4, *64*
Transvaal 123-5, *123*
trapezoids 195, 196, 199
triangles 49, 53-5, 169, 189, 195, 212, 217, 236, 239
tricolor
  Africa 22, 23, 119
  black people's rights and 175-6
  Caribbean 19
  Europe 11-13, 15-16, 22, 83-5, 90
  Latin America 92-3, 96-7, 99-100, 101-5
  origins 11, 122
  revolution and 12, 13, 15-16, 17, 19, 95-7, 100
  stripe width 15, 90, 103
  see also France: flag
trident *236*, 237
Trinidad and Tobago 36, 112, 240
Trujillo, Rafael 71
Trump, Donald 29
TTPI (Trust Territory of the Pacific Islands) 51, *51*
Tunisia 178, 208
Turkey 47, 48, 68, 166, 191, 205, 206-7
Turkmenistan 46, 50, *50*, 80, *137*
Tutsi 227
Tuvalu 7, 29, 40-1, 43, 52, 210

U

UAE (United Arab Emirates) 196-7, *196*, 200
Uganda 229-30, *229*
UK Flag Institute 55
Ukraine
  Austro-Hungarian Empire and 82
  flag 136, *137*, 138, 163, *163*, 164, 237, 240
  history 163-4
  Russian war against 9, 81, 84, 164, 168, 172
  UN member 138
UNIA (Universal Negro Improvement Association) 175, 176
unicorns 32
Union Jack
  Commonwealth and
    Africa 124-5, 155
    Australasia 29, 30, 36, 38-42
    Canada 31-5
    Caribbean 238
    countries getting rid of 29, 31, 238
  development *26, 27*, 27
  etymology 27
  influence 11
  Wales and 29, *29*
Union of African States 179, *179*

Index   **255**

United Arab Republic 192, *192*, 193, *193*
United Kingdom *see* Britain
United Nations
    Bhutan happiness index promoted 133
    Blue 46, 52, 55, 112
    creation 137
    flag 45-6, *46*, 99, 112, 141
    history 45
    Indonesia leaving 117
    influence on other flags 47, 48-52, 54-5
    peace missions 48, 50-1, 52
    USSR and USA seeking power over 137-8
United States
    civil rights movement 175
    Civil War 112
    eagles 46
    flag 110-11, *110*, 112, 119, 186, 218
    foreign policy 67, 104, 114-17, 145, 150, 216, 218
    revolution 109-10
    Second World War 216
    territories 111, 242
    Vietnam War 145
Upper Volta 184, *184*
see also Burkina Faso
Uruguay 98, 99, 100, *100*, 101
USSR (Union of Soviet Socialist Republics)
    atheism 141, 142
    collapse 50, 142-3, 164, 168, 185
    flag 13, 101, 135-8, *135*, *137*
    foreign policy 117, 137-8, 145, 150, 166
Uzbekistan *137*, 207, *207*

V

van der Wal, Julien 239
Vanuatu *241*, 242
Vatican City 9, 62, 68-70, *68*, 212
Venezuela 95, 97-8, *97*, *98*
Vespucci, Amerigo 98
vexillology 9, 11, 34, 40, 54, 55, 90, 107, 173, 181, 245
Vietnam 52, 144-5, *144*, *145*
Voltaire 82

W

Wales 29
Weah, George 113
weapons 37, 53, 139, *139*, 176, *176*, 197, *197*, 201, *201*, 232
wheel 129, 132
Wilhelmina (Netherlands) 121
William of Orange 122, 175
Wilson, Woodrow 115

Wiphala 102, *102*
Wolfsangel 83, 84, 125

Y

Yemen 197, *198*
yin and yang *140*, 141, 142, *142*, 158
yoke and arrows 88, *89*, 90
Yugoslavia 19, 54, 85

Z

Zaire 226, *226*
    see also Congo, Democratic Republic of the
Zambia 128, *128*
Zanzibar 230, *230*
Zimbabwe 53, 186-7, *187*
zodiac signs 97, 207